Marlowe: The Plays

ANALYSING TEXTS
General Editor: Nicholas Marsh

Published

Chaucer: The Canterbury Tales   *Gail Ashton*

Webster: The Tragedies   *Kate Aughterson*

Shakespeare: The Comedies   *R. P. Draper*

Charlotte Brontë: The Novels   *Mike Edwards*

Shakespeare: The Tragedies   *Nicholas Marsh*

Jane Austen: The Novels   *Nicholas Marsh*

Emily Brontë: Wuthering Heights   *Nicholas Marsh*

Virginia Woolf: The Novels   *Nicholas Marsh*

D. H. Lawrence: The Novels   *Nicholas Marsh*

John Donne: The Poems   *Joe Nutt*

Thomas Hardy: The Novels   *Norman Page*

Marlowe: The Plays   *Stevie Simkin*

Analysing Texts
Series Standing Order ISBN 0–333–73260–X
(*outside North America only*)

You can receive future titles in this series as they are published by placing a standing
order. Please contact your bookseller or, in case of difficulty, write to us at the
address below with your name and address, the title of the series and the ISBN quoted
above.

Customer Services Department, Macmillan Distribution Ltd
Houndmills, Basingstoke, Hampshire RG21 6XS, England

Marlowe: The Plays

STEVIE SIMKIN

palgrave

First published 2001 by
PALGRAVE
Houndmills, Basingstoke, Hampshire RG21 6XS and
175 Fifth Avenue, New York, N.Y. 10010
Companies and representatives throughout the world

PALGRAVE is the new global academic imprint of
St. Martin's Press LLC Scholarly and Reference Division and
Palgrave Publishers Ltd (formerly Macmillan Press Ltd).

ISBN 0–333–92241–7 hardback
ISBN 0–333–92240–9 paperback

This book is printed on paper suitable for recycling and
made from fully managed and sustained forest sources.

A catalogue record for this book is available
from the British Library.

Library of Congress Cataloging-in-Publication Data
Simkin, Stevie.
    Marlowe : the plays / Stevie Simkin.
      p. cm. – (Analysing Texts)
    Includes bibliographical references and index.
    ISBN 0-333-92241-7 — ISBN 0-333-92240-9 (pbk)
      1. Marlowe, Christopher, 1564–1593—Criticism and interpretation.
      I. Title. II. Series.

PR2674 .S58 2001
822'.3–dc21   00-048338

10 9 8 7 6 5 4 3 2 1
10 09 08 07 06 05 04 03 02 01

Printed in China

822.3
MARLOWE

For my parents

Contents

General Editor's Preface

This series is dedicated to one clear belief: that we can all enjoy, understand and analyse literature for ourselves, provided we know how to do it. How can we build on close understanding of a short passage, and develop our insight into the whole work? What features do we expect to find in a text? Why do we study style in so much detail? In demystifying the study of literature, these are only some of the questions the *Analysing Texts* series addresses and answers.

The books in this series will not do all the work for you, but will provide you with the tools, and show you how to use them. Here, you will find samples of close, detailed analysis, with an explanation of the analytical techniques utilised. At the end of each chapter there are useful suggestions for further work you can do to practise, develop and hone the skills demonstrated and build confidence in you own analytical ability.

An author's individuality shows in the way they write: every work they produce bears the hallmark of that writer's personal 'style'. In the main part of each book we concentrate therefore on analysing the particular flavour and concerns of one author's work, and explain the features of their writing in connection with major themes. In Part 2 there are chapters about the author's life and work, assessing their contribution to developments in literature; and a sample of critics' views are summarised and discussed in comparison with each other. Some suggestions for further reading provide a bridge towards further critical research.

Analysing Texts is designed to stimulate and encourage your critical and analytic faculty, to develop your personal insight into the author's work and individual style, and to provide you with the skills and techniques to enjoy at first hand the excitement of discovering the richness of the text.

NICHOLAS MARSH

A Note on Editions

All quotations from Marlowe's plays are taken from the Oxford World's Classics version of the plays (*Doctor Faustus and Other Plays*), edited by David Bevington and Eric Rasmussen (Oxford University Press, 1995). The format is I.iii.45, where I indicates act number, iii is scene number, and 45 is line number. A reference to a stage direction is noted as 's.d.'. In the extracts, those stage directions in square brackets [ ] have been added by the editors; all other stage directions are from the original texts. Quotations from Shakespeare's plays are taken from *The Norton Shakespeare*, edited by Stephen Greenblatt, Walter Cohen, Jean E. Howard and Katherine Eisaman Maus (W.W. Norton & Company, 1997).

In the Critical Views chapter, quotations from Harry Levin are taken from the extracts reprinted in the *Doctor Faustus Casebook*, edited by John Jump; quotations from Jonathan Dollimore are from the second edition of *Radical Tragedy* (Harvester Wheatsheaf, 1989); quotations from Stephen Greenblatt and Emily Bartels are taken from *Christopher Marlowe: Longman Critical Reader*, edited by Richard Wilson (Longman, 1999).

Introductory Guidance

Texts

The rationale of this book is based on close analysis of short extracts from Marlowe's five major plays. The bedrock of that analysis has to be *text*: for our purposes, that means the collection of Marlowe's plays we have bought from a bookshop or borrowed from a library, and which should contain (at least) the plays *Tamburlaine Part One*, *Tamburlaine Part Two*, *The Jew of Malta*, *Edward II* and *Doctor Faustus*. The latter is often included in two versions which are given the titles 'A-text' and 'B-text' (or '1604' and '1616' after their publication dates), and I will return to this issue. However, before we proceed any further with an investigation of Marlowe's work, we must take a closer look at what the term 'text' means in this instance.

The notion of a text is always going to be a complex one when we are looking at four-hundred-year-old plays. Elizabethan drama was a performance medium, not a literary one, and if a play appeared on paper it was initially used only as an aid to performance. A playwright would hand over his work to the company and one or two copies would be made by hand (notice the margin for error that opens up here, as the play is transcribed). From the copy, the actors (known then as players) would be given their 'sides' which contained their lines and cues (individuals would not have been given a copy of the entire play). Time pressure would probably have been considerable at all stages of the process, increasing the likelihood of mistakes creeping in during the various transcriptions. It was not until later in the period that the practice of printing plays and selling them became commonplace, once it became clear that there was a market for them amongst the educated, literate classes. Even then, a large number of these editions were unreliable, often 'pirated' versions. In some cases, this meant that they would be copied down from what a player, or a couple of members of the company, could piece together

1

from memory. Inevitably, the result was often a very distorted representation of what the playwright intended.

It is likely that the texts evolved to a greater or lesser extent during the brief rehearsal period, subject as they were to changes by the actors as they rushed to get the play on its feet; improvising here, cutting there, adapting the raw material to their particular needs and strengths. The plays were also subject to censorship by the government official who wielded the title Master of the Revels, and whose intervention is fairly evident between the A- and B-texts of *Doctor Faustus*. We know from a preface that the printed version of *Tamburlaine* we have inherited has had some comic business excised (by its printer, not the Master of the Revels) and the huge differences between the two surviving versions of *Faustus* are perhaps the best illustration in all Elizabethan drama of the fundamental instability of these texts.

Furthermore, play-writing was often a collaborative process between two or more dramatists. Sometimes details of authorship are unclear, and textual critics spend a good deal of time trying to figure out who wrote what. They have even designed computer programs to help them, although opinions vary as to how effective this software can be. In some cases, a play may not be billed as a collaborative effort at all. We think Marlowe's first surviving play, *Dido Queen of Carthage*, which dates from his undergraduate days, was written in collaboration with Thomas Nashe. We know for certain that additions to *Faustus* were made after Marlowe's death by William Birde and Samuel Rowley, although we cannot be sure whether those additions figure in both A- and B-texts. Neither can we be sure what those additions *are*. The differences between the two versions, though, are considerable: the latter is about 600 lines longer, and there are countless minor discrepancies too. *Edward II* is the most 'stable' of all the texts, being printed a couple of years after it was first performed (and just a few weeks after Marlowe's death).

The text of what was probably Marlowe's last play, *The Massacre at Paris*, is the most 'corrupt', an example of the pirated texts mentioned above. It is very probably what we call a 'memorial reconstruction' of the play Marlowe wrote, reproduced some ten years after the first performances, and for this reason, critics do not tend to spend much time discussing it. *Doctor Faustus* remains the most fascinating case, for, as mentioned above, it has come down to us in two distinct versions – what is now referred to as the A-text appeared first in 1604, and the B-text dates from 1616. We cannot be sure which is closest to Marlowe's original, but the key point here is the evidence we have for the playwright's script as a kind of raw material for performance. The two versions suggest that very different performance texts of the same play evolved during the years that the play was in the repertory. There is much to explore in a parallel study of the two versions, but this kind of investigation lies outside the scope of this book. We will focus on the A-text (currently 'in favour' with the critics) with occasional brief references to the B-text.

This is only a brief overview of the textual history of the Marlowe canon. However, it should be enough to make us aware of the dangers inherent in assuming that these plays we are reading are exact representations of the plays that sprung from Marlowe's imagination. Nevertheless, as long as we are using a good modern edition, we can be confident that we are doing the best we can in the circumstances. Except in such extreme cases as *The Massacre at Paris*, where the textual corruption is so evident and so profound, literary critics have made a necessary compromise: while providing the appropriate disclaimers, they proceed to work on the assumption that what we are studying are Marlowe's plays. Meanwhile, textual scholars have proceeded with their own task, battling over each letter and punctuation point as they compare the earliest surviving editions of his works. Within the scope of this book, we will have to be content to make the same compromise as the literary critics.

Verse Form

Christopher Marlowe's body of work is surprisingly slight when set against that of his rival playwright and (now) far more distinguished contemporary, William Shakespeare. However, Marlowe's status as a great innovator secures him a high profile position in the hierarchy of early modern dramatists, and although critical consensus on the quality of his work has varied immensely over the centuries, his significance in the evolution of dramatic form has never really been in doubt. A close contemporary, Ben Jonson, made an admiring reference to Marlowe's 'mighty line', and there is certainly something stately and magisterial in the pace of his verse at times, particularly in the early work *Tamburlaine*. However, there is a recognisable evolution of his style into a more conversational register in the later plays, and this development can be traced in detail if we take on board some fairly straightforward principles of verse analysis.

One of Marlowe's most important innovations was in the area of verse form. Elizabethan plays are written in a combination of poetry and prose, but most of them make much heavier use of the former. The pattern that we are most familiar with from Shakespeare's plays is what is known as blank verse: unrhymed lines each containing five stressed syllables. If we are going to be pedantic about this, the proper term is the **iambic pentameter**: an iamb is a metrical 'foot' or unit, where each unit consists of an unstressed syllable followed by a stressed syllable; for example, in the word 'today', 'to' is unstressed, and 'day' is stressed; these are the two elements of that iambic foot. Pentameter means 'of five measures' so, putting the two halves of the term together, we have the iambic (meaning a unit made up of an unstressed syllable followed by a stressed syllable) and the pentameter (meaning there are five of these units in each line).

Here are two sample lines from *Doctor Faustus*. The first is a typical, regular, iambic pentameter:

> Was this the face that launched a thousand ships
>
> (V.i.90)

The rhythm is a regular, galloping pace: 'Was **this** the **face** that **launched** a **thou**sand **ships**' (de-**dum**-de-**dum**-de-**dum**-de-**dum**-de-**dum***)*. Variation on this rhythm is common, since verse that consistently followed this pattern would not only be monotonous but very restrictive: there are very many words which begin with a stressed syllable, so reversing the iambic pattern. A simple example of a variation, then, comes two lines later:

Sweet Helen, make me immortal with a kiss!

(V.i.92)

The line begins with two stresses, followed by an unstressed syllable: '**Sweet Hel**en', and continues: '**make** me im**mor**tal with a **kiss**'. The variation can be used simply to avoid the monotony that regular iambs imposes on the movement of the verse. However, in some cases, the movement from stressed to unstressed syllables in itself can be expressive, as in the way this line seems to trip over the short, unstressed lines ('-tal with a') to fall heavily on the word 'kiss'.

One more feature of blank verse requires attention. Although the iambic pentameter was familiar in English poetry from the time of Chaucer, dispensing with rhyming couplets was a tremendous innovation, and Marlowe was one of the first to make the break. Hugely liberating, this was a great stride towards what we might call a more 'realistic' representation of human speech. It was already clear that the iambic rhythm most closely replicated a standard speech pattern, and the pentameter (five feet) seemed to suit the English language most comfortably (whereas, for example, the longer twelve-syllable line known as the alexandrine seems to work best for the French language). The use of unrhymed form, introduced by the Earl of Surrey in his translation of the Roman epic *The Aeneid* around 1540, was significant both as another step towards natural speech, and as a release from the bonds of rhyming couplets. Anyone who has tried sustaining composition of a poem where each pair of lines rhymes will know how quickly one is forced either to hunt around desperately for an appropriate rhyming word, or else do strange things to the word order to clinch the couplet.

Character and Convention

Over the past ten years or so, I have directed a number of sixteenth and seventeenth century plays, including several by Shakespeare, as well as tragedies by John Ford, John Webster and Christopher Marlowe (*The Jew of Malta*). One of the most frequent problems in rehearsal would be an actor pulling up short in front of a speech and

complaining that 'my character wouldn't say this' or 'I don't understand my motivation for this line'. At the time, under pressure of
concentrated rehearsal, the easiest way to cope was to play the game
the actors wanted to play – that of 'psychologising' the characters. I
would often find myself inventing the most tortuous narratives to
create what actors call a 'through line of action', a rationale that con-
nects a character's every speech, action and even her unscripted
moves, silences and absences.

The reason why this problem crops up so frequently is because
playwrights like Marlowe did not approach their *dramatis personae* as
'characters' in the sense that we do today. I have explained how
blank verse brought us closer to natural, 'realistic' dialogue, and it
certainly *does* come closer than mechanical rhyming couplets. But
verse form still remains at one remove from natural speech for the
simple reason that it demands a certain number of stresses in a line,
something we obviously don't concern ourselves with in real life.
Similarly, the characters speaking the lines are in some senses 'larger
than life'. The priority for Elizabethan and Jacobean playwrights
seems to have been rhetorical effect rather than psychological
realism, and the structure and direction of the plot was certainly
more important than character consistency. While we would tend to
be driven to interpret what a character says and does by looking for
some form of motivation – perhaps with reference to 'subtext' (what
we can deduce by 'reading between the lines'), for their past, their
emotional ties, their subconscious drives – it is unlikely that actors
in Marlowe's time would have shared such preoccupations, if only
because much of this belongs to a post-Freudian age.

Marlowe is one of the dramatists who represent a turning point in
the development of dramatic character. Although some speech and
behaviour will strike us as remarkably 'naturalistic', at other times we
will be surprised by the appearance of an allegorical figure or else a
fully, explicitly detailed description of a certain emotional or spiritual state from a 'realistic' character, speaking in soliloquy. Hundreds
of books have been written about the title character of Shakespeare's
Hamlet, each one providing a new explanation for his behaviour. It is
tempting to suggest that the existence of so many different (and
often contradictory) accounts says more about misunderstandings of

the construction of dramatic character than it does about the genius of Shakespeare as a creator of lifelike human beings.

I have already mentioned that the Elizabethans used the term 'player' rather than 'actor', and the process of acting was referred to as 'playing'. One of the easiest, 'shorthand' ways of beginning to understand the difference between our current dominant acting style and the Elizabethan style is to consider the terms: Edward Alleyn, in the role of Barabas the Jew of Malta, is *playing* the role, or *playing at* it, we might say. The performer retains some distance between himself and his character. Today, someone like Dustin Hoffman might *act* or *enact* the role of Willie Loman in *Death of a Salesman*. Alleyn displays his character, he *shows* it; Hoffman inhabits the role, and *'becomes'* the character Willie Loman. Crudely speaking, this is the goal of so-called Method acting, and the goal of 'becoming' the character remains the dominant trend in mainstream western theatre. In plays dominated by caricatures (like Barabas), by historical, sometimes semi-mythical figures (like Faustus, Edward II and Tamburlaine), and supernatural beings (like Mephistopheles), the chasm between a modern and an early modern concept of character may seem even wider.

There is a similar adjustment to make in terms of theatrical convention. Chapter 8 discusses in more detail the kind of performance conditions that Elizabethan playing companies were accustomed to. The theatrical experience four hundred years ago was very different from what we tend to expect today. Briefly, the crucial aspects of Elizabethan theatre which we may be less familiar with today include:

1) the acknowledgement of the presence of the audience; actors will frequently address the audience directly, breaking the convention of the 'fourth wall', that imaginary boundary that separates audience from performer;

2) consistency is not prioritized, whether this is in terms of the psychological consistency of 'character', or of mood – plays will often swing abruptly from comic to tragic mode, and from 'realistic' action to allegory;

3) performance style probably relies more on conventions; certain poses, gestures and so on would have been familiar to the audience of the time, and 'decoded' appropriately;

4) the *dramatis personae* may include, alongside 'real' people, allegorical characters (such as Gluttony, of Everyman) or supernatural figures (ghosts, devils and angels);
5) the fact that plays were performed during the day, outdoors,
   meant that there was no artificial lighting to establish, for
   example, a night time scene; similarly, the open style of staging,
   with little or nothing in the way of set, meant that a specific location would be established or evoked in a speech.

Finally, and this is something we will return to continually, there
is the issue of cultural and historical difference. A brief word will
suffice at this point. It is clear that human understanding of the self,
the world around us, and the supernatural realm has altered drasti-
cally over the past four hundred years. Human beings do not remain
'essentially the same', whether we move down through history, or
across the globe geographically. In terms of religious belief, in relations between men and women, in international relations, in the
relationship between the state and the citizen, we are several worlds
away from the Elizabethans. There are of course elements that we
share in common with them; if there were not, Marlowe's plays
would make no sense to us. However, we do need to ensure that the
common elements do not blind us to the huge differences that
divide us. We should always be careful to take full account of social
and historical context when we are interpreting the actions of a character within a play.

Tradition

As we go on to look more closely at Marlowe's work, we will discover different ways in which he can be understood as a pioneer of
early modern theatre. Because of his position in the genealogy of the
drama there will be aspects of his work which strike us as unusual,
bizarre or awkward, even if we are already familiar with plays of the
period from our exposure to some of Shakespeare's work. Marlowe
in some senses stands at a crossroads. He is the inheritor of a classical
tradition, the ancient plays of Greek playwrights like Sophocles
(496–406 BC) and Aeschylus (525–456 BC) and the Roman Seneca

(died AD 65). From them, Marlowe takes the models of tragedy, the tradition of poetic verse form and the convention of the hero or protagonist. However, Marlowe also draws upon the popular European traditions of medieval theatre, in particular the so-called morality plays and mystery plays of the fourteenth, fifteenth and early sixteenth centuries. From this tradition, paradoxically, come both the serious religious subject matter and the commonplace, often bawdy 'low' comedy. The Elizabethan theatre was a hugely creative industry and, we must remember, a hugely commercially successful one – the two aspects are inseparable. In some respects the character of late sixteenth and early seventeenth century English drama was the result of the bringing together of these two strands. A writer like Marlowe was university educated and so very familiar with the classics. But he was writing for companies and audiences reared on a popular theatre that, while based on Bible stories and church teachings, had also come to reflect immediate and local issues and priorities.

The range of Marlowe's subject matter, even within such a relatively small body of work, is remarkable. He embarks on his career as a playwright with a 'safe', classically based piece, *Dido Queen of Carthage*. *Dido* is a dramatic adaptation of books 1, 2 and 4 of *The Aeneid* by the Latin poet Virgil (70–19 BC). *The Aeneid* was an epic that was a staple of university curricula and Marlowe would have known it very well. The historical dramas *Tamburlaine, Edward II* and *The Massacre at Paris* use the ancient genre of tragedy to shape stories ranging from the fourteenth century (the story of the Scythian Timur the Lame and the English King Edward II) to what could be described as current affairs (the St. Bartholomew's Day Massacre took place in Paris in 1572). Even though they are all historically based, each represents a very different kind of history, and each tells its story in a distinctive fashion. There is a decisive swing towards the European tradition with the morality-derived *Faustus,* although its shape remains rooted in classical tragic form. Meanwhile, the savagely satirical *The Jew of Malta* manages to defy categorisation. It remains (for the Elizabethans) perhaps the most 'current' of all Marlowe's work, touching (as *Tamburlaine* does) on English xenophobia – the fear of the Islamic threat in the East as well as the anti-Semitism that would automatically cast Barabas as villainous anti-hero.

Marlowe's work offers many challenges to a modern reader and a modern audience. In his own time, his plays were immensely popular. To capture in our imaginations some sense of that massive popular appeal, we need to bear in mind two things. First of all, the importance of the performative dimension cannot be underestimated. These play-texts are blueprints for spectacular, exciting theatrical experiences, and we need to do our best to visualise them on the stage if we cannot see them in the theatre for ourselves. Tamburlaine's magnificent chariot drawn by conquered kings is one good example, the shooting to death of the governor of Babylon another. In *Faustus*, we have the terrifying sight (for an Elizabethan) of Faustus being dragged down to hell, in *Edward II* and *The Jew of Malta* the gruesome deaths of the protagonists. Secondly, as the *Faustus* example suggests, we need to bear in mind the significance of historical difference, and do what we can to read and see the plays as an Elizabethan might have done. At the same time, the plays continue to provoke because of how they resonate in contemporary society. It is this double focus of 'our time' and 'their time' that lies at the heart of a full appreciation of the plays.

PART 1

ANALYSING MARLOWE'S PLAYS

1

Openings and Entrances

The pattern of this first chapter of extracts will not match the layout of the chapters that follow: rather than looking closely at one passage from each of Marlowe's plays, as most subsequent chapters will, in this opening section we are going to consider **two** extracts from each play, the prologue and the first scene. We will compare the different ways in which the plays begin, and how the prologues function in each case. We will also make some comparisons between the plays.

Three of the four plays we are studying in this book open with a prologue, usually spoken by a 'Chorus' figure. The Chorus can be seen as the equivalent of a narrator; a convenient modern parallel would be the 'voice-over' that sometimes features at the start of a film. At the most elementary level, these prologues help to set the scene, providing what film-makers call the 'backstory', filling in details that the members of the audience need to get their bearings. Shakespeare occasionally uses a Chorus figure, and probably the most famous example is the one that opens *Henry V*. As Elizabethan drama evolved, the Chorus was in effect superceded as playwrights found other, more dramatic ways of providing audiences with the information they required. When I use the term 'dramatic' here, I don't mean in the sense of startling or exciting (though they may be this, too); I am using the term in the sense of *dramatic form* – implying that what evolved was more in keeping with a theatrical form seeking to represent 'real life'. Shakespeare's most familiar tech-

nique is to stage a conversation between a couple of minor characters to provide the necessary plot exposition. The opening of *Edward
II* represents a significant shift in this direction, as we shall see.

The use of a prologue may strike us today as unusual, and somewhat clumsy. An Elizabethan audience would have had no such prejudices. The fact that the prologue often 'gives away the plot' would
not have surprised them either. Indeed, an Elizabethan picking up a
handbill announcing a play called *The Tragical History of Doctor
Faustus* would have a pretty fair idea that it was unlikely to have a
happy ending and, in any case, he may well have been familiar with
the story already, since it had its roots in a popular legend. Today,
when we attend a performance of a new play – or of a play we
haven't seen or read before – part of the appeal is the suspense
derived from not knowing what will happen next. Although some
early modern plays probably worked in this way too, very often the
dramatist was drawing on stories, or on historical sources, that
would have been familiar to some or all of the spectators. The different pleasures an Elizabethan derived from watching a play is a
good example of the kind of cultural differences we need to take into
account when reading early modern dramatic texts.

We are now going to compare the prologues of three plays,
Tamburlaine, *Doctor Faustus* and *The Jew of Malta*, and then
examine the beginning of the first scene proper of each play, where
the protagonists either make their entrances (*Faustus, The Jew*) or are
introduced by others (*Tamburlaine*). The section ends with a consideration of *Edward II*, which dispenses with a prologue: Marlowe has
found a more dramatically effective way of fulfilling the function of
the Chorus, and he uses instead a soliloquy, a speech performed by a
character, on stage alone, as if thinking aloud to the audience.

Tamburlaine I, Prologue and *Tamburlaine II*, Prologue

Tamburlaine the Great (1587 or 1588) was Marlowe's first major play,
and it is the best place to start if we wish to see further evidence of
Marlowe the pioneer dramatist. *Tamburlaine* was preceded by *Dido
Queen of Carthage* which was probably written around 1586 for a

company of boy actors, the Children of the Chapel Royal in Windsor. *Dido*, as its title suggests, reflects the classical strand of the dramatic tradition Marlowe inherited, being an adaptation of part of the epic poem *The Aeneid*, written by the Roman poet Virgil (70–19 BC). *Tamburlaine*, which is actually two plays written several months apart, was Marlowe's calling card on his arrival in London (he had probably written it during his final months at Cambridge University). From what we can deduce, the play was a sensation, and Marlowe became, almost overnight, the star of the Elizabethan theatre industry. What is interesting about this prologue is its brash self-confidence; there is certainly a sense of Marlowe staking out his territory. Let's take a close look at the eight lines that make up this short prologue.

> From jigging veins of rhyming mother-wits
> And such conceits as clownage keeps in pay
> We'll lead you to the stately tent of War,
> Where you shall hear the Scythian Tamburlaine
> Threat'ning the world with high astounding terms
> And scourging kingdoms with his conquering sword.
> View but his picture in this tragic glass,
> And then applaud his fortunes as you please.

Marlowe is announcing himself as a bold innovator in both style and subject matter. He begins by targeting his competition (probably plays by writers such as Robert Greene and John Lyly), pouring scorn on the formal shortcomings of their work: he attacks both its mechanical rhythm ('jigging') and its elementary rhyme scheme ('mother-wits' means common sense, and so implies that the rhymes are overly simplistic). The word 'jigging' is in itself expressive, but may also convey something more precise: although today we go to the theatre expecting to see nothing more than a performance of the play advertised, the Elizabethan custom was rather different. A trip to the theatre was an afternoon out, and the performances of the plays themselves were crowded into a programme that featured other kinds of entertainment, including dances (jigs), performed by 'clowns' like Will Kemp and Richard Tarlton. Marlowe's attack on 'jigging veins of rhyming mother-wits' associates the plays themselves with the frivolous entertainment that preceded them.

The content of these plays is scorned, too: the 'conceits', or tricks, are denigrated, and again are associated with the business of the Kemps and Tarltons ('such conceits as clownage keeps in pay' [2]) and compared unfavourably with Marlowe's own serious subject matter: 'the stately tent of War' (3). Marlowe is promising us, in stark contrast, 'high astounding terms' and a 'tragic glass' (5,7) – the glass is a mirror, in which humankind can see itself reflected. We will return to this in a moment, but for now notice how expressive Marlowe's own verse is: the first three lines are run on, a swift dismissal of the competition:

> From jigging veins of rhyming mother-wits
> And such conceits as clownage keeps in pay
> We'll lead you to the stately tent of War.

The momentum does not let up until the end of that third line: the speaker of the Prologue has to decelerate as he or she reaches 'the stately tent of War', and the rhythmical and linguistic complexity of the following line ('Scythian Tamburlaine / Threat'ning . . .') requires a more careful pace.

The prologue works in a number of different ways. First of all, it functions as a kind of advertisement: Marlowe is calling his audience to attention by issuing a challenge, promising something new, and inviting the spectators to see how he lives up to the task he has set for himself. The prologue also draws the parameters for his play, and introduces a couple of key terms. The notion of the 'scourge' requires some explanation: we can trace it back to the Old Testament (specifically, the book of the prophet Isaiah, chapter X). Here, the prophet depicts God using a heathen Assyrian to punish his (God's) people, the Israelites, for their disobedience. Having used him as a rod with which to strike them, the prophet declares that God will destroy the Assyrian too, but not before he has served his purpose: 'I will send him against an hypocritical nation, and against the people of my wrath [the Israelites] will I give him a charge, to take the spoil, and to take the prey, and to tread them down like the mire of the streets' (Isaiah X.vi). References to Tamburlaine as a scourge of God were familiar in the historical sources that Marlowe drew upon when he wrote the play. The epithet is one that recurs several times in the course of the play (crucially, it is included in Tamburlaine's own final line, as he dies), and the text invests a great deal in the term, as we shall see. The status of the scourge as a tool or a weapon that God uses before discarding, is one of the things that makes Tamburlaine such a fascinating protagonist.

The other key term is 'tragic glass'. As I mentioned above, 'glass' here means mirror. It was a familiar principle of Elizabethan learning that the study of history had a specific purpose, and this is most conveniently summarised and expressed in a collection of historical material known as *The Mirror for Magistrates*, first published in 1559, and frequently reprinted. *The Mirror for Magistrates* depicts the faults and sins of rulers in the past, and shows with grim satisfaction the punishment meted out for their various vices. The authors (or rather editors) of the collection make it clear that they intend these descriptions to act as warnings. The impact is enhanced by a neat device: the dead rulers themselves tell their histories to the poet, who has been led by the allegorical figure Sorrow into the land of the dead. The stories they tell are cautionary tales for those rulers who are wise enough to heed them.

The prologue to *Tamburlaine I* ends with a kind of appeal to the audience, although its tone retains a proud, combative tone: 'applaud his fortunes as you please' (8). It appears that the audiences *were* pleased with what they saw; within a few months, Marlowe had been inspired (presumably by the Elizabethan equivalent of good box office receipts) to write *Tamburlaine II*, which opens with an acknowledgement of the first part's success:

> The general welcome Tamburlaine received
> When he arrivèd last upon our stage
> Hath made our poet pen his second part,
> Where death cuts off the progress of his pomp
> And murd'rous Fates throws all his triumphs down.
> But what became of fair Zenocrate,
> And with how many cities' sacrifice
> He celebrated her sad funeral,
> Himself in presence shall unfold at large.

This prologue promises to chart the second half of the trajectory of the scourge of God, 'Where death cuts off the progress of his pomp / And murd'rous Fates throws all his triumphs down' (4–5). This is only to be expected. The tragic hero will be seen at the pinnacle of success and in a position of great fortune (as he is at the end of *Tamburlaine I*), before an inevitable fall, a descent dictated both by the shape of tragedy as a genre and by Tamburlaine's identity as scourge of God – one who will be used and then himself destroyed. His annihilation is vital, for it is this that underlines the insuperable status of God himself, something Tamburlaine repeatedly challenges during the course of the two plays.

One final point worth noting in *Tamburlaine II*'s prologue is the significance of Zenocrate. Zenocrate is the daughter of the Soldan of Egypt, one of Tamburlaine's early conquests. Tamburlaine takes her in Part I as his concubine, and she later becomes his wife. She fulfils several dramatic functions during the course of the play, as we shall see, but her death is one of the turning points in the action, for it represents a challenge to Tamburlaine that he is powerless to counter. Death, whom Tamburlaine has chosen to see as his servant in Part I, robs him of his beloved wife, and it is at this point that we begin to see the slow decay of his sense of invincibility (and the audience's perception of that invincibility). The prologue, once again, provides an early signal of this vital strand in the narrative that is about to unfold.

Doctor Faustus, Prologue

The prologue to *Doctor Faustus* is more substantial than the *Tamburlaine* prologues. Marlowe was presumably working with a different agenda by the time he wrote *Faustus*, having established a reputation in the London theatrical community (although it is worth noting that the date *Faustus* premiered is uncertain, see p. 3). In any case, the blustering self-promotion has been replaced by something more considered: a careful redrawing of the boundaries marking what is and is not suitable tragic material.

Enter Chorus.

CHORUS   Not marching now in fields of Trasimene
     Where Mars did mate the Carthaginians,
     Nor sporting in the dalliance of love
     In courts of kings where state is overturned,
     Nor in the pomp of proud audacious deeds,   5
     Intends our muse to daunt his heavenly verse.
     Only this, gentlemen: we must perform
     The form of Faustus' fortunes, good or bad.
     To patient judgements we appeal our plaud,
     And speak for Faustus in his infancy.   10
     Now is he born, his parents base of stock,
     In Germany, within a town called Rhode.
     Of riper years to Wittenberg he went,
     Whereas his kinsmen chiefly brought him up.
     So soon he profits in divinity,   15
     The fruitful plot of scholarism graced,
     That shortly he was graced with doctor's name,
     Excelling all whose sweet delight disputes
     In heavenly matters of theology;
     Till, swoll'n with cunning of a self-conceit,   20
     His waxen wings did mount above his reach,
     And melting heavens conspired his overthrow.
     For, falling to a devilish exercise,
     And glutted more with learning's golden gifts.
     He surfeits upon cursed necromancy;   25
     Nothing so sweet as magic is to him,
     Which he prefers before his chiefest bliss.
     And this the man that in his study sits.

Exit

The prologue to the first *Tamburlaine* play begins with a jaunty, mischievous rejection of others' attempts at writing for the stage. It then shifts gear, speaking in more measured verse of the weighty subject matter of an historical figure, a great and terrible ruler and conqueror of nations who was responsible for the deaths of many thousands of people. The Chorus that sets the scene for *Faustus* in a sense

moves in the opposite direction, although it is again beginning with
a list of things that the play will *not* be about: the opening lines
make it clear that the subject matter of this play will not be found
'In courts of kings . . . Nor in the pomp of proud audacious deeds'
(4–5). This is not a play about politics, state conflicts, or the affairs
of kings and queens. The first six lines are in high-flown, elaborate,
and self-consciously poetic language, but these terms are deployed
only to be swept aside. In a mirror image of the opening of
Tamburlaine I, the seventh line of this prologue brings us up short.
The poetry stops dead, as the Chorus drops into something close to
a conversational tone and rhythm: 'Only this, gentlemen: we must
perform / The form of Faustus' fortunes, good or bad' (7–8). After
the poetic flight of the opening lines, the tone is muted, almost perfunctory. In the meantime, we are reminded of the trajectory that
tragedy conventionally follows ('fortunes, good or bad'), the arc it
traces from the height of prosperity to the depths of ruin and misery.
By the end of the prologue, we already have a good idea of Faustus's
fate, which will now be staged for our entertainment. We know that,
having 'mount[ed] above his reach', the heavens conspired his 'overthrow' (21–2). The Chorus then brings us back to the beginning of
the narrative: 'And this the man that in his study sits' (28).

The structure of the prologue allows for a poetic flight in the first
six lines, which it then juxtaposes with the more prosaic account of
Faustus's early life (8–14). As the Chorus goes on to describe his
extensive and profound learning, the poetic terms return ('fruitful
plot of scholarism . . . sweet delight . . . heavenly matters' [16–19]),
and the speech then moves into a metaphor with classical roots
(20–2). The elaborate use of imagery invoking purity and spiritual
health are strongly contrasted with 'cursed necromancy' (25); the
natural bounty of legitimate scholarship is set against forbidden
knowledge, which is cast in terms of sinful excess: 'falling to a devilish exercise . . . glutted . . . He surfeits . . .' (23–5). There is
nothing neutral about the moral tone of the Chorus's speech and,
with this perspective stated in such powerful terms so early on, it is
bound to have a significant impact on the way the members of the
audience are going to interpret Faustus's behaviour as the play
begins.

The Chorus includes a brief description of Faustus's life history. Notice how Marlowe continues the shift away from the nobility (traditionally the only figures worthy of tragic heroic status); Faustus's parents, we are told, are 'base of stock' (11). Faustus travels to Wittenberg and studies theology. The place was significant for its reputation as a stronghold of Protestantism: Martin Luther preached there and taught philosophy at the university, and it was in Wittenberg that he nailed his famous 95 Theses to the door of a church, one of the defining moments in the birth of the Protestant faith. Sharp satire at the expense of the Catholic church feature in several of Marlowe's plays, including *Doctor Faustus*. In any case, it is no surprise to find Marlowe going out of his way to establish his hero's impeccable Protestant credentials: there is a good deal of evidence to suggest that Marlowe, as an undergraduate, worked as a secret agent in the fight against Catholic infiltration (see the discussion of the conflict between Protestants and Catholic in early modern England in Chapter 8, pp. 222–5).

The next part of this prologue shifts the focus onto the pattern of Faustus's tragedy, which is modelled on the story of Icarus. According to Greek myth, Daedalus (Icarus's father) made wings for the two of them to fly from the isle of Crete. But Icarus flew so close to the sun that the wax holding the feathers of the wings together melted, and he fell into the sea and drowned. The myth had a well established moral – the perils of any aspiration that transgresses the boundaries God, or the gods, have established. Icarus's 'self-conceit' spurs him to 'mount above his reach', and the result is that the melting heavens 'conspired his overthrow' (20–2). The final strand the Chorus draws out for us is the dimension of good and evil, salvation and damnation. Faustus, a glutton for learning who remains unsatisfied while confined within the boundaries of what humankind is permitted to know, turns to forbidden knowledge and 'devilish exercise'; 'cursed necromancy' replaces what the Chorus calls his 'chiefest bliss', that is to say, the hope of salvation.

A final note on the prologue: there is a tradition in Marlovian criticism of characterising Marlowe himself as one subject to these dangerous desires, the aspiration to reach beyond legitimate boundaries. The tradition is actually rooted in the stories that circulated around the time of his death: some depicted him as a man of dangerous and heretical opinions, and his early death was seen by some as God's swift judgement on a decadent, immoral atheist (see pp. 233–7). The tradition has lingered, and some literary critics, while dropping the moral opprobrium, have chosen to depict Marlowe as an 'over-reacher'. In this criticism there is an implicit connection made between several of his heroes and Marlowe himself. We will return to this point, and one of the samples of criticism (by Harry Levin) included in the discussion in Chapter 9 takes this further (see pp. 242–6). For now, it is enough to recognise that Marlovian scholars are often tempted to make what we call *ad hominem* judgements, deducing things about the author's own personality by studying his plays. The temptation is particularly strong in Marlowe's case because we know that he had earned a reputation in his own lifetime as an atheist or heretic. We do need to be wary of indulging in this kind of speculation, for it is an attractive but often misleading path to follow. It is usually more helpful to interpret the text on its own terms, and we should be circumspect when reading any attempts to romanticise Marlowe himself as some kind of Elizabethan Faustus figure.

The Jew of Malta, Machiavel's Prologue

[Enter] Machiavel

MACHIAVEL   Albeit the world think Machiavel is dead,
    Yet was his soul but flown beyond the Alps,
    And, now the Guise is dead, is come from France
    To view this land and frolic with his friends.
    To some perhaps my name is odious,   5
    But such as love me guard me from their tongues,
    And let them know that I am Machiavel,
    And weigh not men, and therefore not men's words.
    Admired I am of those that hate me most.
    Though some speak openly against my books,   10
    Yet will they read me and thereby attain

To Peter's chair, and, when they cast me off,
Are poisoned by my climbing followers.
I count religion but a childish toy
And hold there is no sin but ignorance. 15
Birds of the air will tell of murders past!
I am ashamed to hear such fooleries.
Many will talk of title to a crown;
What right had Caesar to the empery?
Might first made kings, and laws were then most sure 20
When, like the Draco's, they were writ in blood.
Hence comes it that a strong-built citadel
Commands much more than letters can import –
Which maximé had Phalaris observed,
He'd never bellowed in a brazen bull 25
Of great ones' envy. O'th'poor petty wits
Let me be envied and not pitièd!
But whither am I bound? I come not, I,
To read a lecture here in Britainy,
But to present the tragedy of a Jew, 30
Who smiles to see how full his bags are crammed,
Which money was not got without my means.
I crave but this: grace him as he deserves,
And let him not be entertained the worse
Because he favours me. 35

[*Exit*]

The prologue to *The Jew of Malta* is perhaps the most fascinating of all Marlowe's openings. Longer still than *Faustus*'s first Chorus speech (clocking in at 35 lines), its speaker is given a name, Machiavel, a name that would have resonated powerfully for an Elizabethan audience, the educated amongst them in particular. The Machiavel Marlowe puts on the stage is a parody of Niccolo Machiavelli (1469–1527), a figure of some significance in European political theory at this time. In short, Machiavelli and his writings had been demonized by Elizabethan culture; even today the term machiavellian is used to denote someone or something that is untrustworthy, manipulative, or in possession of a hidden agenda.

The tendency to identify Machiavelli's political theory in this way was largely based on a reading of his work *The Prince* (1513), a book intended for rulers that purported to guide them in the most effective methods of government, using any means necessary to secure the greatest advantage for the states they governed, and for themselves.

Marlowe's prologue to *The Jew* draws on and contributes to that construction of Machiavelli, perpetuating the stereotype of the evil manipulator. This Machiavel (as Marlowe calls him) acknowledges that 'To some perhaps my name is odious' (5) and he proceeds to alienate his audience by associating himself with 'the Guise' (3): Henri the third Duke of Guise (1550–88) was a French nobleman reviled in Protestant England for his part in the St. Bartholomew's Day Massacre in 1572, in which thousands of Huguenots (French Protestants) were slaughtered at the instigation of the Catholic French royal family. Marlowe, incidentally, depicts the massacre and its political fall-out in his play *The Massacre at Paris*, which survives only in a mangled form. There is some clever irony embedded in Machiavel's description of himself: he claims that he is 'Admired . . . of those that hate me most' (9). 'Though some speak openly against my books,' he claims, 'Yet will they read me and thereby attain / To Peter's chair' (10–12). At a stroke, Marlowe thereby establishes both the hypocrisy of those who follow him (they speak against him, but secretly employ his methods) and their Catholicism (Peter's chair being the Pope's throne). Their hypocrisy is itself Machiavellian and, for a predominantly Protestant audience, their identity as Catholics is further proof, if any were necessary, of their evil and duplicitous nature.

Marlowe in effect creates a personality for his prologue figure: Machiavel is haughty, dismissing his critics at a stroke ('I am Machiavel, / And weigh not men, and therefore not men's words' [7–8]). He is offhand and provocatively dismissive of the enormity of the crimes committed in his name: 'Birds of the air will tell of murders past! / I am ashamed to hear such fooleries' (16–17). The tone of the whole speech is powerfully rhetorical: he states his traits and his opinions bluntly and without concessions, answering his own questions as a matter of course ('What right had Caesar to the empery? / Might first made kings . . .' [19–20]). He also propounds some brutal political theory when he asserts that 'laws were then most sure / When, like the Draco's, they were writ in blood' (20–1). 'Draco' is the root of our term 'draconian' – Draco, in Athens in the seventh century BC, established a code of law that dictated capital punishment for virtually every offence, hence laws that were 'writ in blood'. The prologue walks a narrow margin between what is and is not acceptable when Machiavel announces that 'I count religion but a childish toy / And hold there is no sin but ignorance' (14–15). Both notions would have shocked the average Elizabethan theatre-goer (bearing in mind the dangers of such a generalization). However, Marlowe deftly defuses the controversy, or at least diverts it away from himself, by having them spoken by a Chorus figure that has already identified itself as the spirit of Machiavelli.

From the establishment of Machiavel's credentials, the closing lines of the prologue finally shift our attention to the hero (or anti-hero) of the play itself. The fact that Machiavel spends longer talking about himself than he does about Barabas is instructive. The figure of the Machiavel, or the concept of the self-seeking political manipulator, is central to the play, and one we will return to in our own discussion later in this book: it is crucial in defining the two main characters, the Jew Barabas and the Christian Ferneze, as well as the relationship between them. It also helps to modulate the response of the audience to each of them.

In any case, the representation of Barabas here in the prologue and in the play both draws upon and helps to feed the anti-Semitic prejudice that was very much a part of Elizabethan (and European) culture at this time. Blamed by Christian doctrine for the death of Christ, associated with the devil, feared and hated, the Jewish population scattered across the continent had suffered persecution down through the centuries. All kinds of myths circulated, including stories about Jews poisoning wells (similar to Barabas's poisoning of the nunnery), and Jews crucifying Christian children and drinking their blood (a myth the play makes reference to in III.vi.44–50). The Holocaust of the Second World War was genocide on a scale previously unimaginable, but in the larger perspective of two thousand years of Christianity it is only a chapter in the history of anti-Semitism, not the whole story. The Crusades of the eleventh and twelfth centuries were launched against Islamic nations, but also incorporated widespread slaughter of Jews across Europe as the crusaders made their way towards the Holy Land. When Marlowe wrote *The Jew of Malta* Jews had been officially banned from England for over 300 years, expelled by Edward I in 1290, although a few communities remained, practising their religion in secret. Elsewhere in Europe, Jewish communities were confined to ghettos and suffered high taxation while being denied full citizenship – a context Shakespeare would exploit when writing his *The Merchant of Venice*, which shows evidence of Marlowe's influence. The issue of anti-Semitism in the play is a crucial one that cannot be ignored, and we will return to it in due course.

The prologue quickly establishes Barabas as avaricious (he 'smiles to see how full his bags are crammed' [31]), a characteristic that will be reinforced by our first sight of him '*in his counting house*' (I.i.0, s.d.). Furthermore, Barabas is immediately identified as one of those who follows Machiavelli's teaching – 'Which money was not got without my means' (32). The closing lines are richly ironic, and signal the kind of ironies Marlowe will proceed to set up throughout the play. Machiavel asks that the audience 'grace him as he deserves' (33). The term 'grace' here means 'honour'; Machiavel is craving the audience's indulgence to allow him a fair hearing, but the plea is undercut from the moment it is offered as the idea of honouring a Jew would more than likely have provoked the laughter of an Elizabethan audience. Furthermore, Machiavel, already idenitified as villainous, is a comically unsuitable advocate for a character to whom the audience will already have an instinctive hostility. Machiavel, as if anticipating this response, requests, 'let him not be entertained the worse / Because he favours me' (34–5). The word 'favours' is ambiguous. Today, we are likely to assume it means 'approves of', or 'sides with'. However, editors more often gloss the line with the meaning that would probably have been more familiar to the Elizabethans – 'resembles'. Either way, the irony of one villain craving the audience's indulgence for another is not lost, and is most likely intensified by the wordplay. Machiavel is asking for a fair trial ('grace him as he deserves') but the outcome is never in doubt, even before Barabas steps onto the stage. Nevertheless, as we shall see, the text does manage to pull the rug out from under the audience's predisposed hostility. Barabas is perhaps the most fascinating of all Marlowe's protagonists, mostly on account of the relationship he establishes with the audience. As we shall see later, it is this aspect of his *persona* that makes him such a fascinating and complex figure. We will now take a look at the opening scenes of each of the four plays in relation to their prologues.

Tamburlaine I, I.i.1–80

[Enter] Mycetes, Cosroe, Meander, Theridamas, Ortygius,
Ceneus, [Menaphon,] with others

MYCETES   Brother Cosroe, I find myself aggrieved,
    Yet insufficient to express the same,
    For it requires a great and thund'ring speech.
    Good brother, tell the cause unto my lords;
    I know you have a better wit than I.   5
COSROE   Unhappy Persia, that in former age
    Hast been the seat of mighty conquerors
    That in their prowess and their policies
    Have triumphed over Afric, and the bounds
    Of Europe where the sun dares scarce appear   10
    For freezing meteors and congealèd cold –
    Now to be ruled and governed by a man
    At whose birthday Cynthia with Saturn joined,
    And Jove, the sun, and Mercury denied
    To shed their influence in his fickle brain!   15
    Now Turks and Tartars shake their swords at thee,
    Meaning to mangle all thy provinces.
MYCETES   Brother, I see your meaning well enough,
    And through your planets I perceive you think
    I am not wise enough to be a king.   20
    But I refer me to my noblemen
    That know my wit and can be witnesses.
    I might command you to be slain for this.
    Meander, might I not?

MEANDER   Not for so small a fault, my sovereign lord.   25
MYCETES   I mean it not, but yet I know I might.
    Yet live, yea, live, Mycetes wills it so.
    Meander, thou my faithful counsellor,
    Declare the cause of my conceivèd grief,
    Which is, God knows, about that Tamburlaine,   30
    That like a fox in midst of harvest time
    Doth prey upon my flocks of passengers,
    And, as I hear, doth mean to pull my plumes.
    Therefore 'tis good and meet for to be wise.
MEANDER   Oft have I heard your majesty complain   35
    Of Tamburlaine, that sturdy Scythian thief,
    That robs your merchants of Persepolis
    Trading by land unto the Western Isles,
    And in your confines with his lawless train
    Daily commits incivil outrages,   40
    Hoping, misled by dreaming prophecies,
    To reign in Asia and with barbarous arms
    To make himself the monarch of the East.
    But ere he march in Asia or display
    His vagrant ensign in the Persian fields,   45
    Your grace hath taken order by Theridamas,
    Charged with a thousand horse, to apprehend
    And bring him captive to your highness' throne.
MYCETES   Full true thou speak'st, and like thyself, my lord,
    Whom I may term a Damon for thy love.   50
    Therefore 'tis best, if so it like you all,
    To send my thousand horse incontinent
    To apprehend that paltry Scythian.
    How like you this, my honourable lords?
    Is it not a kingly resolution?   55
COSROE   It cannot choose, because it comes from you.
MYCETES   Then bear thy charge, valiant Theridamas,
    The chiefest captain of Mycetes' host,
    The hope of Persia, and the very legs
    Whereon our state doth lean, as on a staff   60
    That holds us up and foils our neighbour foes:

Thou shalt he leader of this thousand horse,
Whose foaming gall with rage and high disdain
Have sworn the death of wicked Tamburlaine.
Go frowning forth, but come thou smiling home,   65
As did Sir Paris with the Grecian dame.
Return with speed! Time passeth swift away.
Our life is frail, and we may die today.

THERIDAMAS   Before the moon renew her borrowed light,
Doubt not, my lord and gracious sovereign,   70
But Tamburlaine and that Tartarian rout
Shall either perish by our warlike hands
Or plead for mercy at your highness' feet.

MYCETES   Go, stout Theridamas. Thy words are swords,
And with thy looks thou conquerest all thy foes.   75
I long to see thee back return from thence,
That I may view these milk-white steeds of mine
All loaden with the heads of killèd men,
And from their knees ev'n to their hoofs below
Besmeared with blood, that makes a dainty show.   80

The opening of the first *Tamburlaine* play adopts a technique that we may be familiar with from some of Shakespeare's plays. In *Macbeth*, for instance, we hear about the title character some time before we see him, and the impression created is of a brave, resourceful soldier and military leader, an honourable but implacable foe. Part of the skill of the dramatist is the way in which he then proceeds to play with the expectations he has established. Tamburlaine himself does not appear in the first scene of this play, but Marlowe manages to create a strong impression of him by the way in which others speak about him. The chief character in this first scene is the King of Persia, Mycetes. From his first speech, we are alerted to his shortcomings. 'I find myself aggrieved', he tells his brother Cosroe, 'Yet insufficient to express the same' (1–2). This is a king who, far from having mastery of the 'high astounding terms' the prologue has promised us, finds himself unable to muster the 'great and thund'ring speech' required of him. Instead, he orders Cosroe to speak for him, an abdication that is symptomatic of his feeble nature.

Mycetes's opening speech is in halting, broken sentences, petering out into a meek deferral to Cosroe. Mycetes's weakness is signalled by his inability to construct anything substantial in his address to the court. Cosroe, by contrast launches into a speech that stretches one, soaring sentence over ten lines (6–15). The speech is divided almost evenly between a celebration of his nation's past glories and lament for its present predicament (6–11), followed by a damning indictment of Mycetes's failings. According to Cosroe, Persia is a cursed nation, ruled by a king who is weak, lazy, inarticulate and unreliable (these are some of the flaws he identifies in his reading of the astrological signs at Mycetes's birth). Mycetes responds with another deferral, complete with a poor attempt at wordplay ('I refer me to my noblemen / That know my wit and can be witnesses' [21–2]), and a threat to kill Cosroe which has to be propped up by another member of his court ('I might command you to be slain for this. / Meander, might I not?' [23–4]). Meander, metaphorically speaking, kicks away the crutch with his reply: 'Not for so small a fault, my sovereign lord' (25). 'I mean it not, but yet I know I might' Mycetes concludes, lamely (26).

Mycetes proceeds to the business at hand: the threat posed by the Scythian Tamburlaine, the 'fox' preying upon his flocks – his people (31–2). Between them, Mycetes and Meander create a picture of a lawless bandit – he is 'that sturdy Scythian thief', one who 'commits incivil outrages', accompanied by his 'lawless train' of followers (36–41). However, his ambitions are grander than the depiction of him as a kind of land-bound pirate would suggest: Meander claims that prophetic dreams have planted in his mind the notion of ruling all Asia. However, we learn later (II.v.50ff.) that Tamburlaine apparently harbours no such ambitions until after he has defeated Mycetes and handed over the crown to Cosroe, who joins forces with him against his brother. It may be that Marlowe has overlooked this apparent inconsistency. It is equally likely that the notion of inconsistency may not have occurred to him in the first place, as the remarks on dramatic character in the Introductory Guidance section suggest.

The rest of the scene continues to set Mycetes up for a fall: he invests his security in the hands of the captain of his forces 'valiant

Theridamas' (57), and his lines bristle with ironies: his reference to 'Sir Paris' and the 'Grecian dame' (66) evokes the catastrophic Trojan war, and the couplet, 'Return with speed! Time passeth swift away. / Our life is frail, and we may die today' (67–8) is even more ominous. The final lines of the extract comprise a nice example of bathos, an impressively brutal fantasy bungled by an incongruous conclusion that is deployed for comic effect: the 'milk-white steeds' are imagined 'All loaden with the heads of killed men'. Mycetes imagines that the sight of the horses' legs 'Besmeared with blood' will make 'a dainty show' (76–80).

The passage is built, then, upon a series of contrasts between the powerful (offstage) Tamburlaine and the ineffectual (onstage) Persian king. Mycetes is a comically inept ruler ripe for usurpation and Tamburlaine is identified as the one who will topple him. This is an unexpectedly comic opening to a play which has begun with a promise of 'high astounding terms', but these will come soon enough. As an opening, this first scene manages both to disarm and engage an audience (particularly in the wake of the prologue), and makes us impatient for our first glimpse of Tamburlaine himself in the following scene (I.ii).

Doctor Faustus, I.i.1–65

Enter Faustus in his study

FAUSTUS   Settle thy studies, Faustus, and begin
     To sound the depth of that thou wilt profess.
     Having commenced, be a divine in show,
     Yet level at the end of every art,
     And live and die in Aristotle's works.   5
     Sweet *Analytics*, 'tis thou hast ravished me!
     [*He reads*] '*Bene disserere est finis logices.*'
     Is to dispute well logic's chiefest end?
     Affords this art no greater miracle?
     Then read no more; thou hast attained the end.   10
     A greater subject fitteth Faustus' wit.
     Bid *On kai me on* farewell. Galen, come!

Seeing *Ubi desinit philosophus, ibi incipit medicus,*
Be a physician, Faustus. Heap up gold,
And be eternized for some wondrous cure.   15
[*He reads*] '*Summum bonum medicinae sanitas*':
The end of physic is our body's health.
Why Faustus, hast thou not attained that end?
Is not thy common talk sound aphorisms?
Are not thy bills hung up as monuments,   20
Whereby whole cities have escaped the plague
And thousand desperate maladies been eased?
Yet art thou still but Faustus, and a man.
Wouldst thou make man to live eternally,
Or, being dead, raise them to life again,   25
Then this profession were to be esteemed.
Physic farewell. Where is Justinian?
[*He reads*] '*Si una eademque res legatur duobus,*
Alter rem, alter valorem rei', etc.
A pretty case of paltry legacies!   30
[*He reads*] '*Exhaereditare filium non potest pater nisi –*'
Such is the subject of the Institute
And universal body of the Church.
His study fits a mercenary drudge
Who aims at nothing but external trash –   35
Too servile and illiberal for me.
When all is done, divinity is best.
Jerome's Bible, Faustus, view it well.
[*He reads*] '*Stipendium peccati mors est.*' Ha!
'*Stipendium*', etc.   40
The reward of sin is death. That's hard.
[*He reads*] '*Si peccasse negamus, fallimur*
Et nulla est in nobis veritas.'
If we say that we have no sin,
We deceive ourselves, and there's no truth in us.   45
Why then belike we must sin,
And so consequently die.
Ay, we must die an everlasting death.
What doctrine call you this? *Che serà, serà,*

What will be, shall be? Divinity, adieu!   50
                [He picks up a book of magic]
These metaphysics of magicians
And necromantic books are heavenly,
Lines, circles, signs, letters and characters –
Ay, these are those that Faustus most desires.
O what a world of profit and delight,   55
Of power, of honour, of omnipotence
Is promised to the studious artisan!
All things that move between the quiet poles
Shall be at my command. Emperors and kings
Are but obeyed in their several provinces,   60
Nor can they raise the wind, or rend the clouds;
But his dominion that exceeds in this
Stretcheth as far as doth the mind of man.
A sound magician is a mighty god.
Here, Faustus, try thy brains to gain a deity.   65

We have already seen how the prologue of *Faustus* moves in the opposite direction to *Tamburlaine*'s, passing as it does from the serious to the more mundane. The opening scene of *Tamburlaine* has an impressive setting – the court of a king – and, at its centre, a clownish figure metaphorically dwarfed by the throne on which he sits. *Faustus* opens in a location as commonplace as *Tamburlaine*'s is grand: the humble scholar Faustus sits in his study, surrounded by his books. However, whereas the mind of Mycetes is petty, self-centred, witless and weak, Faustus is a man whose imagination seems to be boundless, and whose aspiration reaches far beyond mortal potential. The internal dimensions of these two plays reverse the polarities and, at least at this early point, we see in Faustus the potential for greatness that Mycetes so patently lacks.

Faustus embarks on a whistle-stop tour of different avenues of classical learning, and each one is systematically rejected as inadequate. He rejects the study of logic (Aristotle's *Analytics* [5–10]) when he finds that it does nothing more than teach one to 'dispute well'; medicine is rejected next, having been considered chiefly for its commercial potential – he exhorts himself to 'Heap up gold, /

And be eternized for some wondrous cure' (14–15). But medicine, he decides, which is represented by the ancient Greek physician Claudius Galenus ('Galen' [12]), is worthless if one cannot raise the dead, or grant the gift of eternal life. The sixth century Byzantine emperor Justinian represents the law, which is 'too servile and ill-beral' (36) for Faustus's taste, and divinity is dismissed on what amounts to a rather foolish mismatch of two verses from different books of the Bible: 'The reward of sin is death' (Romans VI.ii) (39–41) and 'If we say that we have no sin, / We deceive ourselves, and there's no truth in us' (I John I.viii) (44–5). Faustus unadvisedly welds the two together and concludes that humankind is doomed either way.

This leads him to another stack of volumes: the 'necromantic books', he finds, are 'heavenly' – an epithet whose irony is evidently lost on him, as he pores over the 'lines, circles, signs, letters and characters' of the demonic spells (52–3). 'Ay', he declares, 'these are those that Faustus most desires' (54). If we had begun to suspect Faustus's motiviation as he dismissed all other types of learning as unprofitable, our suspicions are confirmed when he reveals what attracts him to the magician's books:

> O what a world of profit and delight,
> Of power, of honour, of omnipotence
> Is promised to the studious artisan!
>
>   (55–7)

He goes on to dream of world domination ('All things that move between the quiet poles / Shall be at my command' [58–9]) and ends with an aspiration to divine status: 'A sound magician is a mighty god', he affirms, and, in an ominous climax to this lengthy soliloquy, he exhorts himself to 'try thy brains to gain a deity' (64–5).

All of this would probably have coloured an Elizabethan audience's response to Faustus in a way that we may find hard to comprehend today. In a largely secular age, it may be difficult to imagine the reactions of a population for whom the spiritual realm was as real as the material world: the devils and angels depicted in *Faustus*, and frequently represented in the medieval morality plays, were not figures of fantasy, as they are likely to be for the majority of a present day audience. Today, even religious believers tend to imagine these entities in abstract terms, or else take them as figures of speech for the ways in which the forces of good or evil intervene in human lives. The extent to which the devils were 'real' to a typical Elizabethan is indicated by the stories that circulated about performances of the play: there were reports that the Devil himself appeared on stage during one production; another evocative story tells of a group of actors terrified to discover one too many devils in the troupe, whereupon the players and the audience swiftly evacuated the theatre. The extent to which the passage of time establishes certain mental, social and cultural differences between ourselves and our ancestors is a difficult issue, one that I discuss at greater length in Chapter 9. For now, it is enough to recognise that *Doctor Faustus* is likely to have a very different kind of impact in the theatre today than it did 400 years ago and, inevitably, our response to Faustus is likely to be different, too. At the same time, the enduring popularity of the play both on stage and in the classroom is proof of its resilience to the passing of the centuries. Even in a largely secular age, this profoundly religious play retains the power to engross and move us.

I have spoken in the Introductory Guidance section of the care with which we need to use terms like 'character', and *Doctor Faustus* illustrates the difficulties most starkly, populated as it is not only by human characters like Faustus, Wagner and knights, servants and friars, but also supernatural beings like Mephistopheles, Lucifer, the Seven Deadly Sins and the Good and Evil Angels. Nevertheless, bearing in mind my earlier cautionary notes about assuming that figures like Faustus are 'realistic' characters, we can identify certain moments and lines in this opening scene that give Faustus something at least approximating a set of character traits. As he considers the different kinds of learning he has at his fingertips, from philosophy to medicine, law and divinity, his mind darts from one tradition to the next, and each one is abandoned within the space of half a dozen lines. This sense of perpetual intellectual motion, suggesting a deep-seated sense of dissatisfaction and frustration, is something that plagues Faustus throughout the play. Even when he has made his pact with the Devil, earning the right to question Mephistopheles about all the mysteries of the earth and the heavens, he finds himself blocked at every turn, with each avenue of discovery closed down before he can discover anything of real importance.

As we shall see time and time again, Marlowe often disrupts the steady pattern of the imabic pentameter to achieve certain effects. The Latin quotations, if they are to be rendered accurately, are bound to be unmetrical. Nevertheless, they have a significant impact on the flow of this opening speech. This is most evident when Faustus ponders the verse he quotes from Jerome's Bible (39–43), for the English lines that surround the Latin quotations are similarly uneven. 'The reward of sin is death' begins with two light stresses, followed by heavy stresses on '-ward', 'sin' and 'death', and two more heavy stresses as Faustus allows the meaning to sink in: 'That's hard' (41). His translation of the Latin lines that follow are similarly uneven (eight syllables in line 44, eleven in line 45, seven each in lines 46 and 47, with the rhythm taking something of a tumble in the awkward 'And so consequently die'). Faustus's reflection is grandly fatalistic: 'Ay, we must die an **everlasting death**' (48). As Faustus lays his hands upon his necromantic books, however, the rhythms of the verse settle quickly into a smoother and more ordered metre. The difference is marked. There is a surging confidence in the list recited in line 53 ('Lines, circles, signs, letters, and characters – '), and the verse soars in Faustus's exclamation as he imagines what he might achieve by magic – 'a world of profit and delight' (55). There is something of what has been described as Marlowe's mighty line in the portentous, 'All things that move between the quiet poles / Shall be at my command' (58–9). The verse is measured, stately and proud: notice the carefully balanced 'raise the wind, or rend the clouds' (61), and the sense of surging forward in 'Stretcheth as far as doth the mind of man' (63).

Finally, it is worth noting that Faustus, in his opening soliloquy, sets himself up as a prime target for Mephistopheles. There is a suggestion in the B-text version of the play (in a passage omitted in the A-text) that it is Mephistopheles who directed Faustus's eye as he read the scriptures he cites to justify his rejection of Christian doc-

trine (see B-text, V.ii.89–95). In any case, it is clear from the way
Faustus rushes to transgress the boundary between legitimate human
learning and the forbidden knowledge of black magic that he is an
easy catch for the Devil. Furthermore, it is clear that his ambitions
are self-centred, decadent ones. Notice the way he luxuriates in
learning, and the way he covets it: he talks of how philosophy has
'ravished' him (6); he calls on medicine with a breathless, 'Galen,
come!' (12); and, as we have already seen, he looks upon the study of
medicine as a route to fame and fortune ('Heap up gold, / And be
eternized . . .' [14–15]). The presence of such vices so close to the
surface would not have gone unnoticed by an Elizabethan audience.

The Jew of Malta, I.i.1–48

> *Enter Barabas in his counting-house, with heaps of gold*
> *before him*

BARABAS   So that of thus much that return was made,
    And, of the third part of the Persian ships,
    There was the venture summed and satisfied.
    As for those Samnites and the men of Uz,
    That bought my Spanish oils and wines of Greece,   5
    Here have I pursed their paltry silverlings.
    Fie, what a trouble 'tis to count this trash!
    Well fare the Arabians, who so richly pay
    The things they traffic for with wedge of gold,
    Whereof a man may easily in a day   10
    Tell that which may maintain him all his life.
    The needy groom that never fingered groat
    Would make a miracle of thus much coin;
    But he whose steel-barred coffers are crammed full,
    And all his lifetime hath been tired,   15
    Wearying his fingers' ends with telling it,
    Would in his age be loath to labour so,
    And for a pound to sweat himself to death.
    Give me the merchants of the Indian mines,
    That trade in metal of the purest mould;   20

The wealthy Moor, that in the eastern rocks
Without control can pick his riches up,
And in his house heap pearl like pebble-stones,
Receive them free, and sell them by the weight –
Bags of fiery opals, sapphires, amethysts,   25
Jacinths, hard topaz, grass-green emeralds,
Beauteous rubies, sparkling diamonds,
And seld-seen costly stones of so great price
As one of them, indifferently rated
And of a carat of this quantity,   30
May serve in peril of calamity
To ransom great kings from captivity.
This is the ware wherein consists my wealth;
And thus methinks should men of judgement frame
Their means of traffic from the vulgar trade,   35
And as their wealth increaseth, so enclose
Infinite riches in a little room.
But now, how stands the wind?
Into what corner peers my halcyon's bill?
Ha, to the east? Yes. See, how stands the vanes?   40
East and by south. Why then, I hope my ships
I sent for Egypt and the bordering isles
Are gotten up by Nilus' winding banks;
Mine argosy from Alexandria,
Loaden with spice and silks, now under sail,   45
Are smoothly gliding down by Candy shore
To Malta, through our Mediterranean Sea.
But who comes here?

Like *Doctor Faustus*, *The Jew of Malta* opens with the protagonist seated at a table, poring over a book. Faustus sits amidst his stacks of scholarly tomes while Barabas, the Jew of Malta, is to be found 'in his counting-house, with heaps of gold before him' (I.i.0, s.d.) studying in minute detail the columns of his accounts. Faustus is in raptures over the symbols of the necromantic spells; Barabas over the entries in his book which detail his latest material acquisitions. The parallels between the two plays can be taken further. Faustus hungrily attacks every field of human knowledge and, disappointed at how little they seem to offer, proceeds to reject each one systematically. Barabas begins with a slow, prosaic reckoning of his latest profits (1–3); the lines are surprisingly naturalistic, and it is easy to imagine Barabas checking the columns of his accounts as he speaks them: '**thus** much **that** return . . . **there** . . .' and so on. However, by the seventh line, he has shifted from careful reckoning to irritable impatience: 'Fie, what a trouble 'tis to count this trash!' Just as Faustus turns his back on the 'paltry legacies' of the study of law (I.i.30), so Barabas rejects 'paltry silverlings' (6) and dreams instead of those who deal with the more precious commodity of gold, the Arabians (8), the 'merchants of the Indian mines' (19), the 'wealthy Moor' (21). Later, when his daughter retrieves his hidden resources of gold from his confiscated house he will be in raptures once more over 'My gold, my fortune, my felicity, / Strength to my soul, death to mine enemy!' (II.i.48–9). In this opening soliloquy, as his imagination catches hold, the verse moves into an extraordinary flight of fancy, a vision of a cascade of precious stones: ' . . . opals, sapphires, amethysts, / Jacinths, hard topaz, grass-green emeralds, / Beauteous rubies, sparkling diamonds' (25–7).

The speech is rich in detail, its language sensuous and visually evocative, its geography remarkably exotic ('those Samnites and the men of Uz' [4], 'Spanish oils and wines of Greece' [5], 'Arabians' [8], 'Indian mines' [19]). The sense of precise itemizing and reckoning underpins the movement of the verse, and it concludes with a beautifully compact image that has become one of Marlowe's most famous lines: Barabas's advice to 'men of judgement' is that they should ignore the 'vulgar trade' and instead concentrate on the more refined forms of wealth he has identified, and thereby 'enclose / Infinite riches in a little room' (36–7). Marlowe's poetry is remarkably physical, too, in this speech: phrases such as 'wedge of gold' (9), and the description of the 'needy groom that never fingered groat' (12) with its pinched vowels and repeated hard 'g' sounds, are particularly expressive. Elsewhere, the metrical variations serve different purposes: the barrage of heavy stresses in '**steel-barred coff**ers are **crammed full**' sound as strong and densely packed as the boxes they describe (14), and there is a powerful impression of a mountain of precious jewels being amassed in the crowd of accented syllables in 'And in his house heap pearl like pebble-stones' (23).

This is another substantial soliloquy, almost as long as the one that begins *Doctor Faustus*. It works not only to establish Barabas's defining characteristic (his avarice), although it certainly achieves that, too. What is more important is its evocation of a particular atmosphere. Within the next hundred lines, Barabas's elaborate fantasies and his gloating over news of the success of his latest ventures will be swept away by developments on Malta itself that threaten his prosperity, and which will ultimately rob him of all he possesses. This opening soliloquy has placed material wealth firmly at the centre of the drama. It is around human greed that the narrative will play itself out and in the course of the performance we will be exposed to a harsh stereotype of an avaricious, murderous Jew, as well as the unmasking of the hypocrisy of a Christian governor (Ferneze) and revelations about Catholic friars, who we will find are subject to the same weaknesses (greed, lust, envy) as the rest of humankind.

Edward II, I.i.1–23, 50–72

Edward II is the only one of Marlowe's major plays that does not open with a prologue. It is also the one that seems to have made the most significant progress in terms of its 'realism'. We have moved on from the intersecting natural and supernatural realms of *Faustus* and have left behind the cartoon-like stereotypes that populate *The Jew of Malta*. *Tamburlaine* shows flashes of realism, but it is not until we reach *Edward II* that we (as twenty-first century audience or readers) find ourselves encountering *dramatis personae* that seem to 'breathe', who show some level of complexity in their relationships with other characters and who seem to have a sense of themselves as autonomous beings. (There is also a sense of this happening in *The Massacre at Paris*, although the poor remnant of a text that we have inherited makes it difficult to assess this with any degree of accuracy.)

Enter Gaveston reading on a letter that was brought him from
the King

GAVESTON   [*reads*] 'My father is deceased; come, Gaveston,
And share the kingdom with thy dearest friend.'
Ah, words that make me surfeit with delight!
What greater bliss can hap to Gaveston
Than live and be the favourite of a king?   5
Sweet prince, I come; these, these thy amorous lines
Might have enforced me to have swum from France
And like Leander gasped upon the sand,
So thou wouldst smile and take me in thy arms.
The sight of London to my exiled eyes   10
Is as Elysium to a new-come soul –
Not that I love the city or the men,
But that it harbours him I hold so dear,
The king, upon whose bosom let me die
And with the world be still at enmity.   15
What need the arctic people love starlight,
To whom the sun shines both by day and night?
Farewell, base stooping to the lordly peers;
My knee shall bow to none but to the king.
As for the multitude, that are but sparks   20
Raked up in embers of their poverty,
Tanti; I'll fawn first on the wind
That glanceth at my lips and flieth away.
[. . .]
I must have wanton poets, pleasant wits,   50
Musicians that with touching of a string
May draw the pliant king which way I please.
Music and poetry is his delight;
Therefore I'll have Italian masques by night,
Sweet speeches, comedies, and pleasing shows;   55
And in the day, when he shall walk abroad,
Like sylvan nymphs my pages shall be clad;
My men, like satyrs grazing on the lawns,
Shall with their goat feet dance an antic hay.
Sometime a lovely boy in Dian's shape,   60

With hair that gilds the water as it glides,
Crownets of pearl about his naked arms,
And in his sportful hands an olive tree
To hide those parts which men delight to see,
Shall bathe him in a spring, and there hard by   65
One like Actaeon peeping through the grove
Shall by the angry goddess be transformed,
And running in the likeness of an hart
By yelping hounds pulled down and seem to die.
Such things as these best please his majesty,   70
My lord. Here comes the king and the nobles
From the parliament. I'll stand aside.

Edward II marks a move back into the settings of royal courts and battlefields, the territory that *Tamburlaine* occupies. However, it is also a very personal tragedy: *Tamburlaine* has a few, fleeting moments of intimacy, particularly in the relationships between Tamburlaine and Zeoncrate, and Bajazeth and Zabina, the Emperor and Empress of Turkey. *Edward II* takes seriously certain 'live' issues in state politics, particularly the fraught question of when it might be lawful to rebel against one's own monarch. However, one of the key narrative sequences in the play is the relationship between Edward and his male lover Gaveston. Gaveston's opening soliloquy begins with his reading of a couple of lines from a letter he has received from King Edward, recalling him from his exile (1–2). In the following lines, the eroticism that tones his response is fairly evident, although a closer look at the language, and an under-standing of the different connotations certain words carried four hundred years ago, will make this clearer.

The myth that Gaveston refers to when describing his relationship with Edward (6–9) is the legend of Hero and Leander, an ominously tragic story. Leander swims the Hellespont each night to visit his beloved Hero (a woman) at Sestos. When Leander drowns one night Hero, unable to bear her grief, commits suicide. The fact that Gaveston draws this parallel with an heterosexual couple should make it clear to the audience that his relationship with Edward is also of a sexual nature. If any doubts remain, they are dispelled by his use of a familiar *double entendre* in line 14 ('upon whose bosom let me die'). 'Die' was at this time a familiar euphemism for orgasm (the phrase 'gasped upon the sand' [8] carries similar connotations). The homoeroticism is unmistakable in the description of the kinds of entertainment with which Gaveston plans to entertain the king. I discuss briefly in Part 2 the fact that all roles in the Elizabethan theatre, including female ones, were played by male actors, and the text exploits this when Gaveston talks of the pages (male servants) clad like sylvan nymphs (who, according to Greek legend, are female). The 'lovely boy in Dian's shape' (the Greek goddess Diana) is described as hiding 'those parts which men delight to see' (60, 64) and the playful ambiguity over gender identity means that exactly *what* parts men 'delight to see' is left deliberately, mischievously unspecified. Gaveston also makes suggestive references to the boy's 'naked arms' and 'sportful hands' (62, 63). The reference to Actaeon draws on another Greek legend. Actaeon was a hunter who saw the goddess Diana bathing. As a consequence, he was turned into a stag and then torn to pieces by hunting dogs. As he is pulled down by 'yelping hounds', he 'seem[s] to die' (69): once again, the wordplay on the euphemism for sexual climax is inescapable.

Gaveston's fantasies of a reunion with Edward are swept along on a surging tide of verse, particularly in the Hero and Leander parallel (climaxing with 'gasped upon the sand' (6–8), and 'upon whose bosom let me die' (14). At both points, at the ends of lines 8 and 14, the movement of the verse is momentarily suspended, before each of the two sentences are completed in the following lines (9 and 15). In the description of the entertainment, the rhythm is once again put to good use: there is a noticeable spring in the verse of lines like 'Sweet speeches, comedies, and pleasing shows' (55) and 'with their goat feet dance an antic hay' (59). In other places, the complex variations on rhythm achieve other effects, as in the *rallantando* of 'By yelping hounds **pulled down** and **seem** to **die**' (69). The 'lovely boy in Dian's shape' is evocatively described as having 'hair that gilds the water as it glides', enhanced by the smooth metre and the wordplay of 'gilds' and 'glides' (61).

The stage is set, then, for a personal tragedy that is intricately bound up with the political dimension – the latter is inevitable in a play about a king, although it is also clear that the private drama will be as significant as the political one. Furthermore, the potentially controversial subject of a homoerotic relationship (and, what is more, a relationship between a king and his subject) has been broached. One final note concerns Gaveston himself. The soliloquy is interrupted by the arrival of three beggars, whom Gaveston at first dismisses out of hand before relenting, promising he will do what he can for them, then turning back to the audience with the words, 'These are not men for me', as they shuffle off the stage (49). (The short dialogue between Gaveston and the paupers has been omitted in the extract reprinted above.) Here we are alerted to Gaveston's potential for hypocrisy and we may be inclined to think a little more carefully about what is motivating him in his elaborate plans to entertain the king – he declares that

> I must have wanton poets, pleasant wits,
> Musicians that with touching of a string
> May draw the pliant king which way I please.
>
> (50–2)

As we shall see, the extent of Edward's love for Gaveston is not in dispute. Whether it is requited in equal measure is less certain, and there is room here for interpretation by director and actors in a performance context.

Conclusions

The opening prologues and scenes are, of course, vital to the plays' effectiveness. We have considered the use of a particular convention, the prologue, and seen how it functions in relation to the rest of the play, and in particular to the first scene of each play. The use of the character Machiavel in *The Jew of Malta* helps to establish the credentials of the Jew Barabas and sets in motion a curious, continuously shifting relationship between the protagonist and his audience. In *Faustus* the Chorus establishes the shape of the play before it starts, and we are given a view of Faustus from a specific moral and religious perspective which will inevitably colour our impression of him when he appears in the first scene. *Tamburlaine's* prologue acts more as an advertisement for the playwright himself, as he announces himself to the theatre-going London public. It also sets the tone for the play – the epic, historical mode that the *Tamburlaine* narrative requires. With *Edward II*, Marlowe discards traditional Chorus-led prologues and instead uses a character – Gaveston – to set the scene. This seems appropriate for the kind of drama *Edward II* is: an historical tragedy with a significant private and personal dimension.

Methods of Analysis

1. We have used a number of different kinds of analysis to explore the prologues and opening scenes of these four plays. We have started to trace the 'shapes' of the drama as they are prefigured in the prologues, and considered genre in relation to this: tragedy has a distinct pattern that each of these plays follows. *Tamburlaine* announces itself as a serious, historical drama, and stakes a claim as a dramatized *Mirror for Magistrates*, showing in a 'tragic glass' the fortunes of a great political leader. Its second part foregrounds the arc from prosperity to calamity that the tragic genre demands.

2. We have also considered aspects of language and verse in some detail, and noticed how Marlowe is able to express some of the meaning of his lines through the movement of the verse, or by careful choice of words. This has also alerted us to some of the difficulties inherent in reading four-hundred-year-old plays; there are some connotations familiar to Elizabethans which are lost to us now. So, for example, in the soliloquy that opens *Edward II*, Gaveston considers his love for Edward and then proceeds to plan entertainment to please the king. The subtleties of double meanings in his speech reveal the homoerotic nature of their relationship, and the decadent sport he devises perhaps acts as an early indication of the way in which their love affair will be seen by others: as a self-centred indulgence on the part of the king which blinds him to his political responsibilities.

3. Finally, we have discussed some of the ideological implications of Marlowe's work, in particular the Protestant/Catholic conflict, very much a 'live' issue at the time the plays were written. In addition, we have touched on the very sensitive issue of anti-Semitism, and have discovered something of the chasm of cultural difference that has opened up between us and the writers, performers and audiences of Elizabethan England that first encountered these plays.

Suggested Work

Although we have looked at the opening scene of each play, this does not in every case mark the first appearance of the play's protagonist. We have seen that the things Mycetes, Menander and Cosroe say about Tamburlaine set up audience expectations, some of which will be fulfilled while others may be overturned. Take a look at Tamburlaine's first appearance in act I scene ii, paying particular attention to the way in which others on stage respond to him. Also, try to imagine the visual impact he might have in the scene, and compare his entrance to the first appearance of Mycetes in act I scene i. It is also worth looking at act II scene i of *Tamburlaine I* and analysing in detail Menaphon's description of him as a terrifying demi-god (I.ii.7–49).

In *Faustus* it may be useful to look at the first appearance by the other major 'character', Mephistopheles (I.iii.22.s.d.). The intervening scene is also fascinating (I.ii). This conversation between two scholars functions as a kind of Chorus, commenting on the action so far and giving voice, perhaps, to some of the fears a contemporary audience may have felt: noticing that he keeps company with the sorcerors Valdes and Cornelius, the First Scholar fears 'he [Faustus] is fall'n into that damned art for which they two are infamous throughout the world' (I.ii.30–1). In the same scene, notice how Wagner's mischievous wordplay works as a kind of ironic echo of Faustus's ostentatious learning. The use of Wagner and other minor characters in this way will be commented on in greater detail later.

The Jew of Malta's other key character is the Christian governor Ferneze, and the first staged encounter between him and Barabas is a thrilling one (I.ii.38ff). We will consider these two characters in relation to each other shortly, but act I scene ii is crucial in shifting the ground in terms of the audience's response to Barabas. The shameless hypocrisy of the Christians and their persecution of the Jewish community may have been seen as reprehensible by a contemporary audience: it certainly strikes us that way today. However, it is just as likely that the audience would have found it quite acceptable, and this issue once again alerts us to the significance of historical context when considering something like anti-Semitism.

Finally, we should look at Edward's first appearance in his play (I.i.72,s.d.). He is, from his entrance, quarrelsome, imperious, and unashamed of the way he prioritizes his relationship with Gaveston above all other concerns. This first scene is fraught with the tension that crackles between the king and his barons. Gaveston is caught in the middle, and the scenario that is enacted in this scene will recur many times, as the situation spirals out of control and the nation descends into civil war.

2

Heroes and Anti-Heroes

One of the greatest challenges that Marlowe's plays present is their tendency to centre the narratives around awkward central characters. We discuss Shakespeare's protagonists fairly straightforwardly as heroes: tragic heroes like Macbeth, Hamlet and Othello; comic or romantic heroes like Benedict (*Much Ado About Nothing*) and Petruchio (*The Taming of the Shrew*). Marlowe's protagonists wear the label much less comfortably. As the 'first impressions' discussed in the previous chapter should have made clear, all of Marlowe's protagonists (Tamburlaine, Barabas, Faustus and Edward) set up ambiguous, complex relationships with their audiences. The cruelty of Tamburlaine, the vicious self-seeking of Barabas, the blind arrogance of Faustus; these are characteristics that tend to alienate us. Accustomed as we are to enjoying a play via some kind of sympathetic engagement with the protagonist, an initial encounter with a Marlovian hero can repel us and leave us somewhat bewildered, 'shut out' in some sense from the action of the play. In some cases, the vices of a protagonist can open that character up to us. Perhaps in the fond silliness of Lear, in the agonizing prevarication of Hamlet, we recognise their flawed humanity, and find a way in to a character whose circumstances might otherwise seem alien to us. But the vices of a Marlovian 'hero' are both monumental and fundamental: those vices tend to be each character's *raison d'être*, and they are built on the grandest scale. For this reason (and with only a few exceptions), Marlovian heroes stand apart from us, to be observed with curiosity, bafflement, wonder or dread. They do not tend to invite any kind of 'identification' and understanding or 'sympathy', except in momentary flashes.

In some ways, it is more appropriate to consider them as anti-heroes. Certainly Barabas fits much more easily into this category. We have already noted how he functions as a kind of Elizabethan bugbear, a composite creation of Jewish stereotype and Machiavellian hate figure. Although, as we have seen, he manages to raise difficult questions about Christian civilization at the same time, this does not help to make him any more accessible. On the contrary, his awkwardness in this sense would most likely have provoked an increased sense of discomfort, at least amongst those whose *mores* he may have been seen to challenge. At the same time, we should acknowledge that his subversive power may have been appreciated by others less concerned with preserving the *status quo*. Certainly many contemporary critics like to cast Barabas in this light – as a subversive figure challenging the established order, rather than just as a hate figure inciting the anti-Semitic feeling that was evidently close to the surface in Elizabethan society. Edward and Faustus, as we shall see during the course of this study, are perhaps more ambivalent figures in respect of 'sympathy'; Tamburlaine, on the other hand, is closer to Barabas, although for the most part he lacks the latter's comic edge. It is Tamburlaine we shall look at in more detail first.

Tamburlaine I, V.i.64–134

This incident, placed towards the end of the first *Tamburlaine* play, ranks as one of Marlowe's most shocking scenes. The massacre of the Virgins of Damascus seems to have been adapted from one or more of Marlowe's sources: there is a reference, for example, to an unspecified city besieged by Tamburlaine's forces whose governor sent out a long procession of boys and girls dressed in white and carrying olive branches, begging for mercy. According to the source, the sight provoked in Tamburlaine nothing but fury, and he immediately ordered his cavalry to charge and trample the children to death. Elsewhere, the same source mentions Damascus as a city attacked, captured and looted – but only at great cost to Tamburlaine's own forces (something Marlowe does not pick up on). Marlowe has taken the story of the massacre of the children and sharpened its pathos by devoting a considerable amount of stage-time to it, and allowing the virgins their own voice in pleading for mercy.

> *Exeunt [all except the Virgins. Enter] Tamburlaine, Techelles,*
> *Theridamas, Usumcasane, with others; Tamburlaine all in black,*
> *and very melancholy. [The Virgins make obeisance]*

TAMBURLAINE   What, are the turtles frayed out of their nests?
    Alas, poor fools, must you be first shall feel   65
    The sworn destruction of Damascus?
    They know my custom. Could they not as well
    Have sent ye out when first my milk-white flags
    Through which sweet mercy threw her gentle beams,
    Reflexing them on your disdainful eyes,   70
    As now when fury and incensèd hate
    Flings slaughtering terror from my coal-black tents
    And tells for truth submissions comes too late?
FIRST VIRGIN   Most happy king and emperor of the earth,
    Image of honour and nobility,   75
    For whom the powers divine have made the world
    And on whose throne the holy Graces sit,
    In whose sweet person is comprised the sum
    Of nature's skill and heavenly majesty:
    Pity our plights, O, pity poor Damascus!   80
    Pity old age, within whose silver hairs
    Honour and reverence evermore have reigned!
    Pity the marriage bed, where many a lord,
    In prime and glory of his loving joy,
    Embraceth now with tears of ruth and blood   85
    The jealous body of his fearful wife,
    Whose cheeks and hearts – so punished with conceit
    To think thy puissant never-stayèd arm
    Will part their bodies and prevent their souls
    From heavens of comfort yet their age might bear –   90
    Now wax all pale and withered to the death,

As well for grief our ruthless governor
Have thus refused the mercy of thy hand
(Whose sceptre angels kiss and Furies dread)
As for their liberties, their loves, or lives.   95
O then, for these, and such as we ourselves,
For us, for infants, and for all our bloods,
That never nourished thought against thy rule,
Pity, O, pity, sacred emperor,
The prostrate service of this wretched town;   100
And take in sign thereof this gilded wreath
Whereto each man of rule hath given his hand
And wished, as worthy subjects, happy means
To be investors of thy royal brows,
Even with the true Egyptian diadem.   105
                          [She offers a laurel wreath]
TAMBURLAINE   Virgins, in vain ye labour to prevent
    That which mine honour swears shall be performed.
    Behold my sword. What see you at the point?
VIRGINS   Nothing but fear and fatal steel, my lord.
TAMBURLAINE   Your fearful minds are thick and misty, then,   110
    For there sits Death, there sits imperious Death.
    Keeping his circuit by the slicing edge.
    But I am pleased you shall not see him them there;
    He now is seated on my horsemen's spears,
    And on their points his fleshless body feeds.   115
    Techelles, straight go charge a few of them
    To charge these dames, and show my servant Death,
    Sitting in scarlet on their armèd spears.
ALL THE VIRGINS   O, pity us!
TAMBURLAINE   Away with them, I say, and show them Death!   120
             [Techelles and others] take them away
    I will not spare these proud Egyptians
    Nor change my martial observations
    For all the wealth of Gihon's golden waves,
    Or for the love of Venus, would she leave
    The angry god of arms and lie with me.   125
    They have refused the offer of their lives,

And know my customs are as peremptory
As wrathful planets, death, or destiny.
                    Enter Techelles
What, have your horsemen shown the virgins Death?
TECHELLES   They have, my lord, and on Damascus' walls   130
Have hoisted up their slaughtered carcasses.
TAMBURLAINE   A sight as baneful to their souls, I think,
As are Thessalian drugs or mithridate.
But go, my lords. Put the rest to the sword.
                    Exeunt [all except Tamburlaine]

The extract begins with a startling stage direction. Stage directions
tend to lie thin on the ground in early modern play-texts, and when
they are present, they seldom indicate much more than entrances
and exits and essential stage business. *Tamburlaine* has a couple of
much fuller directions, both of which are interesting for the way in
which they give a firm steer to a director and her actors. So, when
the Virgins of Damascus are abandoned on-stage by the governor of
their city they are alone for a moment, huddled together, stranded,
awaiting Tamburlaine's arrival. When he does appear, attended by
his followers, the stage directions tell us that he is '*all in black, and
very melancholy*'. His black garb is in keeping with a custom that the
play has established (and which is also drawn from Marlowe's
sources): in act IV scene i, a messenger reports that Tamburlaine uses
three colours for his tents and banners. On the first day, white tents
and crests indicate that an offer of immediate surrender will be
accepted mercifully. One the second day, the white banners and
tents are exchanged for red, meaning that only those who do not
bear arms will be spared. Finally, the red is replaced by black: on that
third day, the messenger warns, 'Without respect of sex, degree, or
age, / He razeth all his foes with fire and sword' (IV.i.62–3).

The colour of his costume, no doubt mirrored by his retinue,
reminds an alert audience of Tamburlaine's colour-coded battle campaign (and it also contrasts starkly with the white robes of the
Damascan Virgins). When we bear in mind that we already have
plentiful evidence of Tamburlaine's implacable will, we can predict
fairly confidently that the Virgins are doomed even before they

begin their formal plea. If we have forgotten the significance of his costume, Tamburlaine himself reminds us in the first lines of the extract, contrasting his 'milk-white flags' with his 'coal-black tents'. 'Sweet mercy' which 'threw her gentle beams' through white flags is set against 'fury and incensed hate' which 'flings slaughtering terror from my coal-black tents' (68–72). There is something like tenderness in Tamburlaine's exclamation, 'What, are the turtles frayed out of their nests?' ('turtles' meaning turtle-doves) (64). The simple line 'They know my custom', referring to the rulers of the city, can be interpreted as businesslike and matter of fact, as an expression of puzzlement, or as an exasperated cry, and each interpretation will shed a different light on Tamburlaine.

The First Virgin's plea, some thirty lines long, is formal and measured, lending the impression that it has been carefully scripted. The imprecation begins with a recognition of Tamburlaine, elevating him to near-divine status: he is one 'For whom the powers divine have made the world' (76). Later in the speech, the First Virgin refers to his sceptre that 'angels kiss and Furies dread' (94). The reference to the Furies implies Tamburlaine is a revenger, and draws on the notion of the scourge of God (discussed in more detail on pp. 84–5). For the audience, the lines are sour with irony: for the all-conquering Tamburlaine, the title of 'king and emperor of the earth' (74) may seem like an appropriate title, but 'Image of honour and nobility' (75) is grotesquely inappropriate; 'sweet person' even more so (78).

The speech is built around a refrain that pleads for 'pity': the Virgin solicits pity for 'our plights', for Damascus (80), for old age (81), for the married couples of the city (83–91) and even 'our ruthless governor' (92–4). The speech works by its pictorial, evocative detail. The use of 'silver hairs' for old age is woodenly conventional, but the description of the husband embracing 'the jealous body of his fearful wife' ('jealous' here meaning anxious) their 'cheeks and hearts . . . wax[ing] all pale and withered to the death' is an arresting image (83–92). Unfortunately, the lines that are sectioned off by the dashes form a parenthesis that hampers this part of the speech; it may be easier to catch the sense by skipping from 'cheeks and hearts' (87a) to 'Now wax all pale . . .' (91), returning afterwards to the parenthesis. These lines are simply describing the fear of the lord and his wife: that Tamburlaine will part them and kill them, thus depriving them of the comforts they might expect in old age. The wreath they offer is a sign of victory, a belated acknowledgement of Tamburlaine as the victor and conqueror of their city. There is something desperate about the Virgin's claim that the wreath has been formally acknowledged by all the rulers of the city as a sign of their submission as 'worthy subjects' of Tamburlaine.

The contrast between the pitiable picture painted by the First Virgin's speech and Tamburlaine's stony implacability is chilling. Tamburlaine's reply starts with a kind of disclaimer – that what is going to happen to the Virgins is provoked not by cruelty but is simply 'That which mine honour swears shall be performed' (107). He draws his weapon ('Behold my sword') and asks the Virgins, 'What see you at the point?' (108). When they reply that they see 'Nothing but fear and fatal steel', Tamburlaine corrects them with one of the most striking speeches in the play. 'Your fearful minds are thick and misty, then,' he chides, 'For there sits Death, there sits imperious Death, / Keeping his circuit by the slicing edge' (110–12). This is a graphic portrayal of Tamburlaine's brutality, as well as his belief in his control over life and death. He understands Death to be one who serves him: the reference to 'circuit' forms a metaphor that compares the arc described by his sword to that of a judge, who travels within a certain area ('circuit') to officiate at local courts. According to Tamburlaine, Death is 'my servant' (117), awaiting his orders, depicted 'seated on my horsemen's spears', and 'on their points his fleshless body feeds' (114–15). The image recalls of course the traditional emblem of death, the skeleton, but the phrase 'fleshless body feeds' is a terrifying one, conveying as it does the sense of death as an insatiable force; the further refinement of the picture ('Sitting in scarlet on their armèd spears') of course anticipates blood, and reinforces the sense of Death as being under Tamburlaine's control.

Any further attempts to plead for mercy are cut off: the unison cry 'O, pity us!' (119) is shouted down by Tamburlaine's order for them to be taken away. The expression of resolve is familiar:

Tamburlaine's reference points are 'wrathful planets, death, or destiny' (128). He also talks of Venus, Roman goddess of love, vowing that he would not swerve from his determined course if Venus herself should leave her lover Mars to lie with him (Mars, god of war, is one whom Tamburlaine challenges in rhetorical fashion on several occasions during the course of the two plays). The reference to Venus actually reminds us of Zenocrate: there is an easy parallel to be drawn between Venus and Mars, and Zenocrate and Tamburlaine himself (the governor of Damascus refers to Tamburlaine as 'this man, or rather god of war' at the beginning of the scene [V.i.1.]). Damascus is Zenocrate's own city, and she has already pleaded with him to have mercy on its inhabitants (I, IV.iv.65–94). Tamburlaine at that time promised to spare her father (the Sultan) and his family, and immediately after he has given order for the slaughter of the Virgins, he remembers his vow and, after a lengthy soliloquy (I, V.i.135–90), establishes that he will indeed save the Sultan. Before this, we are told that the massacre has been carried out, and that Tamburlaine's soldiers have 'on Damascus' walls . . . hoisted up their slaughtered carcasses' (130–1). The fact that the killing takes place offstage, for obvious reasons, does not necessarily weaken the dramatic moment. A production is likely to include the sounds of screams; certainly the 1992 Royal Shakespeare Company version, cannily casting pre-teenage girls as the company of Virgins, was harrowing enough: as the order was given for the children to be taken away a chorus of screams, wails and weeping ensued, and Zenocrate tried in vain to intervene (a liberty on the part of the director, since she is not present at the time, according to the stage directions).

Tamburlaine, probably even more so than Barabas, remains a dramatic character very alien to his audience. For Elizabethans, still aware of the threat posed by the threat of Islam in the East, he would in any case have been a figure inspiring a degree of fear and hostility. Our inability to feel 'sympathy' for Tamburlaine is built largely upon our perceptions of his brutality, and the massacre at Damascus provides no better illustration of that brutality given full rein.

Doctor Faustus, I.iii.45–101

In this crucial scene, Faustus has just conjured Mephistopheles, summoning him from hell. The six or seven lines of Latin that comprise
the spell (I.iii.16–22) mix Jewish, Christian and classical theology.
Mephistopheles has appeared in his own shape, a sight too terrible
for Faustus to behold and, with an incidental side-swipe at
Catholicism, Faustus has ordered him to return as 'an old Franciscan
friar' since 'That holy shape becomes a devil best' (I.iii.25–6). He
has marvelled at the 'virtue' in his 'heavenly words' (27), apparently
unaware of the irony of describing a spell conjuring a devil in these
terms. This lack of self-awareness is one of the keys to unlock this
persona; it is not necessarily a signifier of 'character', something we
can understand as a psychological trait. However, Faustus's failure to
understand the implications of his words and actions throughout the
play is crucial to the way in which the narrative operates. The irony
of this is intensified by his tendency to talk about himself in the
third person using 'Faustus' and 'he', rather than 'I'. Although it is
not very unusual to find characters referring to themselves in the
third person in plays of this period, it is remarkable how frequently
Faustus does choose this mode of address. In his case, the lines can
sound over-rhetorical and self-regarding, often self-aggrandizing. At
the same time, he remains astoundingly ignorant of his predicament.

FAUSTUS   Did not my conjuring speeches raise thee? Speak.   45
MEPHISTOPHELES   That was the cause, but yet *per accidens.*
    For when we hear one rack the name of God,
    Abjure the Scriptures and his Saviour Christ,
    We fly in hope to get his glorious soul,
    Nor will we come unless he use such means   50
    Whereby he is in danger to be damned.
    Therefore, the shortest cut for conjuring
    Is stoutly to abjure the Trinity
    And pray devoutly to the prince of hell.
FAUSTUS   So Faustus hath   55
    Already done, and holds this principle:
    There is no chief but only Beelzebub,

To whom Faustus doth dedicate himself.
This word 'damnation' terrifies not him,
For he confounds hell in Elysium. 60
His ghost be with the old philosophers!
But leaving these vain trifles of men's souls,
Tell me what is that Lucifer thy lord?
MEPHISTOPHELES   Arch-regent and commander of all spirits.
FAUSTUS   Was not that Lucifer an angel once? 65
MEPHISTOPHELES   Yes, Faustus, and most dearly loved of God.
FAUSTUS   How comes it then that he is prince of devils?
MEPHISTOPHELES   O, by aspiring pride and insolence,
   For which God threw him from the face of heaven.
FAUSTUS   And what are you that live with Lucifer? 70
MEPHISTOPHELES   Unhappy spirits that fell with Lucifer,
   Conspired against our God with Lucifer,
   And are for ever damned with Lucifer.
FAUSTUS   Where are you damned?
MEPHISTOPHELES   In hell. 75
FAUSTUS   How comes it then that thou art out of hell?
MEPHISTOPHELES   Why, this is hell, nor am I out of it.
   Think'st thou that I, who saw the face of God
   And tasted the eternal joys of heaven,
   Am not tormented with ten thousand hells 80
   In being deprived of everlasting bliss?
   O Faustus, leave these frivolous demands,
   Which strike a terror to my fainting soul!
FAUSTUS   What, is great Mephistopheles so passionate
   For being deprivèd of the joys of heaven? 85
   Learn thou of Faustus manly fortitude,
   And scorn those joys thou never shalt possess.
   Go bear these tidings to great Lucifer:
   Seeing Faustus hath incurred eternal death
   By desp'rate thoughts against Jove's deity, 90
   Say he surrenders up to him his soul,
   So he will spare him four-and-twenty years,
   Letting him live in all voluptuousness,
   Having thee ever to attend on me,

To give me whatsoever I shall ask,   95
To tell me whatsoever I demand,
To slay mine enemies and aid my friends,
And always be obedient to my will.
Go and return to mighty Lucifer,
And meet me in my study at midnight,   100
And them resolve me of thy master's mind.

For his re-appearance, Mephistopheles returns in the garb of a friar, and his first line is plain and matter of fact: 'Now, Faustus, what wouldst thou have me do?' (35). Faustus's response is, as we would expect, a grand and sweeping gesture at omnipotence, demanding that Mephistopheles do whatever he commands. Faustus's ambition encompasses power over the forces of nature, using two feats that were familiar from classical literature about magicians: 'mak[ing] the moon drop from her sphere . . . the ocean to overwhelm the world' (38–9). Mephistopheles's reply undercuts him immediately. Faustus assumes that this evil spirit will be his servant, but Mephistopheles coolly sets the record straight: 'I am a servant to great Lucifer / And may not follow thee without his leave' (40–1). Faustus is stumped, and each time he attempts to reassert his mastery, he is stymied by Mephistopheles's assertions of autonomy; 'I came hither of mine own accord', Mephistopheles announces (44) and, asked if he was raised by Faustus's spells, he responds that 'That was the cause, but yet *per accidens*' (46). The latter term comes from scholastic tradition, and draws a distinction between agents that themselves bring about a certain effect, and incidents that allow another external agency to operate. What Mephistopheles is saying is that he has come not as a direct result of the conjuration, but rather that he has chosen to respond to an opportunity that has presented itself via the conjuration. He remains firmly, stubbornly autonomous. As he goes on to explain further, it is the opportunity to seize Faustus's soul that has stirred him to action.

Mephistopheles's quiet insolence gives the lie to Faustus's confidence, expressed moments earlier as he awaited the Devil's return and marvelled at how 'pliant' he seemed to be: 'Full of obedience and humility!' (29–30). Faustus interpreted this as proof of his power: 'Such is the force of magic and my spells' (31). However, while Faustus understands conjuring as something that invests him with the power to control, Mephistopheles inverts the equation: the quickest way to conjure, he says, is simply to 'abjure [renounce] the Trinity / And pray devoutly to the prince of hell' (53–4). When a man does this, he risks his own salvation, and the devils 'fly in hope to get his glorious soul' (49), a hauntingly predatory turn of phrase.

That little scholastic term, *per accidens*, is crucial, a key to understanding how the initiative rests with the Devil, not with Faustus. But Faustus is oblivious. Although Mephistopheles repeatedly counters his assertions of control, Faustus persists in his familiar, haughty, foolish pride, and this extends to his understanding of the theological implications of his words and deeds. The word 'damnation', he asserts, does not terrify him, 'For he confounds hell in Elysium' (Faustus, using the pronoun 'he', is talking about himself here, a good example of his use of the third person). The talk of hell and Elysium would have caught the attention of an Elizabethan audience, since it is clearly blasphemous. What Faustus is claiming is that there is no distinction ('confounds') between Christian hell (which implies punishment for sins committed on earth that have not been forgiven) and the Elysian fields of classical mythology, where the afterlife is imagined as a paradise (the word 'Elysian' means 'delightful'). He continues with his cavalier rejection of orthodox belief by imagining his spirit being destined to join 'the old philosophers' – the classical (pre-Christian) philosophers such as Plato and Aristotle – and sets a seal on it with a provocatively dismissive rejection of all talk of souls and salvation, 'But leaving these vain trifles of men's souls' (62) choosing instead to demand more knowledge of Mephistopheles's lord, Lucifer.

It is at moments like this that the text comes closest to the Greek tragic model of *hubris*, where the presumptuous human ignores the warnings of the gods and, following his aspiring will, proceeds to transgress divine laws. Finally, he or she is punished for their insolence and pride. In the case of Faustus, of course, we are working within the Christian paradigm, and this makes it more complex. What is crucial, as we shall see at the climax of the play, is Faustus's belief that his sins are finally unforgivable. Having rejected God and embraced the Devil, faced with imminent damnation, his earlier rejection of Christian doctrine is replaced by an unshakable belief that his sins have been so enormous that he has put himself beyond God's grace. This is the sin of presumption – the belief that Christ's death, intended as a ransom for all sinful humankind, cannot atone for the grievous sins he has committed. In this sense, if we accept Marlowe's use of a classical model for a Christian narrative, Faustus provides perhaps the most extreme example of *hubris* one could imagine.

Faustus's ignorance or willful blindness is put into sharper relief by the story Mephistopheles tells of Lucifer – that he became the prince of all devils for 'aspiring pride and insolence, / For which God threw him from the face of heaven' (68–9). The audience would by now be well aware that this is precisely what Faustus is doing himself: endangering his immortal soul. However, there seems to be a fundamental failure of logic on Faustus's part and, given this failure, his inability to match Lucifer's experience to his own is unsurprising. Happily dismissing talk of damnation, he is ready simultaneously to dedicate himself to Lucifer, the prince of that hell he says he 'confounds . . . in Elysium' (60). A little later he talks quite explicitly of his damnation, acknowledging that 'Faustus hath incurred eternal death / By desp'rate thoughts against Jove's deity' (89–90). In this context, when he admonishes Mephistopheles to 'Learn thou of Faustus manly fortitude' in scorning a lost paradise (86), Faustus seems to be parading not so much courage as blind stupidity.

This patronizing attitude towards Mephistopheles is provoked by a conversation in which Faustus questions Mephistopheles more closely about hell. When he asks him how he can be out of hell if he is, as he claims, perpetually damned, the reply is chilling: 'Why, this is hell, nor am I out of it' (77). For Mephistopheles, the torture of hell is contingent upon his awareness of the 'eternal joys of heaven' (79); the torment derives from the memory of the 'everlasting bliss' (81) he enjoyed before he conspired and fell with Lucifer. Even what may strike us as a sudden lapse on Mephistopheles's part, a cracking of that cold, controlled tone, fails to alert Faustus to the gravity of his situation: having endured this interrogation on the subject of hell, Mephistopheles suddenly implores Faustus to 'leave these frivolous demands, / Which strike a terror to my fainting soul!' (82–3). There are several options for the delivery of these lines in performance, but Faustus's response – 'What, is great Mephistopheles so passionate / For being deprivèd of the joys of heaven?' (84–5) – implies that the Devil is unable to hide the fear and remorse that the talk of heaven and hell has provoked.

Faustus now makes his pact, and it is with characteristic arrogance, and that familiar, blind conviction that he remains in control. He orders Mephistopheles to bear a message to 'great Lucifer', offering his soul in exchange for a period of twenty-four years during which Mephistopheles will serve him. Faustus has learned nothing from Mephistopheles's explanation of the relationship between devils and humankind; he remains as convinced of his power as he did when he pronounced himself 'conjurer laureate' after first raising Mephistopheles (32). It is noticeable that Faustus switches from the third to the first person as he reels off his list of demands: 'attend on **me** . . . give **me** . . . tell **me** . . . slay **mine** enemies and aid **my** friends . . . be obedient to **my** will' (94–8). Although we hear mention once or twice of ambitions that extend beyond his own personal gratification, they are few and far between: his talk in the first scene of walling Germany with brass (I.i.90) is replaced by the dream of becoming 'great emperor of the world' (I.iii.105). One of the cruelest ironies of all, which only emerges as the narrative plays out, is the gulf between Faustus's ambitions (as laid out in the early scenes) and what he actually learns and achieves. As the play proceeds, we shall see his desire to seek out forbidden knowledge frustrated by Mephistopheles's refusals and evasions, and his dreams of performing feats to astound the world reduced to party tricks and practical jokes.

The Jew of Malta, II.iii.164–218

This extract from *The Jew of Malta* is significant for a number of reasons. In terms of the progress of the plot, we are introduced here to the Turkish slave Ithamore who will become Barabas's sidekick and partner in crime. Barabas has just purchased Ithamore, one of a troop of Greek, Turkish and African slaves owned by Admiral Martin del Bosco. Ferneze, Christian governor of Malta, has allowed del Bosco to sell his slaves on the island on the condition that the admiral helps him fight the Turkish enemy. Having bought Ithamore, and with the stage cleared, Barabas proceeds to question him about his 'name . . . birth, condition, and profession' (164–5). For our present purposes, the extract is actually more important for what Barabas reveals about himself at this point, as the two of them compare their credentials.

> [*Exeunt Officers with the rest of the Slaves. Barabas and Ithamore remain*]
>
> BARABAS   Now let me know thy name, and therewithal
> Thy birth, condition, and profession.   165
> ITHAMORE   Faith, sir, my birth is but mean, my name's lthamore,
> my profession what you please.
> BARABAS   Hast thou no trade? Then listen to my words,
> And I will teach thee that shall stick by thee.
> First, be thou void of these affections: 170
> Compassion, love, vain hope, and heartless fear.
> Be moved at nothing; see thou pity none,
> But to thyself smile when the Christians moan.
> ITHAMORE   O brave, master, I worship your nose for this!
> BARABAS   As for myself, I walk abroad a-nights   175
> And kill sick people groaning under walls;
> Sometimes I go about and poison wells;
> And now and then, to cherish Christian thieves,
> I am content to lose some of my crowns,
> That I may, walking in my gallery,   180
> See 'em go pinioned along by my door.
> Being young, I studied physic, and began
> To practise first upon the Italian;
> There I enriched the priests with burials,
> And always kept the sexton's arms in ure   185
> With digging graves and ringing dead men's knells.
> And after that was I an engineer,

And in the wars 'twixt France and Germany,
Under pretence of helping Charles the Fifth,
Slew friend and enemy with my stratagems.   190
Then after that was I an usurer,
And with extorting, cozening, forfeiting,
And tricks belonging unto brokery,
I filled the gaols with bankrupts in a year,
And with young orphans planted hospitals,   195
And every moon made some or other mad,
And now and then one hang himself for grief,
Pinning upon his breast a long great scroll
How I with interest tormented him.
But mark how I am blest for plaguing them: 200
I have as much coin as will buy the town.
But tell me now, how hast thou spent thy time?
ITHAMORE   Faith, master,
In setting Christian villages on fire,
Chaining of eunuchs, binding galley slaves.   205
One time I was an ostler in an inn,
And in the night-time secretly would I steal
To travellers' chambers and there cut their throats.
Once at Jerusalem, where the pilgrims kneeled,
I strewèd powder on the marble stones,   210
And therewithal their knees would rankle, so
That I have laughed a-good to see the cripples
Go limping home to Christendom on stilts.
BARABAS   Why, this is something. Make account of me
As of thy fellow; we are villains both.   215
Both circumcisèd, we hate Christians both.
Be true and secret, thou shalt want no gold.
But stand aside, here comes Don Lodowick.

What we are presented with is a Barabas who self-consciously acts out the role of the stereotypical stage villain, with a particular emphasis on his Jewishness. As he begins his virtuoso display, Ithamore exclaims, 'O brave, master, I worship your nose for this!' (174); the actor playing Barabas would most likely have worn a false nose for the role, enforcing the ethnic stereotype. There is another reference later in the play to Barabas as 'bottle-nosed' (III.iii.10). In the speech that follows, the text draws on a familiar set of racial prejudices to create its monstrous protagonist.

Barabas's motivating principle seems to be religious hatred; he exhorts Ithamore to smile to himself 'when the Christians moan' (173), and repeatedly identifies victims of his crimes as Christians. Marlowe draws on current myths about Jews when he has Barabas declare that, 'Sometimes I go about and poison wells' (177): in the middle of the fourteenth century, when Europe was devastated by plague, the massive epidemic was seen as the work of Satan, with Jews operating as his agents. The rumour circulated that Jews were poisoning the water supply and in the aftermath thousands of Jews were burned alive, either at the stake or in their own houses. The familiar close relationship between medicine and the art of the poisoner is also invoked here: 'Being young, I studied physic', Barabas tells Ithamore, and the purposes to which he put his skills are evident ('There I enriched the priests with burials' [182, 184]).

Elsewhere there are the more familiar associations of Jewishness with avarice, and with usury: usury is the loaning of money and charging of interest, a practice which is at the root of capitalist economics, and which is therefore very familiar to us, and taken for granted in the twenty-first century. However, its status in early modern Europe was much more uncertain, for the Christian church, as far back as the twelfth century, had decreed that usury contravened God's law. Since the ban did not apply to practising Jews, they were a convenient source of badly needed credit for the new venture capitalists in prosperous cities across the continent. Shakespeare bases the plot of his play *The Merchant of Venice* on a loan that defaults, the forfeit being a pound of flesh from the body of the Christian merchant who has borrowed money from the Jew Shylock. By the time Marlowe wrote *The Jew of Malta*, a law had been passed in England allowing some carefully controlled lending for interest, and the perception of Jews had subtly shifted, being identified as creditors charging exorbitant rates of interest. Kept on the fringes of Christian European society in ghettoes, they were social outcasts, retained for their economic utility. Barabas talks of driving some of his victims to suicide; the victim would pin 'upon his breast a long great scroll / How I with interest tormented him' (198–9). The speech is rounded off by a final, audacious, self-congratulatory twist, as he remarks on how 'blest' he is 'for plaguing them: / I have as much coin as will buy the town' (200–1). One can almost hear the Elizabethan audiences booing and jeering the stage Jew in a manner akin to a modern audience's reaction to a pantomime villain. An Elizabethan would almost certainly have worked with the assumption that a stage Jew was a figure to be ridiculed, feared and hated. Barabas elicits all of these responses, although at the same time, as we shall see, the real, complex nature of the relationship he builds with his audience means it is rarely this simple.

Marlowe crams a bundle of verbs together in the main speech to characterise Barabas's fiscal practice: the references are to 'extorting, cozening, forfeiting, / And tricks belonging to brokery' (192–3). The sense of overload becomes palpable at this point, with the stacking of repeated 'And's (lines 192, 193, 195, 196, 197) giving the impression of an improvisation motoring out of control. The tone of this monologue, and the dialogue that follows between Barabas and Ithamore, has a darkly comic edge. Part of the humour derives from the ingenious crimes Marlowe has imagined for his villain, and the relish with which Barabas details them. But the lines work mostly via the deliberately poor fit of text and context. The crimes Barabas describes are appalling but the tone in which they are reeled off is morally flippant. The casual phrases that litter the speeches, such as 'As for myself' (175), 'Sometimes I go about' (177), 'And now and then' (197), and the final 'But tell me now, how hast thou spent thy time?' (202), set against the enormity of the havoc he has wreaked, cannot help but provoke laughter.

Ithamore responds with an attempt to outdo Barabas. The hyperbole of his speech is ludicrous, the stories fairly evidently concocted to impress a new master, and, in terms of the theatrical experience, designed to extend the comic dimension of the scene as far as it will stretch. Again, the victims tend to be Christians specifically – he has spent his time 'setting Christian villages on fire' (204) and crippling pilgrims at Jerusalem (209–13). The tone of the speech is breathless (notice the absence of the 'and' one would expect in line 205) and, again, improvisatory: from the list he rattles off in his opening salvo, he moves on to more elaborate stories of slitting travellers' throats (206–8) and poisoning pilgrims (209–13). The hobbled verse of his final two lines here ('That I have laughed a-good to see the cripples / Go limping home to Christendom on stilts') conveys the sense of the lines, and invites the actor to accompany the lines with an imitation of the cripples he is ridiculing.

Barabas is evidently pleased by Ithamore's performance. Whether or not he believes him is immaterial. The response ('Why, this is something' [214]) could as easily be played either as dubious or impressed. The conclusion is what matters: 'Make account of me / As of thy fellow' (214–15). His next lines are probably intended as direct provocation of a roused audience; 'we are villains both', he notes, 'Both circumcisèd, we hate Christians both' (215–16). The passage as a whole represents one of the greatest challenges to critics who would attempt to recuperate the play and defend it against charges of anti-Semitism. Indeed, one of the only ways to short-circuit the argument against the text would be to suggest that its sledgehammer style demands an ironic reading. Although I personally have my doubts about this, and am fairly convinced that much of the play was designed to play off the prejudices of its first audiences, there is potential here to subvert its anti-Semitism by pushing its excesses beyond what can be taken at face value. In Barabas's self-consciousness about his identity as a villain, neatly demonstrated here in his detailed description of his life of crimes against Christianity, there is room for self-parody. In an earlier scene we have seen Barabas on his way to the nunnery to recover some of his hidden treasure, and the self-consciousness of this speech is even more marked (II.i.1–19). Barabas refers to himself here in the third person: ' . . . Vexed and tormented runs poor Barabas / With fatal curses towards these Christians' (II.i.5–6). This is another scene that offers all kinds of opportunities for performance. However it may be used, though, it is fairly intractable material for anyone determined to approach the text with a 'naturalistic' or 'realistic' methodology. Both the opening of act II scene i and the extract under discussion here emphasise the way in which the concept of dramatic character has evolved over the past four hundred years. Barabas is a conglomerate of stereotypes (as Jew, as devil, as Machiavellian), and a persona fulfilling a variety of narrative and conventional theatrical functions (as villain, as protagonist, and so on). However we choose to read, interpret or stage the play, realism is not a viable option.

Edward II, IV.vii.37–98

Barabas rarely provokes the sympathy of his audience, even when he is stripped of his wealth, and the order is given for his house to be confiscated and turned into a nunnery. Even at the lowest ebb of his fortune, Barabas moves swiftly from despair to resolve. Until the final trap he lays is sprung upon himself, he is seldom less than two steps ahead of his opponents, and his dazzling resourcefulness renders the pity of spectators redundant. Edward, on the other hand, is a much more volatile character in terms of his relation to the audience. In some scenes, it can be difficult to see past his arrogance and self-centredness; his treatment of Isabella in particular often strikes us as indefensible. At other points, however, the text seems to be inviting us fairly unequivocally to sympathise with Edward. It is significant that the scene immediately preceding this extract finds Edward's brother, Kent, suffering pangs of remorse for having rebelled against the king. He even calls on God to 'Rain showers of vengeance on my cursèd head', as punishment for 'this unnatural revolt' (IV.vi.7–9). Marlowe departs from his sources here, underlining the significance of Kent's change of heart. The delicate balance in the play between who appears to be right and who appears to be wrong is one of the most intriguing aspects of this complex drama, and the careful placing of Kent's shifting loyalty, together with his demonizing of the rebels ('Mortimer / And Isabel do kiss while they conspire' [4.7.12–13]), prepares us to be more open in our response to the defeated king.

EDWARD   Mortimer! who talks of Mortimer?
    Who wounds me with the name of Mortimer,
    That bloody man? Good father, on thy lap
    Lay I this head, laden with mickle care.   40

           [He rests his head on the Abbot's lap]
      O, might I never open these eyes again,
      Never again lift up this drooping head,
      O, never more lift up this dying heart!
SPENCER   Look up, my lord. Baldock, this drowsiness
      Betides no good; here even we are betrayed.   45
         Enter, with Welsh hooks, [Soldiers,] Rice ap Howell, a
                Mower, and the Earl of Leicester
MOWER   Upon my life, those be the men ye seek.
RICE   Fellow, enough. – My lord, I pray be short,
      A fair commission warrants what we do.
LEICESTER   *[aside]*
      The Queen's commission, urged by Mortimer.
      What cannot gallant Mortimer with the queen?   50
      Alas, see where he sits and hopes unseen
      T'escape their hands that seek to reave his life.
      Too true it is, *Quem dies vidit veniens superbum,*
      Hunc dies vidit fugiens iacentem.
      But, Leicester, leave to grow so passionate,   55
              [To Spencer Junior and Baldock]
      Spencer and Baldock, by no other names
      I arrest you of high treason here.
      Stand not on titles, but obey th'arrest;
      'Tis in the name of Isabel the queen. –
      My lord, why droop you thus ?   60
EDWARD   O day, the last of all my bliss on earth,
      Centre of all misfortune! O my stars!
      Why do you lour unkindly on a king?
      Comes Leicester, then, in Isabella's name
      To take my life, my company from me?   65
      Here, man, rip up this panting breast of mine
      And take my heart in rescue of my friends.
RICE   Away with them.
SPENCER *[To Leicester]*   It may become thee yet
      To let us take our farewell of his grace.
ABBOT   My heart with pity earns to see this sight –   70
      A king to bear these words and proud commands.

EDWARD   Spencer, ah, sweet Spencer, thus then must we part?

SPENCER   We must, my lord; so will the angry heavens.

EDWARD   Nay, so will hell and cruel Mortimer.

    The gentle heavens have not to do in this.   75

BALDOCK   My lord, it is in vain to grieve or storm.

    Here humbly of your grace we take our leaves.

    Our lots are cast; I fear me, so is thine.

EDWARD   In heaven we may, in earth never shall we meet.

    And, Leicester, say, what shall become of us?   80

LEICESTER   Your majesty must go to Killingworth.

EDWARD   'Must'! 'Tis somewhat hard when kings 'must' go.

LEICESTER   Here is a litter ready for your grace

    That waits your pleasure, and the day grows old.

RICE   As good be gone as stay and be benighted.   85

EDWARD   A litter hast thou? Lay me in a hearse,

    And to the gates of hell convey me hence;

    Let Pluto's bells ring out my fatal knell,

    And hags howl for my death at Charon's shore,

    For friends hath Edward none, but these, and these,   90

    And these must die under a tyrant's sword.

RICE   My lord, be going. Care not for these,

    For we shall see them shorter by the heads.

EDWARD   Well, that shall be shall be. Part we must,

    Sweet Spencer; gentle Baldock, part we must.   95

        [*He throws aside his robes*]

    Hence, feignèd weeds! Unfeignèd are my woes.

    Father, farewell. Leicester, thou stay'st for me,

    And go I must. Life, farewell, with my friends.

       Exeunt Edward [guarded] and Leicester

This is a good example of Marlowe's highly imaginative use of his sources. Edward is in flight after his army's defeat at the hands of Mortimer and Isabella's army, and he has taken refuge at Neath Abbey, an episode that Holinshed mentions only briefly in his *Chronicles* (the source names the exact place, Marlowe does not). Here, Edward finds peace and comfort in the arms (quite literally) of the Abbot. In a scene that echoes Shakespeare's *Henry VI Part III*,

Edward marvels, 'Father, this life contemplative is heaven', and sighs, 'O, that I might this life in quiet lead!' (IV.vii.20–1). Earlier, he has denied any sense of responsibility towards his kingdom, asking only for 'some nook or corner left / To frolic with my dearest Gaveston' (I.iv.72–3). In that context, it had sounded like reprehensible, childish recklessness. Here, with Edward's kingship undoubtedly caught in an irrecoverable tailspin, his desire to be free of its burden is readily understood.

Simply hearing the name of Mortimer tortures Edward. There is something masochistic about his response, twisting the knife in his own flesh as he exclaims, 'Mortimer! Who talks of Mortimer? / Who wounds me with the name of Mortimer' (37–8). He turns from his followers to the Abbot, resting on his lap 'this head, laden with mickle care' ('mickle' meaning 'much') (40). It is a striking image: the king, disguised in a monk's habit, defeated, vulnerable and child-like in the arms of a priest. It may be that we recall Edward spitting threats in the first act, resolving to set fire to all churches, and 'With slaughtered priests make Tiber's channel swell / And banks raise higher with their sepulchres' (I.iv.102–3). Edward's despair and defeat is conveyed by the heavy, stumbling pace of the next few lines, in particular 'O, never more lift up this dying heart!' (43). Spencer asks him to look up; his talk of drowsiness betiding no good, based on a familiar superstition, is confirmed by the arrival of a troop of soldiers led by Rice ap Howell and the Earl of Leicester. The 'Welsh hooks' they carry may refer to military pikes, or may be farming tools used as makeshift weaponry. The Mower who has led the soldiers to the fugitives has been mentioned earlier in the scene: Spencer had noted 'A gloomy fellow' that 'gave a long look after us' (IV.vii.29–30). He has a symbolic function here; just as the party's drowsiness has prefigured disaster, so the Mower serves as a symbol of impending doom.

The tension of the scene, when staged, is increased by Edward's reluctance to give himself up. Leicester, functioning here as a kind of choric figure, commenting on Edward's predicament, speaks in an aside to the audience. He invites them to 'see where he [Edward] sits and hopes unseen / T'escape their hands' (51–2). His Latin quotation from Seneca's *Thyestes* translates as 'Whom the breaking of day has seen high in pride, him the dying day sees fleeing the battle'. This ties in with the model of history that Marlowe seems to have adopted, the cyclical pattern that finds the monarch moving from authority and good fortune to a position of abjection and misery. In a widely read collection of stories known as *The Mirror for Magistrates* (first published in 1559) this pattern is repeated time and time again. The collection's express purpose is to warn those in power of the fate of poor rulers. Leicester's commentary on the action leaves us in no doubt that we are now on the downward curve of Edward's trajectory.

We should take note of the character Spencer here. After Gaveston's death, he takes his place as Edward's favourite and, presumably, his lover. If we try to map the act divisions of the play onto Marlowe's historical sources we find that the third act is the one that has 'telescoped' the events of history most radically: it covers a period of approximately twelve years. However, as far as an audience or reader is concerned, Spencer does emerge very rapidly. We have also seen him scheming his way into Edward's affections: act II scene i has revealed him as shallow and self-serving, and the representation of the relationship between him and Edward is very different from the Edward/Gaveston affair. The short exchange here, with Edward's 'Spencer, ah, sweet Spencer, thus then must we part?' and the reply, 'We must, my lord; so will the angry heavens' (72–3), is the closest we get to the tender way in which the love affair with Gaveston is represented. Spencer and Baldock's orchestrated lament after Edward is marched away rings somewhat hollow, rounded off with a rather anti-climactic, choric conclusion that 'all live to die, and rise to fall' (IV.vii.99–111). Once again Marlowe is reminding us of the way in which the play is following established patterns of history and tragedy.

In Edward's surrender he remains fiercely possessive of his royal title, and its connotations. When Leicester informs him 'Your majesty must go to Killingworth' (82) his reply challenges Leicester's authority over him, but it is a gesture at a confrontation that carries with it a recognition of his own powerlessness: '"Must!" 'Tis somewhat hard when kings "must" go' (82). He is no doubt aware of the ironic fashion in which this arrest is being carried out. Leicester

insists on using the term 'Your majesty' (81); a litter awaits him and
he is to be carried (still like a king) to his prison. Edward cannot
resist: he ruefully suggests a hearse as a more appropriate means of
transport, and imagines being carried to the gates of hell. His vision
of hell draws on classical and medieval sources to conjure the picture
of the 'hags' that 'howl for my death at Charon's shore' (89), Charon
being the ferryman who took the dead across the river Styx to Pluto's
kingdom of the dead. As Edward glances around at his followers on
one hand (no friends 'but these') and the monks on the other ('and
these'), he notes how the former 'must die under a tyrant's sword'
(91). Rice Ap Howell's response is vindictive: 'Care not for these, /
For we shall see them shorter by the heads' (92–3).

Edward remains self-conscious about his title, and his impending
loss of his royal status, and the self-dramatizing tendency that we
find elsewhere in the play is evident here too. There is a degree of
bravado in his self-sacrificial gesture, 'Here, man, rip up this panting
breast of mine / And take my heart in rescue of my friends' (66–7).
Later, he seems to be regaining some sense of poise just before his
exit, uttering a philosophical 'Well, that shall be shall be', and taking
his time with his farewells to Baldock and Spencer: 'Part we must, /
Sweet Spencer; gentle Baldock, part we must' (94–5). The short sentences here slow the pace of the scene, making Edward the still
centre of the stage picture, surrounded by friends and enemies. The
editor of the Oxford edition of the plays inserts a stage direction
here ('*He throws aside his robes*') and a theatrical gesture at this point
would be very much in keeping with the moment, further high-
lighting Edward's control of the stage. The discarding of his disguise
(hence 'feignèd weeds') he contrasts with the genuine nature of his
grief ('Unfeignèd are my woes', [96]), and his parting shot predicts
his end: 'Life, farewell, with my friends' (98). From this point on the
character of Edward increasingly invites nothing but sympathy from
the audience. The depiction of his arrest, his elaborate parting from
his faithful followers and the sight of him being marched away,
guarded, prepares us for Edward the prisoner and victim of the fifth
act, and sets us up for the horror of his murder in act V scene v.

Conclusions

1. We have seen that Marlowe does not present us with protagonists who are easily accessible. For the most part, they do not provide us with routes into their plays, as we might expect them to, and we need to find other ways of engaging with the plays and their characters.

2. Marlowe's protagonists have fundamental vices that inform the way they understand themselves, the way they are understood by others, and the way in which the texts represent them. Their essential 'viciousness', with some occasional exceptions, means they remain fundamentally set apart from their audiences.

3. It is essential to consider the theatrical dimension of these plays in this respect, for what is crucial is the way the protagonists work off their audiences. Barabas in particular frequently resorts to aside and soliloquy to draw the audience, willingly or not, into some kind of complicity with his plots. Furthermore, Marlowe's anti-heroes are often more attractive to the audience because they are outsiders in morally and politically corrupt societies: Edward may be a flawed king, but he lacks Mortimer's scheming duplicity; Barabas is at least straightforward with the audience about his villainy (unlike Ferneze). In this respect, there is room for the potential (at least) of something subversive. Dominant critical approaches in recent decades, in particular cultural materialism and new historicism (see pp. 246–8 for a fuller discussion of the terms), have found Marlowe's plays to be fertile ground for their studies. It may be that the transgressive behaviour of figures like Barabas and Faustus provides members of the audience with some kind of vicarious thrill, as those characters draw them into the contemplation of what is forbidden by strict moral, religious and legal codes. Whether this is genuinely oppositional (as a cultural materialist might claim) or simply a way of containing and so neutralizing subversion (the new historicist position) is open for debate.

4. Marlowe's characters often exhibit a self-dramatizing tendency – Tamburlaine is conscious of the significance of his appearance (note his colour-coded siege, as well as his preoccupation with his

sword, and what it signifies to his terrified enemies); Faustus (remember his frequent use of the third person) is both self-conscious and remarkably lacking in common sense and self-awareness; Barabas very self-consciously plays the role of stage villain; Edward is aware of the performative dimension of kingship.

5. Finally, we need to bear in mind that these extracts analysed here are simply that – extracts – and that the pictures we begin to build of the protagonists here have to remain contingent and provisional. During the course of each of the plays, such pictures are likely to be shattered and rebuilt many times over.

Methods of Analysis

1. We have looked closely at the ambivalent responses Marlowe's protagonists tend to provoke, and we have started to find out how and why they do this. The former we have discovered via interpretations of their actions and their words, sometimes paying close attention to their language.

2. We have borne in mind the significance of the dimension of performance, and we have also considered the importance of the historical, social and cultural context to a full understanding of the extracts. While thinking carefully about what the texts mean to us now, we have also thought carefully about the original Elizabethan context, and considered what different lines, actions and characterisations may have meant then, and how they may resonate differently (or not at all) today.

3. We have paid close attention on a number of occasions to details of syntax, language, rhythm and so on, and considered how Marlowe deploys certain linguistic tricks for specific effects.

4. The way in which the protagonists are understood by their audiences is informed by the ways in which the characters around them respond to them. This may seem like an elementary principle, but it is always important to try and imagine these plays being enacted on a stage. When reading the plays, dialogue may be confined to two or three characters, but there may at the same time be any number of other characters, silent witnesses, hidden

observers, or even active (if silent) participants in the action. Remember the presence of Ithamore during Barabas's monologue, the terrified Virgins during Tamburlaine's chilling speech about his servant Death, and the silent, watchful Mephistopheles listening to Faustus's blustering.

Suggested Work

As I have suggested in the discussion of each extract, Marlowe creates awkward protagonists whose relations with their audiences are constantly shifting. Consequently, the extracts quoted above really provide only half (or less than half) of the story. Having followed the analyses above, the next step would be to consider contrasting extracts in each text. For instance, we have seen Tamburlaine at his most brutal: contrast this with the tenderness in some of his dialogue with Zenocrate, and his grief at her death (II.iv). Barabas is a more difficult case, since it is often difficult to determine when (if ever) the emotions he expresses are genuine; his reaction of grief at the loss of his wealth and his home (I.ii.161–214), enacted in the presence of his fellow Jews, seems real until he is left alone, whereupon he promptly scorns 'the simplicity of these base slaves' (I.ii.215). Perhaps his most poignant moment is when he is first stripped of his wealth by Ferneze: 'You have my wealth,' he tells him, 'the labour of my life, / The comfort of my age, my children's hope' (150–1). It is one moment in the play – all too fleeting – when Barabas seems to be a genuine victim, and Ferneze an oppressor.

Edward is undoubtedly a victim in the scene discussed above, and his death is both horrific and pitiable (see pp. 205–12). However, there are other occasions when we witness him behaving recklessly, selfishly and irresponsibly. In particular, his treatment of Isabella is often gratuitously cruel, as we shall see in Chapter 5. If we have seen Faustus in his full-blown, arrogant stupidity, we must also recognise that his eventual fate seems to retain the capacity to shock and horrify an audience. The next chapter looks in some detail at his agonizing over his pact with Lucifer (act II scene i) and Faustus's own terrible fate is likely to have provoked some kind of pity, even from those members of Marlowe's audience who would have been most offended at his blasphemies. Chapter 7 includes an analysis of his final moments (act V scene ii). It is important to read the extract studied above in relation to those later scenes if we are to piece together complete pictures of these protagonists.

3

Devils and Angels

Marlowe lived at a time when religion was both more central to people's everyday lives, and more controversial than it tends to be in western society today. In early modern England any deviation from orthodox thought was branded as heresy or atheism. The discussion of the political and religious situations in Elizabethan England in Chapter 8 provides more detail; we need only note here that the country was still nursing deep wounds from conflict between Catholics and Protestants, and that religion was inextricably bound up with politics in Elizabeth's time. Although it is difficult to assess the extent to which issues of church and state 'trickled down' to impact directly upon people's lives, it seems likely that the old superstitions that had grown up around Catholic belief and culture were not shaken off easily. But, without doubt, in the second half of the sixteenth century, an Elizabethan's understanding of her place in the universe, her relation to the mortal, visible world around her as well as the immortal world beyond, was changing radically.

How does this relate to Marlowe and the theatre of the time? The extent to which culture in general and theatre in particular had any effect on the religious or political beliefs of the people is a vexed question that has preoccupied literary critics and historians in recent years. The existence of a state censor, the Master of the Revels, suggests that the authorities were aware of its potential, as does the fact that a number of playwrights and players were imprisoned for writing and performing 'seditious' material. Play-going was certainly an immensely popular pastime in Elizabethan England,

and the fact that a wide cross-section of society attended plays is also significant, giving them a status more equivalent to the medium of television today, perhaps, than theatre in the twenty-first century, which has become largely (though certainly not entirely) depoliticized.

It is probably true to say that this is all more pertinent to Marlowe than it is to many of his contemporaries. Religion is at the heart of one of Marlowe's plays (*Doctor Faustus*), and a key issue in almost all of his other works. The exception is *Edward II* where its importance is chiefly bound up with the play's politics. *Edward II* is consequently passed over in this section, although some discussion of the relation between God, the monarch and the people can be found on pp. 116–21. The drama of *Faustus* pivots on the concepts of damnation, repentance, redemption and salvation, and so it will be discussed in more detail than the other texts in this particular section. However, religion is also crucial to the narrative patterning of *Tamburlaine*, and *The Jew of Malta* is also fascinating from this perspective, both in terms of satire of Catholicism and for its use of anti-Semitic stereotypes. In terms of dramatic form, it is also worth noting briefly here the debt that *Faustus* owes to the morality play tradition with its pageant of the Seven Deadly Sins and the presence of the Good and Bad Angels. Furthermore, Barabas, the Jew of Malta, has been seen by a number of critics as a direct descendant of the Vice figure, another 'character' familiar from morality plays.

Marlowe's work raises all kinds of questions about religious doctrine, faith, doubt and belief. A number of different perspectives on the relations between God and humankind are presented, and, although many critics have tried to deduce a coherent position, Marlowe still proves resistant to attempts to pin him down. The extent to which contradictions remain unresolved in Marlovian drama may well explain his enduring appeal in the twenty-first century. We certainly need to be prepared to confront unanswered questions when we read and intepret Marlowe's plays, particularly with regard to religion.

Tamburlaine II, V.i.148–220

We begin our investigation of religion in Marlowe's plays with this moment from the second part of *Tamburlaine*. The audience has witnessed a protracted, faintly ritualized scene depicting the Governor of Babylon refusing to listen to the pleas of his citizens to surrender to Tamburlaine's forces, and bravely (but foolishly) turning down a final offer of mercy from Tamburlaine's officer Techelles. The stage directions indicate that a battle follows, and Tamburlaine's soldiers scale the walls of the city. The Governor is 'upon the walls', presumably using the upper gallery at the rear of the stage. Tamburlaine gives the order for the Governor to be hanged in chains on the city walls and shot to death.

[*The Governor of Babylon is discovered hanging in chains. Re-enter Theridamas. Tamburlaine mounts his chariot*]

AMYRAS   See now, my lord, how brave the captain hangs!

TAMBURLAINE   'Tis brave indeed, my boy. Well done!

    Shoot first, my lord, and then the rest shall follow.   150

THERIDAMAS   Then have at him to begin withal.

Theridamas shoots [*and hits the Governor*]

GOVERNOR   Yet save my life, and let this wound appease

    The mortal fury of great Tamburlaine.

TAMBURLAINE   No, though Asphaltis' lake were liquid gold,

    And offered me as ransom for thy life,   155

    Yet shouldst thou die – Shoot at him all at once.

             They shoot

    So now he hangs like Baghdad's governor,

    Having as many bullets in his flesh

    As there be breaches in her battered wall.

    Go now and bind the burghers hand and foot,   160

    And cast them headlong in the city's lake;

    Tartars and Persians shall inhabit there,

    And, to command the city, I will build

    A citadel, that all Africa,

    Which hath been subject to the Persian king,   165

    Shall pay me tribute for, in Babylon.

TECHELLES   What shall be done with their wives and children,
 my lord?
TAMBURLAINE   Techelles, drown them all, man, woman,
 and child.
 Leave not a Babylonian in the town.
TECHELLES   I will about it straight. Come, soldiers.   170
    Exit [*Techelles with Soldiers*]
TAMBURLAINE   Now, Casane, where's the Turkish Alcoran
 And all the heaps of superstitious books
 Found in the temples of that Mahomet
 Whom I have thought a god? They shall be burnt.
USUMCASANE[*presenting the books*]   Here they are, my lord. 175
TAMBURLAINE   Well said. Let there be a fire presently.
    [*Soldiers light a fire*]
 In vain I see men worship Mahomet.
 My sword hath sent millions of Turks to hell,
 Slew all his priests, his kinsmen, and his friends,
 And yet I live untouched by Mahomet.   180
 There is a God full of revenging wrath,
 From whom the thunder and the lightning breaks,
 Whose scourge I am, and him will I obey.
 So, Casane, fling them in the fire.
    [*The books are burnt*]
 Now, Mahomet, if thou have any power,   185
 Come down thyself and work a miracle.
 Thou art not worthy to be worshippèd
 That suffers flames of fire to burn the writ
 Wherein the sum of thy religion rests.
 Why send'st thou not a furious whirlwind down 190
 To blow thy Alcaron up to thy throne
 Where men report thou sitt'st by God himself,
 Or vengeance on the head of Tamburlaine,
 That shakes his sword against thy majesty
 And spurns the abstracts of thy foolish laws? 195
 Well, soldiers, Mahomet remains in hell;
 He cannot hear the voice of Tamburlaine.
 Seek out another godhead to adore,

The God that sits in heaven, if any god,
For he is God alone, and none but he.   200
             [*Re-enter Techelles*]
TECHELLES   I have fulfilled your highness' will, my lord.
    Thousands of men drowned in Asphaltis' Lake,
    Have made the water swell above the banks,
    And fishes fed by human carcasses,
    Amazed, swim up and down upon the waves   205
    As when they swallow asafoetida,
    Which makes them fleet aloft and gasp for air.
TAMBURLAINE   Well, then, my friendly lords, what now
      remains
    But that we leave sufficient garrison
    And presently depart to Persia   210
    To triumph after all our victories?
THERIDAMAS   Ay, good my lord. Let us in haste to Persia,
    And let this captain be removed the walls
    To some high hill about the city here.
TAMBURLAINE   Let it be so. About it, soldiers.   215
    But stay. I feel myself distempered suddenly.
TECHELLES   What is it dares distemper Tamburlaine?
TAMBURLAINE   Something, Techelles, but I know not what.
    But forth, ye vassals! Whatsoe'er it be,
    Sickness or death can never conquer me.   220
               Exeunt.

We have already seen how Marlowe establishes Tamburlaine as a deeply ambivalent figure in the first of the two plays. The massacre of the Virgins of Damascus in act V scene i, discussed on pp. 49–55, can be deeply disturbing in performance. In that scene we do not see the violence, although we may hear it. In this instance, the execution is staged. The impact, though of a different nature, is potentially equally shocking. The commentary on the execution that Tamburlaine provides underscores the violence, with the hard, percussive consonants in his description of the governor's body: 'Having as many bullets in his flesh / As there be breaches in her battered wall' (158–9). We may not feel the pity that the Damascus massacre inspires, although the order Tamburlaine gives here for every 'man, woman, and child' (168) in the city to be put to death may provoke something reminiscent of that response. The casual issue and receipt of the order heightens its savagery: Tamburlaine's line is muted and deadpan: 'Techelles, drown them all, man, woman, and child. / Leave not a Babylonian in the town.' Techelles's reply is equally matter of fact and efficient: 'I will about it straight. Come, soldiers' (168–70).

It is worth pausing briefly to consider the technical demands of staging the spectacle of the execution of the Governor. The editor's stage direction for the appearance of the Governor hanging in chains uses the term 'is discovered', and it may be that this was an effect revealed by the drawing back of a curtain. We cannot be sure of the precise structure of the gallery, but it is also possible that the actor was chained and lowered over the balcony of the gallery. He was probably shot at with muskets; a document dated 16 November 1587 is extant that mentions an accident at the playhouse in which an actor misfired a weapon, killing 'a child, and a woman great with child forthwith', and injuring a third person. The play is not mentioned by name, though the playing company is – it is Marlowe's company, the Lord Admiral's Men. It is quite likely, then, that the accident occurred during a performance of this scene in *Tamburlaine II*. We know that the Elizabethans expected a degree of verisimilitude in the staging of violence, and it is likely that this was also incorporated into the depiction of the Governor's final moments, with pig's blood and other effects most likely to have been deployed to maximize the impact of the scene.

However, the crucial significance of this extract comes after the Governor has been dispatched. Having ordered the massacre of every citizen of Babylon, Tamburlaine now turns on 'Mahomet' (or Mohammed). He calls on Usumcasane to present him with the 'Alcoran' (the Koran) and other religious books (171–2) and orders them to be burnt. We know from Marlowe's sources that the historical Timur the Lame was a devout follower of Mohammed, and the poetic licence Marlowe allows himself should alert us at once to the significance of this moment at the climax of the play. He speaks of 'that Mahomet / Whom I have thought a god?' (173–4), implying a conscious rejection of beliefs previously held.

Throughout the two plays, Tamburlaine has repeatedly pitched himself against the gods, challenging gods of classical antiquity like Mars, the god of war (see *Tamburlaine I*, II.vii.58–61) and finally even Jove himself, the king of the Graeco-Roman gods. Jove is in some respects more suitable as a role model than an adversary for Tamburlaine: Tamburlaine defeats Mycetes the King of Persia at the beginning of Part I, handing over the crown to Mycetes' brother Cosroe. But a taste of power leaves Tamburlaine thirsty for more, and he challenges Cosroe, who is outraged at the 'giantly presumption' of 'this devilish shepherd' (Part I, II.vi.1–2). In a similar fashion, according to ancient myth, Jove (or Jupiter) established his supremacy by dethroning the titan Saturn. By the end of the first part, Tamburlaine is even ready to challenge Jove, imagining

> Jove, viewing me in arms, looks pale and wan,
> Fearing my power should pull him from his throne . . .
> (Part I,V.i.451–4)

It is hard to judge how Elizabethan audiences would have interpreted this. The figure of Jove or Jupiter (Greek Zeus) in Renaissance culture was the one most closely related, in conceptual terms, to their Christian God: the name of Jove is clearly related to the Hebrew almighty God Jehovah. Tamburlaine's act of blasphemy, however, is committed against Mohammed (and Islam) and consequently an Elizabethan audience's response would probably have been complex. Tamburlaine was a monstrous figure in the annals of history and, as a follower of Islam, a heathen. Marlowe evokes the Islamic prophet Mohammed only to have Tamburlaine blaspheme against him; in so doing, Marlowe was simultaneously raising a spectre that an Elizabethan audience would have instinctively reacted against (Mohammed) and depicting Tamburlaine as a heretic to his own religion. As so often, Marlowe seems to be playing a double game: it is likely that the Elizabethans may have enjoyed hearing a heathen religion attacked, but at the same time it is likely that many would have been shocked by Tamburlaine's godlessness.

Tamburlaine offers another challenge: for him, Mahomet's failure to respond to the outrages he has committed against Islam is proof of his non-existence, or at least of his powerlessness. With typically

inflated rhetoric, he boasts of his deeds ('My sword hath sent millions of Turks to hell' [178]) declaring, 'And yet I live untouched by
Mahomet' (180). The burning of the books is an act of provocation:
'Now, Mahomet, if thou have any power, / Come down thyself and
work a miracle' (185–6). The challenge may actually be a sly (and, if
detected, deeply shocking) reference to the crucifixion, when Christ
was mocked by those standing around and told to save himself and
come down from the cross (Gospel of Mark, XV.xxix–xxxi). When it
seems that Mahomet will neither save his holy books from the
fire nor send 'vengeance on the head of Tamburlaine' (193),
Tamburlaine turns to those standing around him and advises them
to seek out another god to worship (if they must worship any god) –
the 'God that sits in heaven' (199). This is presumably the god he
refers to earlier, the 'God full of revenging wrath, / From whom the
thunder and the lightning breaks' (181–2). The challenge may recall,
for the audience, the moment in *Tamburlaine I* when the Turkish
emperor Bajazeth, taken prisoner and humiliated by Tamburlaine,
calls out for divine intervention: 'O Mahomet, O sleepy Mahomet!'
(Part I, III.iii.269). When Mahomet fails to act, his wife Zabina
decides 'Then is there left no Mahomet, no God' (Part I, V.i.239).
Finally, despairing, they both commit suicide.

Tamburlaine has declared on several occasions that he is this
vengeful god's 'scourge' (183) and this is a term that requires some
explanation (other references to Tamburlaine as scourge include Part
I, IV.ii.31–2; Part II, IV.i.147–8 and IV.i.153, and his final line in
the play: 'For Tamburlaine, the scourge of God, must die' (II,
V.iii.248). The concept of the scourge is rooted in the words of the
prophet Isaiah in the Old Testament: the Jewish people, the children
of Israel, disobey Jahweh, who uses a heathen enemy to punish
them. Subsequently this scourge, an Assyrian, is himself killed by
God, once he has carried out the divine will in the chastisement of
God's chosen race. There is an incident earlier in *Tamburlaine II*
which works as an object lesson in this respect: the Christian King
Sigismund of Hungary breaks a truce with the Moslem Orcanes
which he has sealed by a Christian oath. Orcanes deduces that 'If
there be Christ, we shall have victory', since Christ will be obliged to
avenge the broken truce on Sigismund (Part II, II.ii.63–4), and

Sigismund is indeed defeated in the ensuing conflict (II.iii). It seems indicative of the ironic strategies that underpin the *Tamburlaine* plays that the Moslem Orcanes triumphs via the intervention of a god he does not believe in. However, it is also possible to see this as another instance of God making use of a 'scourge' to carry out his will; Orcanes is triumphant in the second act, but is himself defeated by Tamburlaine in the fourth.

Some critics have seen Tamburlaine's sickness at the end of this scene as punishment for his presumption and his persistent blasphemies, culminating in the burning of the Koran. It certainly seems to be a sudden attack, catching Tamburlaine as he fires off orders and prepares to leave: 'Let it be so. About it, soldiers. / But stay. I feel myself distempered suddenly' (215–16). When Techelles asks what ails him, Tamburlaine is uncharacteristically hesitant and at a loss: 'Something, Techelles, but I **know not what**', the final three syllables falling in three clumsy, heavy stresses (218). The line brings the rhythm of the scene to a shuddering halt, particularly after the energetic, forward movement of the previous speeches made by Tamburlaine (208–11) and Theridamas (212–14), as they gear up to march to Persia. Tamburlaine shakes off his sudden sickness almost immediately, declaring that 'Sickness or death can never conquer me' (220), although the next time we see him he will enter in his chariot, attended by physicians (Part II, V.iii.42). It is perhaps significant that there he assumes that some 'daring god torments my body thus / And seeks to conquer mighty Tamburlaine' (42–3). It may be that, as he staggers, the fire that has been laid to burn the Moslem holy books is still burning, or smoking. If the books have been hurled into a trapdoor in the stage (as seems most likely), Tamburlaine may stagger or fall towards the opening in the floor of the stage. As so often, the extent to which we may wish to read this dramatic incident as divine retribution, or just desserts, remains open to readers, audiences and theatre practitioners. In any case, this is clearly a pivotal moment in the play, representing the toppling of the all-conquering Tamburlaine from his seemingly unassailable status.

The Jew of Malta, IV.i.49–100

This extract is one of the best examples of Barabas's capacity for mischief, enacted in such a way that an audience is as likely to engage
with him as they are to be alienated by it. Cornered by the Friars
Barnardine and Jacomo, he suspects they have discovered that it was
he who poisoned and killed the inhabitants of the nunnery
(including his daughter Abigail). In fact, it is not clear at this stage
that they are aware of this particular crime, though they know, from
Abigail's dying confession, that he is implicated in the deaths of her
suitors Lodowick and Mathias. While it shows Barabas in fine,
manipulative, comic form, the extract is noticeable chiefly for the
comedy it deploys at the expense of the friars.

BARABAS   (*Aside* [*to Ithamore*])
　　　She has confessed, and we are both undone,
　　　My bosom inmate! But I must dissemble.　　　　　　　50
　　　[*To them*] O holy friars, the burden of my sins
　　　Lie heavy on my soul. Then pray you tell me,
　　　Is't not too late now to turn Christian?
　　　I have been zealous in the Jewish faith,
　　　Hard-hearted to the poor, a covetous wretch,　　　　55
　　　That would for lucre's sake have sold my soul.
　　　A hundred for a hundred I have ta'en,
　　　And now for store of wealth may I compare
　　　With all the Jews in Malta. But what is wealth?
　　　I am a Jew, and therefore am I lost.　　　　　　　　60
　　　Would penance serve for this my sin,
　　　I could afford to whip myself to death –
ITHAMORE   [*aside*] And so could I; but penance will not serve.
BARABAS   To fast, to pray, and wear a shirt of hair,
　　　And on my knees creep to Jerusalem.　　　　　　　65
　　　Cellars of wine, and sollars full of wheat,
　　　Warehouses stuffed with spices and with drugs,
　　　Whole chests of gold, in bullion and in coin,
　　　Besides I know not how much weight in pearl,
　　　Orient and round, have I within my house;　　　　　70

At Alexandria, merchandise unsold.
But yesterday two ships went from this town;
Their voyage will be worth ten thousand crowns.
In Florence, Venice, Antwerp, London, Seville,
Frankfurt, Lubeck, Moscow, and where not,   75
Have I debts owing; and in most of these,
Great sums of money lying in the banco.
All this I'll give to some religious house,
So I may be baptized and live therein.

JACOMO   O good Barabas, come to our house!

BARNARDINE   O no, good Barabas, come to our house!   80
    And Barabas, you know –

BARABAS   [*to Friar Barnardine*]
    I know that I have highly sinned.
    You shall convert me; you shall have all my wealth.

JACOMO   O, Barabas, their laws are strict.   85

BARABAS [*to Friar Jacomo*]   I know they are, and I will be
    with you.

BARNARDINE   They wear no shirts, and they go barefoot too.

BARABAS [*to Friar Jacomo*]   Then 'tis not for me; and I am
    resolved
    You shall confess me, and have all my goods.

BARNARDINE   Good Barabas, come to me.   90

BARABAS [*to Friar Jacomo*]   You see I answer him, and yet he
    stays;
    Rid him away, and go you home with me.

JACOMO   I'll be with you tonight.

BARNARDINE [*to Friar Jacomo*]   Come to my house at one
    o' clock this night.

JACOMO [*to Friar Barnardine*] You hear your answer, and you
    may be gone.   95

BARNARDINE   Why, go get you away.

JACOMO   I will not go for thee.

BARNARDINE   Not? then I'll make thee, rogue.

JACOMO   How, dost call me rogue?

               [*The Friars*] *fight*

ITHAMORE   Part 'em, master, part 'em.   100

The first part of this scene is very funny slapstick, with Barabas repeatedly interrupting the friars (who are themselves falling over each other in their attempts to be the first to accuse him); the exchange culminates with Friar Barnardine's climactic challenge 'Thou has committed' and Barabas's interjection, 'Fornication? But that was in another country; and besides, the wench is dead' (41–3). The line is a wonderful expression of the Barabas persona, or what Bertolt Brecht might term his *gestus*; a sudden crystallising of his attitude: the fornication is discounted because it happened in a foreign country (and so presumably Barabas cannot be prosecuted for it). Furthermore, the woman with whom he committed the act is dead; the use of the term 'wench' expresses contempt and utter disregard. The second line is variously interpreted by different actors ('besides, the wench is dead' . . . 'and so it doesn't matter'; or '. . . so how could they have found out?'). It doesn't take very much to imagine that the 'wench', having served his needs, ended up as another of Barabas's victims.

Barabas, the consummate performer, chooses another role from his huge repertoire in order to extricate himself from a new crisis (his aside to Ithamore, 'But I must dissemble', is a clear sign for the audience that the performance is about to begin [50]). Here, he is the miserable penitent and potential convert. His summary of his sins is a standard litany of anti-Semitisms: being 'zealous in the Jewish faith', apparently consists of being 'Hard-hearted to the poor' and 'covetous' (54–55). A Jew is one who would not only willingly sell his soul for money (56), but also charges exorbitant rates of interest – one hundred per cent, as he admits ('A hundred for a hundred I have ta'en' [57]). The loaning of money for interest, 'usury', was a forbidden practice in the Christian community. However, it was permissable under Jewish law. Consequently, usury was sanctioned in Jewish ghettos, since Europe was developing an ever increasing dependency upon it, vital as it was to the nurturing of a nascent capitalism. Being a Jew, according to Christian teaching at the time, meant eternal damnation ('I am a Jew, and therefore am I lost' [60]). Barabas vows penitence, evoking familiar scenarios of self-flagellation ('I could afford to whip myself to death –' [62]) and pilgrimage ('on my knees creep to Jerusalem' [65]).

And then, abruptly, Barabas spins on a sixpence, turning from visions of repentance and acts of self-abnegation to a new horizon of dazzling opulence. In a speech that surely consciously recalls his opening soliloquy (see discussion on pp. 37–40), Barabas parades before these ascetic clerics a mountain of wealth. And not only gold and jewels: the temptations are designed to appeal to their palates and their stomachs as much as their pouches. Furthermore, the talk of ships setting sail (72–3), and of money owed to him in financial capitals around the world (74–7), is a promise of a limitless supply of goods. If the friars are going to swallow this much, they are presumably not going to think twice about the means by which such wealth has been procured, including usury, a practice outwardly despised by the Christian community (no doubt these supposed sums of money owed to Barabas have been loaned at high rates of interest). The speech climaxes with a declaration that he will give all this 'to some religious house', (78) so that he may be baptized and live there.

The comic pay off, of course, is in the friars' response. A beat (a short pause) in the timing of the reply is called for, before Jacomo explodes with his desperate plea ('O good Barabas, come to our house!' [80]) and Barnardine shouts him down with his own invitation. Echoing the device above, Barabas picks up on Barnardine's unfinished line ('And Barabas, you know – '), finishing it with a frank assent ('I know that I have highly sinned') and an agreement to throw in his lot with him. The prosaic matter of fact tone of 'You shall have all my wealth' is another deft comic touch (82–4). The strictness of the two friars' houses, no doubt a cause of pride and competitiveness under normal circumstances, becomes a weapon they wield against each other as they try to sway the supposed convert. Barabas's whimsical switch from one to the other mirrors their own lack of dedication to their faith when faced with such a tempting, blatant bribe.

Marlowe now daringly edges the farce one stage further. At Barabas's prompting, Jacomo, the victor, turns on Barnardine: 'You hear your answer, and you may be gone' (95). A quarrel ensues, with an infantile batting back and forth of dismissals, and the insults and threat of force ('then I'll make thee, rogue' [98]) precipitating physical violence: the stage direction clearly indicates that a fight breaks out between them, and Ithamore's request that Barabas 'Part 'em' suggests that it is quite a tussle. Staged properly, this is one of the funniest moments in this darkly comic play. It also anticipates the escalation of the enmity between these two men of God that culminates in Jacomo's second attack on Barnardine at the end of the scene. By that time, Barnardine has actually been slain already by Barabas and Ithamore. They then engineer Jacomo's attack on Barnardine by propping up the corpse with a staff, and make his death seem Jacomo's doing. This completes the plot against the friars, Barabas's masterpiece.

Much of the comedy comes, of course, from the satire on the friars. It is this kind of thing which some have chosen to interpret as evidence of Marlowe's disregard or even disrespect for religion. Marlowe had certainly gained a reputation as a free thinker (or heretic, or atheist) and in a society where men and women were still being imprisoned and killed for their beliefs this was a dangerous game to be playing. More radical critiques of religious belief can be detected in *Doctor Faustus* by those who wish to find them; here we are concerned with the representation of two clerics who are deployed chiefly as the butt of Barabas's jokes. Elsewhere, they are established as foolish and gullible, easily duped by Abigail's pretence as she begs to be accepted into the nunnery (I.ii.327–31). There are sly remarks from others, and lines of their own, that cast doubt on their integrity as men of God, even before they fall for the temptation Barabas lays before them in this scene. As Abigail, a true convert to Christianity by this time, confesses all to Friar Barnardine, she asks with her dying breath that he witness 'that I die a Christian'. Barnardine replies, 'Ay, and a virgin, too; that grieves me most' (III.vi.40–1). Furthermore, though Barnardine is bound to keep Abigail's dying confession secret (''Twas told me in shrift; / Thou know'st 'tis death an if it be revealed' [III.vi.50–1]) it is clear that by the following scene he has revealed all to Jacomo. The satire is neatly rounded off at the end of IV.i, after Jacomo has been framed for Barnardine's murder. As he and Ithamore exchange moral platitudes over the friar's predicament, Barabas declares that 'for this example I'll remain a Jew. / Heaven bless me! What, a friar a murderer? / When shall you see a Jew commit the like?' (IV.i.197–9).

We have already established how anti-Semitism lies deep in the marrow of *The Jew of Malta*. It may be that Marlowe is raising questions about all kinds of religious belief in this play, revealing how it can be used as a mask to hide hypocrisy, greed and malice. We do have to remember, however, that the state religion of Marlowe's England was Protestant. Anti-Catholicism was rife and appeared in many forms, and it is unsurprising to find Marlowe ridiculing Catholic friars in his play. Anti-clerical feeling can be traced back to Chaucer's *Canterbury Tales* and beyond, and it is fairly likely that Marlowe is indulging in some gallery-pleasing bigotry. Our initial response to this daring satire may be to assume Marlowe was taking a significant risk in ridiculing Christianity so openly and viciously. It may be closer to the truth to interpret his satirical attack as a safe and conservative option that would have raised an easy laugh amongst a predominantly Protestant audience.

Doctor Faustus, II.i.1–82

The issue of whether Marlowe's supposed atheism can be traced in what he wrote has, for obvious reasons, been most prominent in discussions of his tragedy of damnation, *Doctor Faustus*. There are a number of crucial scenes where the implications of Faustus's pact with the Devil are explored in dramatic mode. The dynamics of scenes like these (act II scene i is one of the best examples) are determined in part by the difference between what the audience knows and what the Faustus persona realises, or fails to realise, about himself and his predicament. The gap between audience awareness and a character's awareness generates dramatic irony, a fundamental element of any kind of drama, from a stage thriller to a pantomime. The ways in which Marlowe uses dramatic irony in *Faustus* depend to an extent on details of Christian doctrine, and it is worth bearing in mind what I said earlier about how understandings of ourselves and the world around us have changed over the past four hundred years. It is likely that the technicalities of doctrine that we learn by reading the research of scholars, literary and biblical, would have been much more familiar to an Elizabethan audience.

Enter Faustus in his study

FAUSTUS   Now, Faustus, must thou needs be damned,
         And canst thou not be saved. [?]
         What boots it then to think of God or heaven?
         Away with such vain fancies and despair!
         Despair in God and trust in Beelzebub.   5
         Now go not backward. No, Faustus, be resolute.
         Why waverest thou? O, something soundeth in mine ears:
         'Abjure this magic, turn to God again!'
         Ay, and Faustus will turn to God again.
         To God? He loves thee not.   10
         The god thou servest is thine own appetite,
         Wherein is fixed the love of Beelzebub.
         To him I'll build an altar and a church,
         And offer lukewarm blood of new-born babes.

Enter Good Angel and Evil [Angel]

GOOD ANGEL   Sweet Faustus, leave that execrable art.   15
FAUSTUS   Contrition, prayer, repentance – what of them?
GOOD ANGEL   O, they are means to bring thee unto heaven.
EVIL ANGEL   Rather illusions, fruits of lunacy,
         That makes men foolish that do trust them most.
GOOD ANGEL   Sweet Faustus, think of heaven and heavenly things. 20
EVIL ANGEL   No, Faustus, think of honour and wealth.

Exeunt [Angels]

FAUSTUS   Of wealth?
         Why, the seigniory of Emden shall be mine.
         When Mephistopheles shall stand by me,
         What god can hurt thee, Faustus? Thou art safe;   25
         Cast no more doubts. Come, Mephistopheles,
         And bring glad tidings from great Lucifer.
         Is't not midnight? Come, Mephistopheles!
         Veni, veni, Mephistophile!

Enter Mephistopheles

         Now tell, what says Lucifer thy lord?   30
MEPHISTOPHELES   That I shall wait on Faustus whilst he lives,

So he will buy my service with his soul.

FAUSTUS   Already Faustus hath hazarded that for thee.

MEPHISTOPHILES   But, Faustus, thou must bequeath it solemnly,
And write a deed of gift with thine own blood,   35
For that security craves great Lucifer.
If thou deny it, I will back to hell.

FAUSTUS   Stay, Mephistopheles, and tell me what good will
my soul do thy lord?

MEPHISTOPHILES   Enlarge his kingdom.   40

FAUSTUS   Is that the reason he tempts us thus?

MEPHISTOPHILES   *Solamen miseris socios habuisse doloris.*

FAUSTUS   Have you any pain, that tortures others?

MEPHISTOPHILES   As great as have the human souls of men.
But tell me, Faustus, shall I have thy soul?   45
And I will be thy slave, and wait on thee,
And give thee more than thou hast wit to ask.

FAUSTUS   Ay, Mephistopheles, I give it thee.

MEPHISTOPHILES   Then stab thine arm courageously,
And bind thy soul that at some certain day   50
Great Lucifer may claim it as his own,
And then be thou as great as Lucifer.

FAUSTUS [*cutting his arm*]   Lo, Mephistopheles, for love of thee
I cut mine arm, and with my proper blood
Assure my soul to be great Lucifer's,   55
Chief lord and regent of perpetual night.
View here the blood that trickles from mine arm,
And let it be propitious for my wish.

MEPHISTOPHILES   But, Faustus, thou must write it in manner
of a deed of gift.   60

FAUSTUS   Ay, so I will. [*He writes*] But Mephistopheles,
My blood congeals and I can write no more.

MEPHISTOPHILES   I'll fetch thee fire to dissolve it straight.
Exit [*Mephistopheles*]

FAUSTUS   What might the staying of my blood portend?
Is it unwilling I should write this bill?   65
Why streams it not, that I may write afresh?
'Faustus gives to thee his soul' – Ah, there it stayed!

Why shouldst thou not? Is not thy soul thine own?
Then write again: 'Faustus gives to thee his soul.'
    Enter Mephistopheles with a chafer of coals
MEPHISTOPHILES   Here's fire. Come, Faustus, set it on.   70
FAUSTUS   So. Now the blood begins to clear again.
    Now will I make an end immediately.
                    [*He writes*]
MEPHISTOPHILES [*aside*]   O, what will not I do to obtain his
    soul?
FAUSTUS   *Consummatum est.* This bill is ended,
    And Faustus hath bequeathed his soul to Lucifer.   75
    But what is this inscription on mine arm?
    '*Homo, fuge!*' Whither should I fly?
    If unto God, he'll throw thee down to hell. –
    My senses are deceived; here's nothing writ. –
    I see it plain. Here in this place is writ   80
    '*Homo, fuge!*' Yet shall not Faustus fly.
MEPHISTOPHILES [*aside*]   I'll fetch him somewhat to delight
    his mind.

Faustus has conjured Mephistopheles once before, in act I scene iii.
In a vividly theatrical scene, amidst chanted spells, reams of Latin
and, almost certainly, spectacular stage effects, Mephistopheles has
appeared, apparently at Faustus's bidding. His first appearance was
so terrifying that Faustus bid him return in a human shape, as 'an
old Franciscan friar; / That holy shape becomes a devil best' (another
anti-Catholic jibe, and another instance of a dramatic moment
being complemented by a sly witticism) (I.iii.24–5). Enthralled by
his own power and by visions of what he will conjure when
Mephistopheles becomes his servant, he eagerly awaits news from
the evil spirit, who has carried his proposed bargain to Lucifer:
Faustus will give up his soul to Lucifer in exchange for twenty-four
years of service from Mephistopheles.

    This scene, however, finds Faustus in a very different frame of
mind. The opening lines would seem to imply that he has already
given up hope of salvation, although the punctuation of the lines is
uncertain, and crucially important in this instance. Different editors

have chosen to punctuate the second line in different ways: the Oxford edition that has been used as the standard text for this book prints it as, 'And canst thou not be saved.' The full stop clearly signals that this is a statement of fact, as Faustus understands it. However, the original text (in both A-text and B-text versions) ends the line with a question mark. The B-text also puts a question mark at the end of the first line. The editors of another modern version (Revels Plays series, edited by David Bevington and Eric Rasmussen) explain that question marks were often used instead of exclamation marks in early texts; they also suggest that the question mark at the end of the second line is a mistake, a transposition from the third line. It is true that the third and fourth lines read as a conclusion: 'What boots it then to think of God or heaven? / Away with such vain fancies and despair!' – since he is damned, he should give up any thoughts of God or heaven. This would imply that the opening lines should be taken as an assessment of his situation, rather than as an interrogation of it.

However, the syntax of these lines do not give the impression of a man resigned to his fate and prepared to face the consequences of his choice. After the brave gesture, 'Away with such vain fancies and despair:' (4), he continues: 'Now go not backward. No, Faustus, be resolute' (6). The hesitancy, and the effort involved in keeping himself on his chosen course, is obvious. Infuriated with his own lack of resolve, he chastises himself: 'Why waverest thou?' (7). The reason for his uncertainty is another voice that plants doubts in his mind. The voice actually anticipates the Good Angel, who enters five lines later: '"Abjure this magic, turn to God again!"' (abjure meaning to renounce an oath) (8). The plea is met by a swift rejoinder, this one spoken as if by the Evil Angel, also currently off-stage: 'To God? He loves thee not' (10). This unusually truncated line (only six syllables) is scornful, probably with three (or even four) heavy stresses falling at the end to hammer home the hopelessness of his situation ('**He loves thee not**').

A later play, like Shakespeare's *Macbeth*, would use the convention of the soliloquy to dramatize the conflicted psyche. Marlowe uses soliloquies to allow Faustus to explore his predicament, too, but he also uses the manifestations of the Good and Evil Angels to externalize the debate raging inside Faustus. One impulse pulls him back towards god-fearing orthodoxy, while the other plays the role of tempter and, significantly, always manages to have the last word before it and its Good Angel counterpart leave the stage. Deployed carefully in performance, the angels can be positioned to help illustrate how Faustus stands poised between heaven and hell. He has not yet signed away his soul, and it should be fairly clear to the audience (if not to Faustus himself) that he can still be saved. Nevertheless, some of his pronouncements here would have disturbed an audience of his contemporaries: the shocking inversion 'Despair in God and trust in Beelzebub' (5); his declaration that, 'When Mephistopheles shall stand by me, / What god can hurt thee, Faustus?' (24–5); the assertion that God 'loves [him] not' (10); and finally the resolution to build an altar to Beelzebub and offer there 'lukewarm blood of new-born babes' (14). The latter is a familiar instance of Faustian bravado. Elsewhere he talks of a vow 'To burn his [God's] Scriptures, slay his ministers, / And make my spirits pull his church down' (II.iii.96–7). In fact, the most destructive thing we see Faustus do in this respect is cause mayhem at the Pope's banquet. The rest is nothing but idle and empty boasts. His inflated rhetoric, bristling with threats, measured against what we see him do, is a constant reminder to the audience of the extent of Faustus's self-delusion. The moments of illumination, when Faustus has sudden, brilliant insights into his condition, are passed over as soon as they appear: the acutely perceptive line 'The god thou servest is thine own appetite' might make a fitting epitaph for him (11).

The inversions continue: the summoning of Mephistopheles here is very clearly a parody of Christian traditions; as the angels brought 'glad tidings' of Christ's birth (Luke II.x) Faustus expects Mephistopheles to bring glad tidings from Lucifer (25–6); the Latin invitation to Mephistopheles to come ('*Veni, veni, Mephistophele!*' [29]) recalls the Christian 'O come, O come, Emmanuel'; and his pronouncement, after he has signed the contract, '*Consummatum est*' is an echo of Christ's dying words on the cross according to the gospel of John (XIX.xxx). The shedding of his blood to sign the document is itself an horrific parody of the Christian sacrament of Holy Communion, and could be interpreted as a deliberate rejection of

Christ's sacrificial death, replacing the spilling of the redemptive blood of Christ with the shedding of his own blood.

Faustus's blindness and stupidity is very much in evidence here, as elsewhere at critical points in the play. Mephistopheles, more often that not, is quite direct and straightforward in response to Faustus's questions. So when Faustus asks why Lucifer desires his soul (38–39), Mephistopheles replies, baldly, that it will 'Enlarge his kingdom' (40). The Latin phrase (42) translates as the familiar modern saying, 'Misery loves company', and Mephistopheles goes on to admit that those who torture the souls in hell feel pain as great as those they torment (44). He then shifts abruptly ('But tell me, Faustus, shall I have thy soul?' [45]), and the ease with which Faustus assents ('Ay, Mephistopheles, I give it thee' [48]) borders on the comic. The fact that Faustus's own body rebels against him as he prepares to seal the pact with Lucifer is further proof both of his foolishness and the terrible danger he is courting. His blood congeals, preventing him from signing the contract in blood, as he has been ordered to do. It clearly panics him, and the sudden flurry of question marks in lines 64–69 signals his consternation. His petulant 'Is not thy soul thine own?', an impatient address to himself, is neatly ironized by Mephistopheles in an aside four lines later: 'O, what will not I do to obtain his soul?' (73) (according to Christian doctrine, the soul in fact belonged not to the human but to God). But even once Mephistopheles has fetched fire to cause the blood to flow again, Faustus's body refuses to behave: this time, the Latin inscription '*Homo, fuge!*' appears on his arm: the words 'Fly, O man!' are another quotation from the Bible (II Timothy VI.xi). If this is another sign from God, perhaps the Good Angel at work, for Faustus it comes too late: 'Whither should I fly?' he asks. 'If unto God, he'll throw thee down to hell' (77–8) – words that sound as if they could have come quite easily from the persuasive tongue of the Evil Angel. Faustus is already convinced that he has cut himself off from the possibility of redemption, and his conclusion is a bull-headed, stubborn, 'Yet shall not Faustus fly' (81). Mephistopheles then leaves, only to return at once with a procession of devils carrying crowns and rich gowns for Faustus. By the time they depart, Faustus, enthralled, is ready to give up the soul that Lucifer so covets.

Doctor Faustus, V.i.35–80

We jump now to the penultimate scene of the A-text version of the play. Faustus is measuring out his final hours on earth before he will be compelled to fulfil the terms of the contract he signed in his own blood in act II scene i. He is visited by a holy man; the Old Man's words, assembled largely via direct quotations or paraphrases of Bible verses, represent a final chance of forgiveness, and at the same time display Faustus's unwillingness to accept, or even to see, the proffered hand of redemption.

OLD MAN   Ah, Doctor Faustus, that I might prevail   35
    To guide thy steps unto the way of life,
    By which sweet path thou mayst attain the goal
    That shall conduct thee to celestial rest!
    Break heart, drop blood, and mingle it with tears –
    Tears falling from repentant heaviness   40
    Of thy most vile and loathsome filthiness,
    The stench whereof corrupts the inward soul
    With such flagitious crimes of heinous sins
    As no commiseration may expel
    But mercy, Faustus, of thy Savior sweet,   45
    Whose blood alone must wash away thy guilt.
FAUSTUS   Where art thou, Faustus? Wretch, what hast thou done?
    Damned art thou, Faustus, damned! Despair and die!
    Hell calls for right, and with a roaring voice
    Says, 'Faustus, come! Thine hour is come.'   50
            Mephistopheles gives him a dagger
    And Faustus will come to do thee right.
          [*Faustus prepares to stab himself*]
OLD MAN   Ah, stay, good Faustus, stay thy desperate steps!
    I see an angel hovers o'er thy head,
    And with a vial full of precious grace
    Offers to pour the same into thy soul.   55
    Then call for mercy and avoid despair.
FAUSTUS   Ah, my sweet friend, I feel thy words
    To comfort my distressèd soul;

Leave me a while to ponder on my sins.

OLD MAN   I go, sweet Faustus, but with heavy cheer, 60
Fearing the ruin of thy hopeless soul.

FAUSTUS   Accursèd Faustus, where is mercy now?
I do repent, and yet I do despair.
Hell strives with grace for conquest in my breast.
What shall I do to shun the snares of death? 65

MEPHISTOPHELES   Thou traitor, Faustus, I arrest thy soul
For disobedience to my sovereign lord.
Revolt, or I'll in piecemeal tear thy flesh.

FAUSTUS   Sweet Mephistopheles, entreat thy lord
To pardon my unjust presumption, 70
And with my blood again I will confirm
My former vow I made to Lucifer.

MEPHISTOPHELES   Do it then quickly, with unfeignèd heart,
Lest greater danger do attend thy drift.
    [*Faustus cuts his arm and writes with his blood*]

FAUSTUS   Torment, sweet friend, that base and crooked age 75
That durst dissuade me from thy Lucifer,
With greatest torments that our hell affords.

MEPHISTOPHELES   His faith is great. I cannot touch his soul.
But what I may afflict his body with
I will attempt, which is but little worth. 80

The Old Man is, in effect, a human embodiment of the Good Angel that featured in the first half of the play. The blood imagery, which we have already noticed is central in the signification of Faustus's damnation, resurfaces here. The Old Man seems to spell out the terms by which Faustus may still be saved: Faustus must break his heart (his will) (39), and the blood from his heart, mingled with tears of repentance (39–40) may provoke Christ's mercy (45). Christian doctrine identifies the blood of Christ as redemptive: it washes away the guilt of the sinner (46). The vehemence of the Old Man's tone would have been familiar to an Elizabethan audience from church teaching: the concentration on the sinner's 'vile and loathsome filthiness, / The stench whereof corrupts the inward soul' (41–2) is designed to strike terror in the heart of the sinner, and lead him to repent: the Old Man talks of Faustus's 'flagitious crimes of heinous sins', piling up the expressions of disgust until they are almost tautologies (flagitious essentially means the same as heinous). As we would expect, Faustus's response is despair. He is deaf to the Old Man's insistence on the mercy of 'thy Saviour sweet' (45) and can only conclude, 'Damned art thou, Faustus, damned! Despair and die!' (48). Lucifer needs no Evil Angel to counter this final invitation to seek grace; Faustus has such a deep conviction of his own damnation that he can see no prospect of salvation. All he can hear is hell's 'roaring voice' (49) demanding satisfaction: the roar is an appropriate image for hell, which will soon be seen opening its jaws to receive Faustus. Indeed, the imagery is in one sense quite literal: lists of stage properties from this time include a hell's mouth which would almost certainly have been used in performances of the play.

The imagery of blood, filth and corruption in the Old Man's first speech is replaced in his second entreaty with starkly contrasting images: 'an angel hovers o'er thy head, / And with a vial full of precious grace / Offers to pour the same into thy soul' (53–5). It is an intensely dramatic moment. The lines are delicately poised, expressive of Faustus's own soul wavering in the balance. But Faustus seems unable to find a way out of his despair, and his desperate, sobbing cries ('Despair and die!' [48]) and his imitation of hell's roar, 'Faustus, come! Thine hour is come' (50) are matched by the stage action (Mephistopheles handing him the dagger, Faustus preparing to stab himself). The Old Man's speech is imploring, and overflows with images of purity and gentleness; the crowds of sibilants and other soft consonants reinforce those images: 'hovers o'er thy head . . . vial full of precious grace . . . offers . . . same . . . soul.' Finally, the Old Man's speech seems to begin to have an impact on Faustus, although his request that he be left alone to 'ponder on my sins' (59) is undercut by the reply: the Old Man leaves, telling Faustus that he goes reluctantly, 'Fearing the ruin of thy hopeless soul' (61).

Faustus's 'I do repent, and yet I do despair' (63) is a wonderfully compact, concentrated assessment of his spiritual status, and at the same time contains a hornets' nest of theological debate. Faustus's references to 'despair' are crucial, both here and in his earlier

'Despair and die' (48) since they almost certainly refer to the sin of despair that was understood to be one of the temptations that afflicted those approaching death: the enormity of one's past sins weighed so heavily on the heart that it led to a conviction that forgiveness was impossible. The familiar battle that we have seen embodied in the Good and Evil Angels, and now in the Old Man and Mephistopheles, Faustus here locates within himself. 'Hell strives with grace for conquest in my breast' (64) he declares, and Mephistopheles acts quickly to intervene, terrifying Faustus into a rededication of his soul to Lucifer. Faustus fears for his soul, but his response is not a turn to God; instead, he pleads with Mephistopheles to 'entreat thy lord / To pardon my unjust presumption' (69–70), an indication of the extent to which his understanding of salvation and damnation has been inverted and distorted. Mephistopheles advises him to recommit himself to Lucifer 'Lest greater danger do attend thy drift' (74), but the members of the audience are well aware of the fact that the re-inscription of the pact, once again written in Faustus's own blood, is only moving him further and further away from God's saving grace; at the end of the scene, the Old Man will reappear to despair at how Faustus excludes from his soul 'the grace of heaven / And fliest the throne of his Tribunal seat!' (V.ii.111–12).

The extent to which Faustus remains ensnared by Mephistopheles is evident in his terms of address: he calls him 'sweet friend' (75), which ironically echoes the use of the same form of address to the Old Man (57). He asks Mephistopheles to punish the Old Man 'With greatest torments that our hell affords' (77), and the use of the word 'our' signifies the extent to which Faustus now associates himself with the damned. Mephistopheles's response actually serves to hammer home the irony for the audience (though not for Faustus): having threatened to tear Faustus 'piecemeal' for his disobedience (68), he admits that the damage he can inflict on the Old Man is limited: 'His faith is great, I cannot touch his soul' (78). He promises to do what he can to afflict the holy man's body, but is unable to refrain from adding that it is 'but little worth' (80). In one sense, Mephistopheles's threats against Faustus are as hollow as Faustus's threats against the church in act II scene i. It is only

Faustus's own determined rejection of salvation that makes him vulnerable to demonic attack. Here as elsewhere, the text seems to identify Faustus's own wilfulness and stupidity as the determining factors of his destiny.

Conclusions

1. We have seen how Christian theology underpins (and often determines) the action of Marlowe's plays. Although some quite specific points have been made about issues such as salvation and damnation, it is important to bear in mind that the church's teaching was in flux (and factionally split) at this volatile point in ecclesiastical history, and aspects of theological controversy bleed into texts like *Doctor Faustus*.
2. The scepticism and satire that seem to emerge from Marlowe's plays have been interpreted by some as keys to Marlowe's own psyche: it is easy to understand how one might be tempted to associate these elements with the beliefs of a writer who had, by the time of his death, established something of a reputation as a free thinker, heretic or atheist. However, we need to take care in rushing to make *ad hominem* judgements: the debate about the personal heresy dates back to the 1930s, and we should remember C. S. Lewis's caveat that not every work of art can be read as an expression of the artist's personality. This is especially true of the early modern period, since the understanding of the artist as individual creative genius would not fully emerge until the late eighteenth century. It is also particularly relevant to the drama, where work is by its very nature collaborative, and where the creations of the playwright, his *dramatis personae*, are created only to be interpreted by others in performance.
3. Nevertheless, there are examples in Marlowe's work of some unorthodox perspectives on issues such as salvation and the ways in which God intervenes in human affairs (see the discussion of Tamburlaine's burning of the Moslem holy books at the beginning of this chapter).
4. In addition, there are passages in some of the plays, *The Jew of*

Malta and *Doctor Faustus* in particular, which bear the scars of contemporary religious controversy – the anti-Catholic satire in the portrayal of the friars Barnardine and Jacomo in *The Jew of Malta* is the obvious example. Anti-Semitism is rife, too, in that play, and the fact that the text pokes fun at the Catholic faith as well as the Jewish faith does nothing to diminish the troubling stereotypes that the play deploys.

5. Finally, it is probably unhelpful to try and pin down Marlowe's perspective on religion either as orthodox or as subversive. What is certain is that the plays provide a number of opportunities for readers or performers to open up the relations between God and humankind to scrutiny, and to interrogate the ways in which societies have engineered human understandings of those relations, sometimes for less than godly motives.

Methods of Analysis

1. We have looked closely at each extract in the context of the play as a whole, taking account, for example, of what we have learned about Tamburlaine's attitude towards God or the gods up the point in act V scene i when he blasphemes against Mahomet, and reading Faustus's predicament, trapped between hell and heaven, in the light of what he has previously said and done as he has negotiated his way towards the pact with Lucifer.

2. Analysis of the passages has taken full account of what we know about sixteenth century religious belief. It has been necessary to provide some specific details of doctrine at times, although this has been kept to a minimum.

3. We have paid close attention to the movement of the verse in each extract; note the variety of ways in which it can be used. It is as important in the measuring of comic timing (as in Barabas's interruptions of the friars in *The Jew*, IV.i) as it is in the expression of Faustus's spiritual crisis. There is much to discover of the dynamics of a scene via attention to its variations in rhythm and timing.

4. Dramatic irony is one of the playwright's most frequently used

tools, and Marlowe often exploits the gap between the knowledge his audience has gathered, and the flawed perceptions of his characters (our view of Faustus is heavily influenced by the use of dramatic irony). He uses a similar technique at other times, particularly in *The Jew of Malta*, when he allows Barabas to exploit repeatedly his advantage of superior knowledge over others on the stage.

5. We have also seen how clusters of images can be used to enhance the impact of a scene. This applies particularly to the more 'poetic' passages, and these are most common in *Faustus*, which explores the most extreme situations and states of mind we can imagine. We have also noted how the sounds of words, carefully placed, can have a similar effect.

Suggested Work

Tamburlaine certainly provides scope for a closer consideration of those relations between God and humankind, and is seen by some as Marlowe's most deeply pessimistic work. *Tamburlaine II* opens with the Moslems Orcanes (King of Natolia) and Gazellus (Viceroy of Byron) discussing the necessity of a truce with the Christian King Sigismond of Hungary, in order to combat the greater, common threat of Tamburlaine. Sigismond swears by Christ and Orcanes by Mahomet as they arrange their truce. In act 2 scene 1, Frederick of Buda and Baldwin of Bohemia persuade Sigismond to break the truce and launch a surprise attack on the heathen Orcanes who, having sent most of his troops to deal with Tamburlaine, is vulnerable. Orcanes is incensed by the Christians' treachery, but prepares to meet them in battle, and defeats Sigismond's army. Sigismond dies in battle. Orcanes, the Moslem, attributes his victory to Christ's fury at the Christian king breaking his promise. The scenario in which a Moslem triumphs over a Christian, although apparently as a result of Christ's (rather than Mahomet's) intervention, seems very much in keeping with the ambivalent attitude towards religion that emerges elsewhere in the play. Further investigation of this sub-plot, as well as the presentation of Tamburlaine as 'scourge of God', will reveal more of the complex interaction of God and humankind in the play.

A number of critics have focused on the figure of Ferneze in *The Jew of Malta*, even going so far as to suggest that the true Machiavellian in the play is not Barabas at all, but the duplicitous Christian governor of the island. For some, Marlowe's apparent attack on Christian hypocrisy seems to defuse that play's anti-Semitism, though quite why this must follow is unclear. Any amount of Christian (or Catholic) satire does not make a text any less anti-Semitic. Nevertheless, the satire is undeniably a significant element of *The Jew of Malta*, and any reading or performance of the play must take full account of the ways in which Marlowe allows room for critiques of religious belief and its institutions.

Doctor Faustus is the one that remains the most troubling text, however. Its uneven tone is disorientating, for it veers between knockabout comedy and tragedy of the most serious kind – after all, it deals not only with life and death but with eternal salvation and damnation. The text picks up on and participates in theological debates that were current at the time, particularly in terms of free will and determinism. It may be that the play is an indictment of Calvinist theology, where humans are predestined for heaven or hell. It can also be read as a furious, fire-breathing attack on human sinfulness, a stark reminder of the inevitable fate of anyone who rejects God and embraces the Devil. A number of critics have compared the A-text and B-text versions of the play and attempted to prove how the two versions adopt very different theological perspectives, and deeper research in this area can be followed up via the guide to further reading at the end of the book. In the meantime, a review of the play, tallying the number of times Faustus seems to be offered the chance of salvation only – apparently – to reject it, would be instructive in any attempt to establish the text's shifting perspectives. Finally, a last, reiterative word of advice would be to avoid trying to pin down any of Marlowe's works to specific perspectives, either in terms of doctrine, or else in terms of belief and unbelief. The texts have long since proven their resistance to such attempts.

4

Power and Politics

The principle of the 'will to power' can be applied to interpretations of every one of Marlowe's protagonists. In their different ways, Faustus, Barabas, Tamburlaine, Edward and Mortimer (in *Edward II*) are driven by a desire for control. In Faustus's case, it is a desire to determine his own destiny; for the others, the struggle is a more directly political one. Issues of state politics are crucial to all Marlowe's plays, with the exceptions of *Doctor Faustus* and the early work *Dido Queen of Carthage*. *Edward II* intervenes in Elizabethan debates over the divine right of the monarch. In *The Jew of Malta*, the politics of Machiavelli are put under the microscope (another fashionable debate in Elizabethan England); in the end, some critics argue, the Christian Ferneze proves a more able Machiavellian than the Jew Barabas, and we have already seen the implications of this ironic twist for how we read attitudes to religion in the play. The clearest example of all, however, is *Tamburlaine*, which charts the career of a ruthless, all-conquering soldier and king. There are very few plays from this period that present such an unflinching portrayal of the use and abuse of power: Tamburlaine's brutal savagery, which even extends to the execution of his own son for cowardice, is shocking and at the same time curiously enthralling in performance.

Tamburlaine I, II.v.50–105

The extract below finds Tamburlaine on the cusp of his career as the 'scourge and terror of the world'. Enlisted by Cosroe to overthrow the weak king of Persia, Mycetes (Cosroe's brother), Tamburlaine has won an easy victory over the Persian army. Tamburlaine is rewarded by Cosroe and made regent of Persia. Immediately before the extract, Cosroe has swept off the stage with his followers, to 'ride in triumph through Persepolis'. That final, fateful line is echoed by Tamburlaine and what follows is remarkable for the way it dramatizes the birth of Tamburlaine's ambition. It is important to pay close attention in particular to Tamburlaine's interaction with his followers as the scene proceeds.

TAMBURLAINE   'And ride in triumph through Persepolis'?   50
    Is it not brave to be a King, Techelles?
    Usumcasane and Theridamas,
    Is it not passing brave to be a king
    And ride in triumph through Persepolis?
TECHELLES   O my lord, 'tis sweet and full of pomp.   55
USUMCASANE   To be a king is half to be a god.
THERIDAMAS   A god is not so glorious as a king.
    I think the pleasure they enjoy in heaven
    Cannot compare with kingly joys in earth:
    To wear a crown enchased with pearl and gold,   60
    Whose virtues carry with it life and death;
    To ask, and have; command, and be obeyed;
    When looks breed love, with looks to gain the prize –
    Such power attractive shines in princes' eyes.
TAMBURLAINE   Why, say, Theridamas, wilt thou be a king?   65
THERIDAMAS   Nay, though I praise it, I can live without it.
TAMBURLAINE   What says my other friends? Will you be kings?
TECHELLES   Ay, if I could, with all my heart, my lord.
TAMBURLAINE   Why, that's well said, Techelles. So would I.
    And so would you, my masters, would you not?   70
USUMCASANE   What then, my lord ?
TAMBURLAINE   Why then, Casane, shall we wish for aught
    The world affords in greatest novelty,
    And rest attemptless, faint and destitute?
    Methinks we should not. I am strongly moved   75
    That if I should desire the Persian crown

I could attain it with a wondrous ease.
And would not all our soldiers soon consent,
If we should aim at such a dignity?
THERIDAMAS   I know they would, with our persuasions.   80
TAMBURLAINE   Why then, Theridamas, I'll first essay
To get the Persian kingdom to myself;
Then thou for Parthia, they for Scythia and Media.
And if I prosper, all shall be as sure
As if the Turk, the pope, Afric, and Greece   85
Came creeping to us with their crowns apace.
TECHELLES   Then shall we send to this triumphing king
And bid him battle for his novel crown?
USUMCASANE   Nay, quickly then, before his room be hot.
TAMBURLAINE   'Twill prove a pretty jest, in faith, my friends.   90
THERIDAMAS   A jest to charge on twenty thousand men?
I judge the purchase more important far.
TAMBURLAINE   Judge by thyself, Theridamas, not me,
For presently Techelles here shall haste
To bid him battle ere he pass too far   95
And lose more labour than the gain will quite.
Then shalt thou see the Scythian Tamburlaine
Make but a jest to win the Persian crown.
Techelles, take a thousand horse with thee
And bid him turn him back to war with us   100
That only made him king to make us sport.
We will not steal upon him cowardly,
But give him warning and more warriors.
Haste thee, Techelles. We will follow thee.

Crowns are powerful signifiers in this play. Mycetes tries to hide his when he realises that he is about to lose the battle against Tamburlaine and Cosroe (act II scene iv). Tamburlaine finds him, and they squabble over it, Tamburlaine ridiculing the petrified king, and eventually letting him keep it, but only so he can find a more public moment to take it from him. Now, having seen the victory that he himself has won transformed into a celebration of Cosroe's coronation as the new King of Persia, Tamburlaine is left with the phrase ringing in his ears: 'And ride in triumph through Persepolis?' (50). He muses on it, and his first words to Techelles may well be casual; simply idle conversation: 'Is it not brave to be a King, Techelles?' (51). His followers pick up on it, however, with a good deal of enthusiasm. As Techelles, Usumcasane and Theridamas respond, each one outdoes the other: Techelles seems to respond by rote, but Usumcasane declares that 'To be a king is half to be a god', and Theridamas outdoes him by insisting that 'A god is not so glorious as a king' (55–7). One can easily imagine the three of them shooting each other challenging looks while Tamburlaine, self-absorbed, muses on their replies. Theridamas provides the most elaborate meditation so far on kingship, and central to his meditation is power, the power over 'life and death', where to ask is to have, and to command is to be obeyed (59–60). The sharp insight that the looks of a king 'breed love' is in fact an accurate assessment of the relationship Tamburlaine enjoys with these followers of his: he commands the unwavering loyalty of his officers and soldiers, a fact about the historical figure Timur the Lame that is noted by a number of early chroniclers of his life.

The conversational tone is signalled by the use of prose: immediately after Theridamas's discourse on kingship, the text falls out of pentameters as Tamburlaine turns to each of his followers: 'What says my other friends?' he asks. 'Will you be kings?' (67). Theridamas, having rhapsodised over the prospect, has responded with a non-committal shrug – 'Nay, though I praise it, I can live without it' (66). The contrast between his eloquent discourse and the abrupt dismissal may provoke laughter – from the audience, from his companions, or both. The others seem to detect that there is something more serious stirring in the conversation, and Techelles's response is an earnest, 'Ay, if I could, with all my heart, my lord' (68). Usumcasane wants to understand exactly what Tamburlaine is contemplating, and his response is a prompting for his leader to say more: 'What then, my lord?' (71). As Tamburlaine replies, the text breaks out of the conversational prose and back into iambic pentameters. His challenge is rhetorical: the idea that he should ever 'rest attemptless, faint and destitute' (74) is not to be countenanced, particularly when he is so confident that the Persian crown is there for the taking (76–7).

Within the space of thirty or forty lines, Tamburlaine shifts from a casual musing on the pleasures of kingship to a resolution that he will have the Persian crown for himself – the very crown he handed over to Cosroe just moments earlier. By including 'the Turk, the pope, Afric, and Greece' in his prospective conquests (85), Tamburlaine manages to encompass all the known world. His confidence is already transporting him from the anticipation of his first conquest to dizzying heights of power. Tamburlaine's grim humour as he anticipates recovering the crown he has just handed over is characteristic. In victory, Tamburlaine's triumph over his enemies is usually accompanied by inventive, playful, but frequently savage acts that humiliate those he has defeated. With Techelles and Usumcasane relishing the prospect of unseating Cosroe even before he has had a chance to warm his throne (88–9), Tamburlaine evidently finds the prospect amusing: his ''Twill prove a pretty jest, in faith, my friends' (90) may be read as an indication of how whimsical his decision to betray Cosroe really is. The impact is given added weight by Theridamas's response, a demurring 'A jest to charge on twenty thousand men? / I judge the purchase more important far' (91–2). It may be meant by Theridamas as an aside, but Tamburlaine evidently overhears him, and brushes him off ('Judge by thyself, Theridamas, not me' [93]). As he begins to issue orders, he shoots another rebuttal at Theridamas: 'Then shalt thou see the Scythian Tamburlaine / Make but a jest to win the Persian crown' (97–8). If Tamburlaine wishes to term it a jest, then that is what it will be. Here and elsewhere, any challenge to Tamburlaine's authority in any form – even a dispute over semantics – will not be countenanced. At the same time, the repetition of the word 'jest' is characteristic of Tamburlaine's imperviousness to the savagery and tragedy of war.

By the time the scene concludes the tone has shifted dramatically. The beginning of the scene has featured a crowded stage of triumphant soldiers, and Mycetes's crown will have been handed over to Cosroe amidst the pageantry of military flags and armoured men. Now Tamburlaine is alone with his closest companions, and the stage becomes a more intimate and informal space. From the joy and release of triumph after battle, the energy of the scene has been allowed to drop as it passes from public celebration to private rest and relaxation, and the characters have lapsed into idle chat and reflection. But the first stirrings of a new impetus have been awoken in Tamburlaine by the lure of a crown and all it symbolizes. Two scenes later, the crown has become an obsession for Tamburlaine: he describes it as 'the ripest fruit of all, / That perfect bliss and sole felicity, / The sweet fruition of an earthly crown' (I.II.vii.27–9). From that point on, having triumphed over Cosroe, Tamburlaine's career is directed at one single goal – the possession of power.

The Jew of Malta, V.ii.26–46, 110–123

The figure of Niccolo Machiavelli loomed large in Elizabethan culture, and the significance of his appearance as the prologue to *The Jew of Malta* cannot be underestimated. Machiavel is, after all, the one who introduces Barabas the Jew to the audience, and both what he says about Barabas, and the way he says it, demand close attention (see pp. 22–7 for a close discussion of the play's prologue). What we see here is Barabas acting upon the principles established in Machiavelli's political writings (or at least one inter-pretation of those writings). Having betrayed Ferneze and his knights to the Turkish enemy, Barabas has been made governor of Malta by the Turkish leader Calymath. Barabas now takes stock of what he has achieved.

BARABAS   Away, no more! Let him not trouble me.
    Exeunt [Turkish Janizaries with Ferneze and Knights.
    Barabas remains alone]
    Thus hast thou gotten, by thy policy,
    No simple place, no small authority.
    I now am governor of Malta. True,
    But Malta hates me, and, in hating me,   30
    My life's in danger; and what boots it thee,
    Poor Barabas, to be the governor,
    Whenas thy life shall be at their command?
    No, Barabas, this must be looked into;

And since by wrong thou got'st authority,   35
Maintain it bravely by firm policy,
At least unprofitably lose it not.
For he that liveth in authority,
And neither gets him friends, nor fills his bags,
Lives like the ass that Aesop speaketh of,   40
That labours with a load of bread and wine
And leaves it off to snap on thistle tops.
But Barabas will be more circumspect.
Begin betimes; Occasion's bald behind;
Slip not thine opportunity, for fear too late   45
Thou seek'st for much, but canst not compass it.
[. . .]

We are witnessing Barabas at a turning point: having been reduced from a position of great prosperity to abject poverty, and having rebuilt his fortune only to be betrayed by his own slave, his plots have finally brought to him the position where he is in total control of Ferneze, the Christian governor who was responsible for his ruin. The Turk Calymath, whose victory over Ferneze has been engineered by Barabas's cunning, has left him to use them at his discretion (V.ii.11). He has certainly made the most of the reversal of fortunes in the preceding encounter with Ferneze, relishing the opportunity to send the governor and his confederates to prison (V.ii.22–4).

Left alone, he congratulates himself, reflecting that he has got 'No simple place, no small authority' by his 'policy' (27–8). He allows himself only the shortest time to gloat, however, for he is suddenly, vivdly aware of the precariousness of his position; there may even be room for humour in the juxtaposition of a triumphant 'I now am governor of Malta' with 'True, / but Malta hates me' (29–30). Recognizing the precariousness of his position, he begins to plot again. Now installed as governor of an island whose inhabitants despise him, he decides to plot with Ferneze to return the island to the Christians. It is quite likely that Marlowe has Machiavelli's writings in mind at this point in the play: in *The Prince*, Machiavelli addresses specifically the complications that follow when a ruler has gained power by the intervention of others.

The key word in Barabas's deliberations is the term 'policy', which recurs at several points in the play, and refers to Ferneze's behaviour as much as it does to Barabas's. Having been deprived of his wealth by Ferneze and his knights, Barabas launches a bitter attack on their hypocrisy: 'Ay, policy! That's their profession, / And not simplicity as they suggest' (I.ii.161–2). At the end of this scene, Barabas talks of 'Making a profit of my policy' when describing how he intends to co-exist with the opposing Turkish and Christian forces (V.ii.112). Here again, his priority is to 'Maintain it [his position] bravely by firm policy' (36). The reference to Aesop turns out to be a false trail – there is no sign of such a story in Aesop's writings, but the resort to ancient fable is conventional, and the depiction of the ass 'That labours with a load of bread and wine / And leaves it off to snap on thistle tops' (41–2) is easily interpreted: the animal carries rich food but does not benefit from its labours, eating thistles instead. Barabas is determined to ensure that he will profit from his careful and daring conspiracies. The second fable refers to the idea that the allegorical figure of Occasion (that is to say, opportunity) has a long forelock, but the rest of her head is bald: consequently, she must be caught hold of as she passes, since when she has gone by there is no way of catching her.

The rhythm of this speech perfectly captures the evolution of Barabas's thoughts. The opening lines are calm, resolved and satisfied (27–8). The realization of his perilous position, however, unsettles him, and the next few lines are choppy and agitated (29–33) – notice the profusion of commas and semicolons. He settles himself to find a solution (34) and the deployment of the fable allows time for him to reassess his status (38–42). The lines in the final section of the speech (43–6) are somewhat clipped, energized, demonstrating how quickly Barabas can adapt and prepare himself for his next challenge. Having met Ferneze again and agreed to betray the Turk to the Christian, this is the speech that follows, where he summarizes how he will make 'a profit of . . . policy' (112).

> And thus far roundly goes the business.   110
> Thus, loving neither, will I live with both,
> Making a profit of my policy;

And he from whom my most advantage comes
Shall be my friend.
This is the life we Jews are used to lead,   115
And reason, too, for Christians do the like.
Well, now about effecting this device:
First, to surprise great Selim's soldiers,
And then to make provision for the feast,
That at one instant all things may be done.   120
My policy detests prevention.
To what event my secret purpose drives,
I know, and they shall witness with their lives.

Both the line 'Thus, loving neither, will I live with both' (111) and its corresponding maxim, 'he from whom my most advantage comes / Shall be my friend' (113–14), are thoroughly Machiavellian: it was fundamental to Machiavelli's policies that the successful ruler would not keep promises or maintain truces when to do so would be to the disadvantage either of himself or of his people.

What follows is an odd aside that begins as a standard anti-Semitism on the part of the playwright, but which may on closer inspection be interpreted as an attempt at justifying villainous, duplicitous behaviour. Barabas notes that 'This is the life we Jews are used to lead,' and adds, 'And reason too, for Christians do the like' (115–16). As noted above, a number of critics have remarked on Ferneze's behaviour, and have seen him as the true Machiavellian in the play. Barabas seems to be recognizing something similar when he notes Christian hypocrisy; certainly his own experience as a subject on the island ruled by Ferneze and his knights has borne this out. The two lines actually anticipate a longer speech in Shakespeare's *The Merchant of Venice*, where Shylock remarks that his thirst for revenge he learnt from Christian example. The first half of Shylock's speech is frequently cited as proof that Shakespeare wished to represent Jews as humans on an equal footing with Christians: 'Hath not a Jew eyes? . . . If you prick us, do we not bleed?' (III.i.49–50, 54). However, the climax of that speech does not centre around suffering, but on mutual aggression:

And if you wrong us, shall we not revenge? If we are like you in the rest, we will resemble you in that. If a Jew wrong a Christian, what is his humility? Revenge. If a Christian wrong a Jew, what should his sufferance be by Christian example? Why, revenge.

(III.i.55–9)

Whether or not this speech, and the lines in Barabas's speech, can be taken as attempts to justify what was commonly perceived at the time as customary Jewish behaviour, or whether it is simply an attack on Christian hypocrisy and vengefulness, they are significant in any debate of the two plays' status in terms of anti-Semitism.

The scene's closing lines are once again distinctly Machiavellian. They are also to become fairly conventional expressions of the stage villain's desire to keep his plans hidden until the plot comes to fruition. A number of editors note how closely they parallel a similar speech by another Machiavellian type, the plotting Lorenzo in Thomas Kyd's *The Spanish Tragedy*, where a couple of lines in Spanish that Lorenzo speaks translate as 'And what I wish, no-one knows; I understand, and that suffices me' (III.vi.87–8). Whether or not it is a conscious tip of the hat to his friend Tom Kyd, Marlowe is clearly intent on establishing Barabas's Machiavellian credentials.

Finally, we should note Barabas's continuing dynamic relationship with the audience. Throughout the play, he has indulged in asides and substantial soliloquies that have detailed the skill and ruthlessness of his plots for the benefit of the audience. As I have noted already (p. 73), this leaves the audience in an ambivalent position, inevitably drawn in by the cunning and the humour of a character they would automatically identify as a villain. Barabas directs the audience's attention to the fact that he is keeping his plans secret from everyone but them, and makes them complicit in his villainy. As the play enters its final stage, it is most likely that a modern audience (or reader) will be rooting for Barabas. We can only speculate how Elizabethans, steeped in prejudice against the Jewish people and suspicious of Machiavellian politics, would have reacted in this respect. The potential gap between the audiences, over four hundred years apart, reminds us both of cultural and historical difference, and of the unique nature of drama, forever open to reinterpretation.

Edward II, I.ii.33–83

Enter the [Arch]bishop of Canterbury [and an Attendant]

WARWICK   Here comes my lord of Canterbury's grace.

LANCASTER   His countenance bewrays he is displeased.

CANTERBURY [*to his Attendant*]
   First were his sacred garments rent and torn,   35
   Then laid they violent hands upon him, next
   Himself imprisoned and his goods asseized.
   This certify the pope. Away, take horse.
                  [*Exit Attendant*]

LANCASTER   My lord, will you take arms against the king?

CANTERBURY   What need I? God himself is up in arms   40
   When violence is offered to the Church.

MORTIMER   Then will you join with us that be his peers
   To banish or behead that Gaveston?

CANTERBURY   What else, my lords? For it concerns me near;
   The bishopric of Coventry is his.   45
                  Enter the Queen

MORTIMER   Madam, whither walks your majesty so fast?

QUEEN   Unto the forest, gentle Mortimer,
   To live in grief and baleful discontent,
   For now my lord the king regards me not
   But dotes upon the love of Gaveston.   50
   He claps his cheeks and hangs about his neck,
   Smiles in his face and whispers in his ears,
   And when I come he frowns, as who should say,
   'Go whither thou wilt, seeing I have Gaveston.'

MORTIMER SENIOR   Is it not strange, that he is thus bewitched?   55

MORTIMER   Madam, return unto the court again.
   That sly, inveigling Frenchman we'll exile
   Or lose our lives; and yet ere that day come
   The king shall lose his crown, for we have power,
   And courage too, to be revenged at full.   60

CANTERBURY   But yet lift not your swords against the king.

LANCASTER   No, but we'll lift Gaveston from hence.

WARWICK   And war must be the means, or he'll stay still.

QUEEN   Then let him stay, for rather than my lord
    Shall be oppressed by civil mutinies,   65
    I will endure a melancholy life,
    And let him frolic with his minion.
CANTERBURY   My lords, to ease all this, but hear me speak.
    We and the rest that are his counsellors
    Will meet, and with a general consent   70
    Confirm his banishment with our hands and seals.
LANCASTER   What we confirm the king will frustrate.
MORTIMER   Then may we lawfully revolt from him.
WARWICK   But say, my lord, where shall this meeting be?
CANTERBURY   At the New Temple.   75
MORTIMER   Content.
CANTERBURY   And in the meantime I'll entreat you all
    To cross to Lambeth, and there stay with me.
LANCASTER   Come then, let's away.
MORTIMER   Madam, farewell.   80
QUEEN   Farewell, sweet Mortimer, and for my sake
    Forbear to levy arms against the king.
MORTIMER   Ay, if words will serve; if not, I must.
                [Exeunt]

Marlowe's *Edward II* is a provocative text in a number of ways. The following chapter will look in more detail at its representation of homosexuality. Here, the focus is on the issue of kingship, and, more specifically, this potentially subversive question: when is it lawful for a subject to rebel against his or her monarch? In 1533, about sixty years before Marlowe wrote *Edward II*, Henry VIII had established himself as Supreme Head of the church via the Act of Appeals and Supremacy. The act established that the monarch was endowed with all God's power and authority, a principle which conflicted directly with Rome's teaching that the Pope was to be regarded as the supreme authority. It was a crucial development in the history of the Reformation – Europe's break with the Catholic church – and had enormous implications for the relations between church and state.

    Edward has already launched a direct, symbolic attack on the church by the physical humiliation of the Bishop of Coventry, an attack we have witnessed for ourselves in the previous scene. The assault on the bishop is described at the beginning of this extract, when we overhear the Archbishop of Canterbury ordering his attendant to convey the news to the Pope. The Archbishop's report reinscribes the event on the minds of the audience, underlining its significance. It also allows the audience to see how the barons (and the Archbishop) react to the news. All the speeches preceding Canterbury's entrance have consisted of threats against Gaveston. Now, with the head of the English church clearly incensed by the attack on one of his bishops, Lancaster gives voice to what all the barons are thinking: 'My lord, will you take arms against the king?' (39), and the rest of the extract stages the debate that follows from this singular suggestion. The agitation that the proposed action provokes is signalled by the profusion of questions marks (lines 39, 40, 43, 44). This is a critical moment in the play, and the pace is quick and the tension high.

Canterbury's first response seems to give assent, but he cannily shifts the onus away from human agency with his assertion that 'God himself is up in arms / When violence is offered to the Church' (40–1). When Mortimer alters the terms of the proposal to focus on Gaveston – either to banish or behead him – Canterbury is less hesitant. The debate is interrupted by Isabella's appearance at line 45. When it is taken up again, and Mortimer talks in fairly direct terms about a revolt against Edward, the Archbishop pipes up again: 'But yet lift not your swords against the king' (61). The queen is closer to Canterbury than the mutinous barons with regard to the prospect of a revolt, and Canterbury lobbies hard to deal with the situation by banishing Gaveston rather than attacking the king himself. Lancaster is unconvinced ('What we confirm the king will frustrate' [72]) and when Mortimer asserts that a failure on Edward's part to consent to the banishment would mean that 'Then may we lawfully revolt from him' (73), this is pointedly ignored by the Archbishop, who remains on the safe side of the fence in terms of action against the monarch. The queen ends the scene with a final plea to Mortimer to 'Forbear to levy arms against the king' (82). Mortimer makes no promises: 'Ay, if words will serve' he offers, but 'if not, I must' (83). Mortimer's ambivalent final line strikes an ominous note at the end of this scene, and the barons will indeed act quickly: after the five line speech by Gaveston that makes up act I scene iii, the next scene finds Edward confronted with the document decreeing Gaveston's exile. Edward, having signed it, turns on the barons with a petulant, sarcastic invitation for them to take action against him too:

> Nay, then lay violent hands upon your king.
> Here, Mortimer, sit thou in Edward's throne;
> Warwick and Lancaster, wear you my crown.
> Was ever king thus overruled as I?
>
> (I.iv.35–8)

Lancaster's blunt and impertinent response ('Learn then to rule us better, and the realm' [39]) is an indication of just how far, and how quickly, the balance of power has shifted. Edward has already shown himself a failure in 'ruling' his baronial class, and from this point on the erosion will only accelerate.

Clearly, thoughts of rebellion against the monarch come more easily to some than to others. Note Canterbury's response when Mortimer delivers the most rebellious lines yet: contemplating the consequences of Edward's refusal to agree to Gaveston's banishment, Mortimer asserts that 'The king shall lose his crown, for we have power, / And courage too, to be revenged at full' (59–60). Canterbury's swift response is close to a rebuttal: 'But yet lift not your swords against the king' (61). Lancaster, who elsewhere appears even more eager for a revolt than Mortimer, seems to offer some concession, which may be simply political ('No, but we'll lift Gaveston from hence' [62]). When Warwick supports Mortimer ('And war must be the means, or he'll stay still' [63]), the queen steps up alongside Canterbury, protesting that she would rather Gaveston stay than see her 'lord . . . oppressed by civil mutinies' (64–65). It is at this point that the Archbishop plays politician, and fashions a compromise that will keep the mutinous barons satisfied, at least in the short term. Compromise, however, will be short-lived in this volatile situation.

The role played by Isabella in the scene is a crucial one. Her appearance is couched in a conventional mode, that of the spurned lover. When Mortimer asks where she is going, she replies, 'Unto the forest . . . / To live in grief and baleful discontent', now that her lord the king has rejected her for love of Gaveston (47–50). The language she uses to describe that relationship is notable for its sensuousness: '. . . claps his cheeks and hangs about his neck, / Smiles in his face and whispers in his ears' (51–2). Their idyllic and very physical love is set against her 'grief and baleful discontent' (48). Edward 'smiles' on Gaveston (52) but 'frowns' on her (53). Her stated destination is almost certainly a metaphorical one; we should certainly not expect to see her as if preparing to leave the court. The forest is a symbol that could imply a number of things, including seclusion, abandonment, and possibly renewal. This is Isabella's first appearance in the play, and she cuts a weak and melancholy figure, driven to despair, not anger, by Edward's favouring of Gaveston. As Edward's wife, she is as much a subject of the king as anyone else; furthermore, both the society Marlowe wrote about (early fourteenth century) and the society he lived through (late sixteenth) were starkly patriarchal, and the submission of the wife to the will of the husband was understood as part of the natural order. Gender relations will be studied in more depth in the next chapter, but for now it is worth taking note of Isabella's first appearance, for the contrast between her behaviour here with her words and actions in the second half of the play is striking.

The extract is a good example of Marlowe's gift for exciting, intensely dramatic dialogue. After Canterbury's speech to the Attendant, which itself ends with two clipped commands ('This certify the pope. Away, take horse' [38]), the extract consists of two passages that are remarkably conversational (39–45, and a longer one between lines 72 and 83), sandwiching a set of more conventional, longer speeches between lines 46 and 71. The conversational passages are made up of speeches no longer than two lines each, and at the end of the scene they are single lines, some only a word or two long. After Canterbury's speech, there is another clear demarcation between lines 46 and 71 and the rest of the extract in that the conversational parts are in prose, and the former is in verse. Lines 39 to 45 are interrogative, as the barons attempt to assess the Archbishop's stance, in the wake of the humiliation of the Bishop of Coventry. After the interlude with the queen, Canterbury takes the initiative ('My lords, to ease all this, but hear me speak' [68]) and makes a decisive proposal for action. The tone of the scene is now determined, almost businesslike: ' . . . where shall this meeting be? / At the New Temple. / Content' (74–76) and Lancaster hurries everyone along ('Come then, let's away' [79]), almost as if he is concerned that a delay may weaken this newly forged resolve. It is significant that, as everyone prepares to leave (or perhaps even vacates the stage), Queen Isabella and Mortimer are left to deliver their final exchange. Mortimer is the only one who says farewell directly to the queen (it is likely that the others would at least make a bow), and her reply should be noted: 'Farewell, sweet Mortimer' (81) and read in relation to her first address to him, as 'gentle Mortimer' (47). It may be that the relationship that will develop between Isabella and Mortimer is signalled as early as their first appearance on stage together.

Finally, it is important to try and visualize the scene being played out on stage as you read the extract. The dynamics of power – whether in gender relations, or in terms of relative positions in the social hierarchy – may be conveyed very starkly by a gifted director. In this passage, the Archbishop of Canterbury is likely to be the still figure around whom the others orbit. He is the one who ostensibly holds the balance of power as the talk of rebellion ripples around him. On her entrance, Isabella becomes the primary focus, and the martyred woman perhaps edges the authoritative bishop out of the frame. He makes one attempt to recover his central position (line 61), before regaining control with a more domineering interruption at line 68 ('My lords, to ease all this, but hear me speak'). Then, after a rapid exchange involving most of the characters on stage, the group of actors disperse. The significance of the church (and at the same time its precarious grip on the spiral of events) is underlined by Canterbury's position on stage, and the relative positions of the barons who address him.

Edward II, V.ii.1–56

This second extract from the play finds Edward imprisoned and
Mortimer in control, accompanied by a very different Queen
Isabella. Edward has now relinquished his crown, and the symbolic
transference of power is evident in the stage prop of the crown itself,
brought on by the Bishop of Winchester.

> *Enter Mortimer [Junior] and Queen Isabel.*
> MORTIMER   Fair Isabel, now have we our desire:
> The proud corrupters of the light-brained king
> Have done their homage to the lofty gallows,
> And he himself lies in captivity.
> Be ruled by me, and we will rule the realm.   5
> In any case, take heed of childish fear,
> For now we hold an old wolf by the ears
> That, if he slip, will seize upon us both,
> And grip the sorer, being gripped himself.
> Think therefore, madam, that imports us much   10
> To erect your son with all the speed we may
> And that I be Protector over him,
> For our behoof will bear the greater sway
> Whenas a king's name shall be under writ.
> QUEEN   Sweet Mortimer, the life of Isabel,   15
> Be thou persuaded that I love thee well;
> And therefore, so the prince my son be safe,
> Whom I esteem as dear as these mine eyes,
> Conclude against his father what thou wilt
> And I myself will willingly subscribe.   20
> MORTIMER   First would I hear news that he were deposed,
> And then let me alone to handle him.
> *Enter Messenger [with a letter, and then the Bishop
> of Winchester with the crown].*
> Letters, from whence?
> MESSENGER   From Killingworth, my lord.
> QUEEN   How fares my lord the king?
> MESSENGER   In health, madam, but full of pensiveness.   25

QUEEN   Alas, poor soul, would I could ease his grief. –
    Thanks, gentle Winchester. [*To the Messenger*] Sirrah,
      be gone.
                [*Exit Messenger*]
WINCHESTER   The king hath willingly resigned his crown.
QUEEN   O happy news! Send for the prince my son.
WINCHESTER   Further, ere this letter was sealed, Lord Berkeley
    came,   30
    So that he now is gone from Killingworth,
    And we have heard that Edmund laid a plot
    To set his brother free; no more but so.
    The lord of Berkeley is so pitiful
    As Leicester that had charge of him before.   35
QUEEN   Then let some other be his guardian.
MORTIMER   Let me alone. Here is the privy seal.
    [*Exit the Bishop of Winchester. Mortimer calls offstage*]
    Who's there? Call hither Gurney and Matrevis. –
    To dash the heavy-headed Edmund's drift,
    Berkeley shall be discharged, the king removed,   40
    And none but we shall know where he lieth.
QUEEN   But, Mortimer, as long as he survives,
    What safety rests for us, or for my son?
MORTIMER   Speak, shall he presently be dispatched and die?
QUEEN   I would he were, so it were not by my means.   45
           Enter Matrevis and Gurney
MORTIMER   Enough.
        [*He speaks out of the Queen's hearing*]
    Matrevis, write a letter presently
    Unto the Lord of Berkeley from ourself,
    That he resign the king to thee and Gurney,
    And when 'tis done we will subscribe our name.   50
MATREVIS   It shall be done my lord.
        [*Matrevis writes the letter*]
MORTIMER   Gurney.
GURNEY   My lord.
MORTIMER   As thou intendest to rise by Mortimer,

Who now makes Fortune's wheel turn as he please,
Seek all the means thou canst to make him droop,
And neither give him kind word, nor good look.   55
GURNEY   I warrant you my lord.

Mortimer is now the power-broker, and his opening speech acts
partly as exposition and partly as a reinforcement of the position of
authority he occupies over the country, and over Edward and the
queen in particular. His opponents are dismissed as 'proud corrup-
tors', and Edward himself as 'light-brained' (2). This kind of political rhetoric continues his largely successful efforts to control the
discourse which has been used in the play's political debates: just as
before he was able to justify his actions against the king by convincing his fellow barons and key church leaders that their rebellion
was lawful, he now works to establish the legitimacy of his position.
'Be ruled by me,' he advises Isabella, 'and we will rule the realm' (5).
The most common meaning of the first phrase, 'be ruled by me', is
'take my advice'. However, the pun (on 'rule the realm') carries an
obvious second meaning, which is reiterated when the next stage of
his plan unfolds: he warns her of the dangers, of the need to steel
herself against fears and misgivings, and of the urgency of crowning
her son as the new king, at the same time installing himself as Lord
Protector – the last move effectively giving him full authority.
(Incidentally, this is, strictly speaking, an anachronism; the title of
Lord Protector does not seem to have come into use until the fifteenth century.) Even though the deposed king has been dismissed
as 'light-brained', Mortimer is aware that he remains a potential
danger: the characterization of Edward as an 'old wolf' (7) is an
interesting distortion of Edward's own use of the more kingly 'lion'
metaphor in describing himself (see II.ii.203 and V.i.11).

Isabella is now devoted to Mortimer (she calls him 'Sweet
Mortimer, the life of Isabel' [15]) but this is not the ineffectual,
dependent Isabella of the first half of the play: she has been transformed into a scheming and cold-hearted woman, and it seems to be
she who suggests the assassination of her husband. Her words to
Mortimer ('Conclude against his [the prince's] father what thou wilt,
/ And I myself will willingly subscribe' [19–20]) are fairly unam-

biguous. It is also important to notice how she bases the suggestion on an expression of her devotion to Mortimer ('Be thou persuaded that I love thee well' [16]) and her son ('And therefore, so the prince my son be safe' [17]). In performance, there may be a significant pause before Mortimer's reply, a moment for the two of them to exchange glances, sustained long enough for the actors to convey an unspoken mutual understanding. Again, their relative positions on stage are crucial in conveying the dynamics of power: a still Isabella and an agitated, pacing Mortimer might portray her as the dominant one. On the other hand, an image of Isabella seated and subdued, and Mortimer standing, still and centred, towering above her as he advises her, gives Mortimer the higher status.

The extent to which Isabella has altered, taking on the nature of a political animal, is underlined almost immediately when she asks the messenger, 'How fares my lord the king?' (24). At the messenger's reply, she responds, 'Alas poor soul, would I could ease his grief' (26), a line which could be taken as cruelly ironic, in view of the apparent decision to do away with him (his death would be one way in which his grief might quickly be eased). A few lines later, when the Bishop of Winchester reports that both Berkeley and Leicester have expressed pity for the imprisoned king, Isabel's solution is simple: 'Then let some other be his guardian' (36). Whether she barks the order, or calmly and coolly responds to Winchester's musings, it is further evidence of Isabella's transformation, and confirms the impression of Isabella that Edward has already created in his speech at his abdication: '. . . Isabel, whose eyes, being turned to steel, / Will sooner sparkle fire than shed a tear' out of pity for him, he maintains (104–5). Once Mortimer and Isabella are alone again, it is the queen who turns their discussion back to the issue of Edward's fate. She confronts Mortimer with the same potential threat that he raised himself earlier in the scene: 'as long as he survives, / What safety rests for us, or for my son?' (42–3). In response, Mortimer articulates what has up to now remained unspoken between them: 'Speak, shall he presently be dispatched and die?' (44). Mortimer's plain terms, preceded by the challenge, 'Speak', are aggressive, and Isabella's reply is a crafty one, partly evasive, but still unequivocal: 'I would he were, so it were not by my means' (45). Mortimer's response is swift. Gurney and Matrevis are employed to take the king into their custody, so that Mortimer may do what he (and Isabella) please with him.

The Bishop of Winchester is also deeply implicated in the plot against the king; although regicide is probably far from his mind, the role he has played in the abdication in the previous scene has been a prominent one. The fact that he enters this scene carrying the crown is easily skipped over in a reading of the play, but is a powerful moment in performance. In the previous scene, we have seen Edward, after much hesitation, remove the crown and hand it over to Winchester. The bishop is now on stage with Isabella and Mortimer, and the presence of the crown signifies the power that is now invested in them. Mortimer makes reference to the 'privy seal', the official stamp of the king's authority (37). With this, Mortimer will authorize the letter demanding that the king be handed over to Matrevis and Gurney, thus delivering him finally and completely into his hands – 'none but we shall know where he lieth', he tells Isabella (41). Mortimer's (effective) possession of crown and seal is staged very explicitly; these are powerful visual cues that reinforce the extent of his power.

One of the traditional ways of reading of Marlowe's plays has been to identify one or more specific characters as 'overreachers' – those who aspire to power, or greatness, or wealth – only to find that their vaulting ambition 'o'erleaps itself' (to steal a metaphor from Shakespeare's *Macbeth*) and falls on the other side. The extract shows this play's overreacher at the height of his fortune, success and prosperity. The extract gives a very powerful impression of the extent of his control, but there are also hints of the risk of *hubris,* signalled by his over-confidence. His words to Matrevis are particularly revealing: he brags that he, Mortimer, 'now makes Fortune's wheel turn as he please' (53); his turn of phrase draws on familiar sixteenth-century iconography which depicted Fortune turning the wheel that determined human fate. He advises Matrevis to follow his orders closely, if he wishes to advance himself. Mortimer's excessive pride may be identified as the cause of his downfall, and we see the image of Fortune's wheel return at the moment his fortunes are reversed (V.vi.59–63). Tamburlaine claims a similar power over fate when he brags that 'I hold the Fates bound fast in iron chains / And with my hand turn Fortune's wheel about' (Part I, I.ii.174–5). Both Tamburlaine and Mortimer's arrogant and extravagant claims, however, are challenged by the conclusions to the plays.

The scene is important in its context: we have witnessed the agonizing pain and humiliation that Edward has endured in being forced to give up his crown. Edward has ended the scene ineffectually tearing to shreds a letter from Mortimer. Now we witness the Bishop of Winchester bringing the crown to an exultant Mortimer and Isabella. Mortimer also receives the royal seal and, by the end of the scene, he has arranged to take under his control not just the crown and the prince, but the king too. It may seem that Isabella is already dancing to his tune, but things may not be so simple. Her subtly evasive response to Mortimer's invitation to do away with Edward, and her simultaneous manipulation of Mortimer to ensure Edward *is* dispatched indicates that she retains greater autonomy than we might have expected, particularly in view of her earlier insipid behaviour.

Conclusions

1. This chapter has revealed the centrality of politics in much of Marlowe's dramatic work. *Tamburlaine* and *Edward II* are the two most overtly political plays, and we have found some parallels between them in terms of the powerful political figures that drive their narratives.

2. The focus on politics in the plays has required some more detailed knowledge of the Elizabethan context in order to understand the subtleties of some of the plays, in particular *Edward II* (for relations between monarch and subjects) and *The Jew of Malta* (with reference to Machiavelli).

3. Can we identify a coherent view of power and politics in Marlowe's plays? I think it would be unwise to deduce any kind of Marlovian philosophy from the drama we have looked at, but it may be that we can identify certain issues recurring in different texts. Certainly there is a focus on the will to power and the ways in which power is seized, maintained, and lost. Marlowe also

anatomizes the hypocrisy and duplicity that is often a key element in those processes.

4. Marlowe's texts analyse with startling clarity the corrosive effect of political struggle on individuals, and on the relations between individuals. He analyses and dramatizes the effect that the thirst for (or possession of) total power can have on people. The plays also alert their audiences to the arbitrary nature of authority: the extent to which it resides in symbols, and the ease with which it may be transferred from one individual to another.

Methods of Analysis

1. The significance of physical *signs* of power and authority are crucial, and the most important signifier is the crown. The crown as a symbol of power is particularly potent in a performance context, and directors and designers have often been imaginative in the ways in which they have deployed it on stage. I have particularly vivid memories of a Royal Shakespeare Company production of *Tamburlaine*, where the squabble between Tamburlaine and Mycetes over the crown in act II scene iv (part I) was staged like a playground fight. Marlowe's treatment of the crown as a symbol reveals the extent to which humans can become enthralled by the lure of power. Often, the hollow nature of ambition for ambition's sake is exposed at the same time.

2. Some knowledge of Elizabethan politics is required to appreciate fully the implications of some key scenes, and this is particularly relevant to our reading of *Edward II*. In particular, debates about the relations between God and the monarch, about God, church and state, and the vexed question of when it may be permissible to revolt against the monarch are crucial to a full understanding of the way in which *Edward II* intervenes in those debates. The figure of Machiavel is central to a full understanding of the satirical edge of *The Jew of Malta*, and so some familiarity with the tone and content of the writings of the historical Machiavelli, and of the way he was represented in Elizabethan culture is required.

3. We have seen the need to pay close attention to the dynamics of the relationships between characters during these scenes where subtle (and sometimes not so subtle) negotiations of power are being staged. A sharp director will pick up on the cues that are present in the text, and use familiar conventions to signify particular status relations (for instance). When reading the plays, we need to imagine as fully as possible how the action might be played out on stage.

4. Close attention to the movement of the verse, and in particular shifts from prose to verse and back again can provide clues to the progression and pace of a scene. Furthermore, we need to be very sensitive to the way characters address one another during these scenes where political intrigue is to the fore.

Suggested Work

Although it is not essential, familiarity with the historical sources Marlowe used when writing *Edward II* can be useful for a closer study of the play. An awareness of Marlowe's adherence to or departure from the stories told in these sources can be revealing in terms of the dynamics of the play, and the way the audience relates to it. The same is true, to a lesser extent, of *Tamburlaine*.

Of the other passages that closely relate to the extracts explored here, the most important is probably Tamburlaine's famous speech celebrating 'The sweet fruition of an earthly crown' (Part I, II.vii.12–29). In *Edward II*, take a closer look at the scenes in which Mortimer manoeuvres his way into a relationship with Isabella and then takes on the role of Lord Protector, ending up (however fleetingly) as the effective ruler of England. In *The Jew of Malta*, a closer exploration of the contrast between the two Machiavellians, Ferneze and Barabas, is rewarding. Pay particular attention to the amount of times that alliances are forged and broken as the play reaches its climax, as Barabas in particular makes strategic moves to maximize profits for himself and, as things deteriorate, merely to survive (see, for example, V.i.59–95, V.ii.49–109, and the final scene).

5

Gender and Sexuality

The reading of gender relations in texts that are over four hundred years old is fraught with difficulties. Similarly, the problems that emerge from attempts to categorise sexuality in the early modern context are considerable. In Marlowe's plays, issues of gender are rarely central in the way that they frequently are in Shakespeare's work, the comedies in particular. Marlowe's plays do not contain very challenging roles for women (with the sole exception of Isabella in *Edward II*). Zenocrate in the *Tamburlaine* plays has some fine speeches, but she could hardly be described as a detailed character study. Abigail has some nice comic moments in *The Jew of Malta*, but is essentially lightweight, rarely much more than a foil for her father Barabas (there is some discussion of her death scene in the next chapter; see pp. 176–81). Nevertheless, the female characters in Marlowe's plays are not totally devoid of interest: the figure of Helen in *Faustus* is a curious, conflicted *persona*: a paragon of beauty, but seen as an insidiously destructive force, both in history and, possibly, in terms of her role in Faustus's damnation. Abigail is apparently a 'good' Jew (as opposed to the irredeemably evil Barabas) because she converts to Christianity. Zenocrate is idealized and deified by Tamburlaine; at the same time, she works at crucial moments in the plays to invite the audience to critique her husband's behaviour. In *Edward II*, Isabella plays a number of different 'roles' (female stereotypes), shifting from passive dependence, to wronged wife, to deceitful adulteress, to vengeful predator.

Sexuality is more crucial to an understanding of Marlowe's work, and this has as much to do with his biographical legacy as the plays themselves. The section of this book which reviews Marlowe's life and times (see pp. 219–40) considers the mass of stories that proliferated in the wake of the scandal of his death. It is enough to note here that Marlowe acquired a reputation as a homosexual, certainly after his death and, we can safely assume, before: the rather facile quotation attributed to him by one Richard Baines, that 'all they who love not tobacco and boys are fools', is fairly familiar. The fact that the eponymous hero of Marlowe's *Edward II* was recorded by historians as having been a homosexual has made Marlowe's own sexuality a crucial factor for many critics in interpretation of the play. As we shall see, the temptation to understand the play as some kind of *roman á clef* is one to be resisted. At the same time, the representation of Edward's sexuality is a complex and provocative matter than requires close attention. The centrality (or otherwise) of gender and sexuality to the understanding of each of Marlowe's plays determines how the discussions in this chapter are set out. There are some relatively short extracts from the first part of *Tamburlaine* and from *Doctor Faustus*. *Edward II*, by contrast, is examined in greater depth and with longer extracts, since it is the one play where both issues are crucial.

Tamburlaine I, III.iii.166–211

This extract depicts the clash between Tamburlaine's concubine Zenocrate and Zabina, wife of the Turkish emperor Bajazeth. Bajazeth is represented as a significant threat to Tamburlaine, and the conflict that follows is unusually protracted. There is even space for the creation of some dramatic tension in the struggle – something largely absent from Tamburlaine's customary easy victories. Bajazeth's basso has confronted Tamburlaine with a boastful account of the strength of the Turkish forces, which leaves Tamburlaine massively outnumbered. Techelles's response could as easily have come from Tamburlaine himself: 'The more he brings, the greater is the spoil' (Part I, III.iii.23). Tamburlaine, typically speaking in the third person, is confident that his 'smiling stars give him assured hope /

Of martial triumph ere he meet his foes' (42–3). As they prepare to
lock horns in battle, the two leaders hand over their crowns to their
women until the conflict is over.

ZABINA   Base concubine, must thou be placed by me
    That am the empress of the mighty Turk?
ZENOCRATE   Disdainful Turkess and unreverend boss,
    Call'st thou me concubine, that am betrothed
    Unto the great and mighty Tamburlaine?   170
ZABINA   To Tamburlaine, the great Tartarian thief!
ZENOCRATE   Thou wilt repent these lavish words of thine
    When thy great basso-master and thyself
    Must plead for mercy at his kingly feet
    And sue to me to be your advocates.   175
ZABINA   And sue to thee? I tell thee, shameless girl,
    Thou shalt be laundress to my waiting-maid. –
    How lik'st thou her, Ebea? Will she serve?
EBEA   Madam, she thinks perhaps she is too fine.
    But I shall turn her into other weeds   180
    And make her dainty fingers fall to work.
ZENOCRATE   Hear'st thou, Anippe, how thy drudge doth talk,
    And how my slave, her mistress, menaceth?
    Both, for their sauciness, shall be employed
    To dress the common soldiers' meat and drink,   185
    For we will scorn they should come near ourselves.
ANIPPE   Yet sometimes let your highness send for them
    To do the work my chambermaid disdains.
        They sound [to] the battle within, and stay
ZENOCRATE   Ye gods and powers that govern Persia   190
    And made my lordly love her worthy king,
    Now strengthen him against the Turkish Bajazeth,
    And let his foes, like flocks of fearful roes
    Pursued by hunters, fly his angry looks,
    That I may see him issue conqueror.
ZABINA   Now, Mahomet, solicit God himself,   195
    And make him rain down murdering shot from heaven
    To dash the Scythians' brains, and strike them dead

That dare to manage arms with him
That offered jewels to thy sacred shrine
When first he warred against the Christians.   200
      [*They sound within*] *to the battle again*
ZENOCRATE   By this the Turks lie welt'ring in their blood,
And Tamburlaine is Lord of Africa.
ZABINA   Thou art deceived. I heard the trumpets sound
As when my emperor overthrew the Greeks
And led them captive into Africa.   205
Straight will I use thee as thy pride deserves;
Prepare thyself to live and die my slave.
ZENOCRATE   If Mahomet should come from heaven and swear
My royal Lord is slain or conquerèd,
Yet should he not persuade me otherwise   210
But that he lives and will be conqueror.

In one sense, the verbal battle between Zenocrate and Zabina 'replaces' the clash of the armies that takes place offstage. It is also serves as a comic interlude, much as the Clown scenes do in *Faustus* (see discussion in Chapter 6, pp. 163–70). The exchanges preceding battle almost always take the form of 'vaunts' – the two leaders face off and bellow boastful threats at each other, before leaving the stage to do battle. As was the custom in the early modern theatre, military warfare was generally conducted as off-stage action. Often protagonists would take the stage for single combat, their duels being taken to represent the armies' progress toward victory or defeat. Shakespeare's *Macbeth* is perhaps the best example, from the appearance of the wounded captain in the second scene, who provides a detailed report of the battle (I.ii.1–44), to the final showdown between Macbeth and Macduff (V.vii.31–64).

In this instance, we have already witnessed the vaunting as Bajazeth and Tamburlaine square up to each other (I, III.iii.61–165). Tamburlaine has left with the parting shot, 'The field is ours, the Turk, his wife, and all' (163), and Bajazeth with an exhortation to his own troops: 'Come, kings and bassoes, let us glut our swords / That thirst to drink the feeble Persians' blood' (164–5). Left alone, the two women take up where their men left off. Zabina begins by attacking Zenocrate's status: she, Zabina, is the 'empress of the mighty Turk', far superior to Zenocrate, a mere 'base concubine' (167, 166). Physical position is also significant, and related to status: earlier in the scene, Zabina and Zenocrate take their respective places on their thrones (I, III.iii.116 s.d., 132 s.d.) and Zabina interprets it as an affront that Zenocrate should be 'placed by me' (166). There is an analogous scene in *Edward II* when the rage of the barons is provoked by Edward's act of seating his favourite, the 'base-born' Gaveston *'beside him on the throne'*, according to the stage direction [I,IV.vii s.d.]. The extent of the provocation is clear in Edward's taunting, 'What, are you moved that Gaveston sits here? / It is our pleasure; we will have it so' [I.iv.8–9]). The occupation of a particular space can be highly charged, particularly in performance where positions on stage (both in terms of level as well as up and downstage, and stage right and stage left) can be ranked in terms of their relative strength and weakness.

Zenocrate counters the 'concubine' charge aimed at her by Zabina, asserting herself as Tamburlaine's 'betrothed' (169). Against Zabina's implicit claim of legitimate royal status, Zenocrate sets Tamburlaine's strength and power – 'the great and mighty Tamburlaine' (170). Tamburlaine is king of Persia, though Zenocrate is well aware of the means by which he has risen to power, and Zabina's mocking laugh hits the nail on the head: 'Tamburlaine, the great Tartarian thief!' (171). When Zenocrate predicts the outcome of the battle, she imagines Zabina and Bajazeth pleading for mercy at Tamburlaine's 'kingly feet' (174) and the tussle over status, real and imagined, continues as Zabina proposes that Zenocrate (whom she addresses now as 'shameless girl') will, in defeat, 'be laundress to my waiting-maid' (176–7). What is essentially an imaginative game continues as they both draw their waiting women into the argument. These are self-conscious performances, with both women attempting to assert authority over each other via imagined reconfigurations of the power relations that exist between them. Zenocrate is most adventurous in this respect, casting Zabina's maid Ebea as her own servant Anippe's 'drudge' (182), and referring to Zabina herself as 'my slave' (183). With another audacious leap, she declares that 'for their sauciness', they shall be assigned 'To dress the common soldiers' meat and drink' (184–185). Anippe willingly joins in the game, requesting that they be made to do 'the work my chambermaid disdains' (188). If their abilities as performers are any index of the progress of the battle, it would seem that the smart money is on Tamburlaine.

Zenocrate does indeed emerge triumphant. Shortly after the extract printed here, she humiliates Zabina by carrying out the threats she has rehearsed in the performance described above. Theridamas takes Zabina's crown and gives it to Zenocrate; his line, 'Here madam, you are empress, she is none' (227) is a direct reference back by Marlowe to Zabina's brandishing of her title in the extract (167). The next time we see Bajazeth and Zabina, Zabina has been installed in her lowly position: Tamburlaine orders Zenocrate to 'look better to your slave' when Zabina rails against him. Zenocrate coolly passes the order further down the hierarchy: 'She is my handmaid's slave,' she corrects him, 'and she shall look / that these abuses flow not from her tongue – / Chide her, Anippe' (I,IV.ii.69–71). The cruel humiliation of Bajazeth and Zabina will end in the deaths of both of them, driven to suicide by the shame heaped upon them.

The extract represents one of the more exciting opportunities for actresses playing the roles of Zenocrate and Zabina. Zabina will have a very dramatic scene in the next act, as her imprisonment and then Bajazeth's suicide drive her insane with grief and shame. Here, though, there is room for more subtle acting, as the two women exchange insults. Looked at from one angle, the exchange seems like a fairly tame echo of the military vaunting Tamburlaine and Bajazeth have indulged in. While the men threaten to 'glut their swords' on each other's blood, the women bicker over titles and status – Zenocrate's use of the term 'boss' to describe Zabina is, another insult, a 'boss' being a fat woman (168). Viewed from another perspective, however, the quarrel between the women can be interpreted as a critique of the parade of aggression indulged in by their kings. In the same way that the struggle over the crown between Tamburlaine and Mycetes in act II scene iv can be seen as an ironic swipe at the fetishizing of these symbols of power, the exchange between Zenocrate and Zabina could be read as another of the means by which the text interrogates the construction and performance of power.

The presentation of female conflict inevitably means that the battle has to be fought out in the domestic arena, the only space in which women are generally allowed to operate. The use of slaves and maids, real and imagined, and the designation of household chores, are their weapons. Just as the comic scenes in *Faustus* can be interpreted as ironic reflections upon the tragic progress (or regress) of Faustus's soul, so the conflict between Zenocrate and Zabina can be read as a travesty, a mockery of the male conflict being conducted off stage. At the same time, we have to recognise that both of them, at the end of the extract, defer to the men, and they are at least metaphorically (and probably literally) swept aside as the warriors return to the stage.

The argument modulates into a different tone after the trumpets '*sound* [signal the start of] *the battle*'. The trumpet reminds them of the military conflict itself, and each of them offers up a prayer. Zenocrate's is ironic, considering Tamburlaine's customary scornful disdain for all deities. However, we see here and elsewhere that Zenocrate does not share his agnosticism and irreverence. Later in the play, we witness her articulating her fears for Tamburlaine in the wake of the deaths of Bajazeth and Zabina, fearing his cruelty will provoke divine retribution: 'Ah mighty Jove and holy Mahomet, / Pardon my love, O pardon his contempt / Of earthly fortune and respect of pity' (I, V.i.364–6). Here, she prays to the 'gods and powers that govern Persia' (190) while Zabina invokes Mahomet specifically. Zenocrate's prayer is more conventionally poetic and fanciful – the dirty reality of combat is represented in a hunting metaphor, with Tamburlaine's forces as the hunters and the Turkish soldiers as 'flocks of fearful roes' (192–3); the soft tones are enhanced by the sibilant 'f' and 's' sounds in line 193 in particular. Zabina's invocation is jagged and violent by comparison: 'make him rain down murdering shot from heaven / To dash the Scythians' brains, and strike them dead' (196–7). The women then turn their attention back to one another. At the second trumpet blast they each take flight on imaginative fancy once more: Zabina is convinced that it signals victory for the Turks, and warns Zenocrate to 'Prepare thyself to live and die my slave' (207). Zenocrate's riposte challenges both Zabina and Mahomet: if Mahomet himself were to announce Tamburlaine's defeat and death, she would not believe it. Zenocrate and Tamburlaine, in effect, deify one another; her faith, it seems, is in Tamburlaine himself, not in any divine power, and Tamburlaine eulogizes her as 'divine Zenocrate' (I,V.i.135).

Finally, we should note how the action of the battle itself is massively compressed – between battle being joined at the first blast of the trumpet (188) and broken off at the second (200) there are only a dozen lines; after another dozen lines, Bajazeth *'flies [across the stage], and [Tamburlaine] pursues him [offstage]'*. The stage directions tell us that *'battle'* is *'short'*, and when they re-enter, Bajazeth has been *'overcome'* (211 s.d.). There is evidently dramatic licence in the speed with which the battle has been fought, but its speed is also testimony to Tamburlaine's skill and might. Some directors have chosen to extend the battle, even staging single combat between the Turkish emperor and his Persian challenger, but these choices need to be judged carefully when what is most important is the sense of Tamburlaine's apparent invincibility.

Doctor Faustus, V.i.81–118

The fifth act of *Doctor Faustus* depicts his final hours on earth. Abruptly, following his performance for the Duke and Duchess of Vanholt, Faustus's servant Wagner appears to announce, bluntly, that 'I think my master means to die shortly' (V.i.1). His parting line, at the end of a short eight-line speech is ostensibly a superficial comment on the action, setting the scene for the entrance of Faustus and the scholars. To an attentive ear, however, his remark that 'Belike the feast is ended' works as a grim, ironic judgement on Faustus's position, as he rushes towards his fate. Faustus conjures for the amusement of his colleagues, as he did in the previous scene for the Duke and Duchess of Vanholt. If the previous scene played out the sin of gluttony, then this spell is cast for lust – the ghost of Helen of Troy, 'that peerless dame of Greece' (V.i.13,20) represented in Greek and Roman mythology as the most beautiful woman in the history of the world. The scholars wonder at the apparition of a woman 'Whose heavenly beauty passeth all compare' (30). The vision dies, the scholars leave, and Faustus, approached by a holy man who attempts to convince him that he can still be reconciled to God, tries to repent, only to be threatened by Mephistopheles for his thoughts of reneging on his pact with Lucifer. Having recommitted himself to hell via a bond written in his own blood, he asks Mephistopheles to give him Helen of Troy as his lover.

FAUSTUS   One thing, good servant, let me crave of thee
    To glut the longing of my heart's desire:
    That I might have unto my paramour
    That heavenly Helen which I saw of late,
    Whose sweet embracings may extinguish clean   85
    These thoughts that do dissuade me from my vow,
    And keep mine oath I made to Lucifer.
MEPHISTOPHELES   Faustus, this, or what else thou shalt desire,
    Shall be performed in twinkling of an eye.
           Enter Helen [brought in by Mephistopheles]
FAUSTUS   Was this the face that launched a thousand ships   90
    And burnt the topless towers of Ilium?
    Sweet Helen, make me immortal with a kiss.
           [They kiss]
    Her lips suck forth my soul. See where it flies!
    Come, Helen, come, give me my soul again.
           [They kiss again]
    Here will I dwell, for heaven be in these lips,   95
    And all is dross that is not Helena.
           Enter [the] Old Man
    I will be Paris, and for love of thee
    Instead of Troy shall Wittenberg be sacked,
    And I will combat with weak Menelaus,
    And wear thy colours on my plumèd crest.   100
    Yea, I will wound Achilles in the heel
    And then return to Helen for a kiss.
    O, thou art fairer than the evening air,
    Clad in the beauty of a thousand stars.

Brighter art thou than flaming Jupiter
When he appeared to hapless Semele,   105
More lovely then the monarch of the sky
In wanton Arethusa's azured arms;
And none but thou shalt be my paramour.
        Exeunt [*Faustus and Helen, with Mephistopheles*]
OLD MAN   Accursèd Faustus, miserable man,   110
That from thy soul exclud'st the grace of heaven
And fliest the throne of His tribunal seat!
Enter the Devils, [*with Mephistopheles. They menace the Old Man*]
Satan begins to sift me with his pride.
As in this furnace God shall try my faith,
My faith, vile hell, shall triumph over thee.   115
Ambitious fiends, see how the heavens smiles
At your repulse and laughs your state to scorn!
Hence, hell! For hence I fly unto my God.
                        Exeunt.

At the beginning of the extract, Faustus is seemingly casting about for a distraction to divert him from thoughts of salvation and damnation. In act II scene i, having signed the initial pact with Lucifer, he asks for a wife and receives instead a hideous, fiery devil. So again, at a corresponding moment, he asks for something to 'glut the longing of my heart's desire' (82), demanding that he be given the legendary beauty Helen of Troy as his lover. Just as his mind has been preoccupied with wealth and sensual pleasure during the period of Mephistopheles's service, so now he hopes to 'extinguish clean / These thoughts that do dissuade me from my vow' (85–6).

He explains his request for a wife in act two by admitting that he is 'wanton and lascivious and cannot live without a wife' (II.i.140–1). The justification is illogical – someone who was truly 'wanton and lascivious' would request anything but a marriage partner, with the implications of monogamy that entails. Mephistopheles, with typical, cynical wit, responds by presenting him with *'a Devil dressed like a woman, with fireworks'* (II.i.146,s.d.). If we view the 'bargaining' that takes place in act II scene i and here in act V in ideological terms, we can see two ways of representing women that are familiar in literary and other texts of the sixteenth century. First of all, these women are seen as property and as objects that service the needs of their 'owners', the men. In act V scene i, Helen is part of the 'spoils' brought back to Dardenia (V.i.23). Faustus demands a wife to sate his lust ('I am wanton and lascivious and cannot live without a wife' [II.i.140–1]) and when Mephistopheles hesitates, his demands become more strident, petulant, almost childish: 'Nay, sweet Mephistopheles, fetch me one, for I will have / one' (143–4). Secondly, they are associated with death, disease and damnation. The 'woman' Mephistopheles offers Faustus is in fact '*a Devil dressed like a woman, with fireworks*' (146 s.d.), the fireworks most likely signifying venereal disease. In act IV scene ii, the Duchess has a craving for grapes. Her language is sensuous and intimate – 'I will not hide from you the thing my heart desires', she tells Faustus (IV.ii.8–9). An imaginative director wishing to exploit the potential of the text, perhaps to critique the representation of the female figures in the play, would have scope to set up associations in the minds of the audience between the Duchess, Helen of Troy, and perhaps even the Devil of act II scene i. The belief that women were incapable of controlling their urges and appetites was widespread in Elizabethan society (the inevitable corollary was the need for men to control those appetites for them).

Just as the devil in the second act represents the perils of sexual temptation, Helen of Troy signifies the fatal woman. She is seen as the root cause of dreadful calamity: a long, terrible military campaign that ended in the sacking of the great city of Troy: 'Was this the face that launched a thousand ships / And burnt the topless towers of Ilium?' (90–1). The plea, 'Sweet Helen, make me immortal with a kiss' (92) is richly ironic, for Faustus has already made it clear that awakening his desire is intended to 'extinguish' thoughts of redemption (and immortality). At the kiss, Helen 'suck[s] forth' his soul (93), for she is a *succubus*, or *succuba*, an evil spirit that, according to legend, had sexual relations with men. The movement of the verse in these lines is carefully modulated, expressing the sensual and sexual overtones of the gasping 'Her lips suck forth my soul', and the release of 'See where it flies!' (93). There is a sense of doom shrouding the next line – 'Come, Helen, come, give me my soul again' (94). The sense of hopelessness and ephemeral pleasure is compounded by his declaration that she is 'fairer than the evening air, / Clad in the beauty of a thousand stars' (103–4). It is a couplet that expresses the transience of the experience, but it is nevertheless more evocative than the conventional, classical expressions that follow. At the same time, these too are apt references for those familiar with the classics – Semele asked Jupiter to appear before her in his true likeness, and she was consumed by lightning. Faustus is enraptured, but will likewise be destroyed by his contact with Helen. The story of Semele was also traditionally used as a tale of human presumption punished by divine power. Arethusa was turned into a fountain (hence her 'azured' [blue] arms [108]) after fleeing the river-god Apheus (not Jupiter, as Marlowe suggests here).

Helen's appearance provokes two of the most famous lines in the Marlowe canon, quoted already: 'Was this the face that launched a thousand ships / And burnt the topless towers of Ilium?' (90–1). They are thrillingly heroic, part of the great classical tradition of epic poetry that Marlowe knew so well. The hyperbole ('topless towers') is very much in keeping with classical figures of speech, while at the same time remaining true to what we understand about Faustus, forever self-aggrandizing. Faustus has characteristically sought his salvation in earthly (or probably devilish) pleasures and it is here, in his final hours, that he invests his soul: 'Here will I dwell, for heaven be in these lips, / And all is dross that is not Helena' (95–6). Before he leaves the stage with Helen he delivers a speech in heroic fashion, pitting himself against Greek mythological heroes: Paris (son of Priam, king of Troy, and the one who seduced and stole Helen away from her husband), Menelaus (king of Sparta, Helen's husband) and Achilles (the great Greek hero, his body made invincible save for his heels when his mother dipped his body in the River Styx, which divided the living from the land of the dead). Once again, the stage image is in direct contrast with the empty boasts. Faustus imagines himself as a conquering warrior; what the audience sees is a weak, ageing scholar finding solace in the arms of the mirage of a beautiful woman as his final hour approaches.

The reappearance of the Old Man at the end of the scene serves a number of purposes. We hear Faustus's vindictive demand that the

Old Man be punished for trying to dissuade him from his pact with Lucifer acted upon. The Old Man is also a choric figure, operating in a similar fashion to Wagner at the beginning of the scene, and lending the scene a kind of symmetry in this sense. In both cases, the characters transcend the limitations of the Chorus by their direct involvement in the action of the play, and their relationships with Faustus himself, Wagner his faithful servant and the Old Man as one who seeks to save Faustus's soul. Most importantly, however, the Old Man serves as a point of comparison for the audience. Faced with the threats of the devils, he does not surrender, as Faustus has done, but instead places his faith in God: 'As in this furnace God shall try my faith,' he declares, 'My faith, vile hell, shall triumph over thee' (114–15). It may be that this is staged as a triumph for the holy man, the devils unable to come near him with their weapons. Another option would be to stage the confrontation as a martyrdom: this would climax with the man's dying cry, 'Hence, hell! For hence I fly unto my God' (118). However it is directed, what is crucial is the display of the gulf that separates Faustus (doomed) and the Old Man (destined for salvation). The Old Man remains immediate, physical proof of the alternative that Faustus has repeatedly rejected.

Edward II, I.iv.74–143

Marlowe's *Edward II* has been seen as a remarkable play for its frank depiction of a homosexual relationship. Furthermore, many critics would define the text's representation of the love between Edward and Gaveston as a positive portrayal. Since speculation about Marlowe's own sexuality was common and widespread shortly after his death (and probably before that, though the documents we have inherited mostly post-date the inquest) the idea that the playwright had a major personal and emotional (rather than simply intellectual) investment in the story has preoccupied critics, particularly more recently. We have to be aware of the dangers of this kind of criticism: aside from frequently rehearsed debates about the autonomy of a text – the idea that it is how it is *read* that is most important, not the intentions of the author – we also have to remember that understandings of sexuality have altered profoundly over the past four hundred years (see discussion in the Context section, pp.237–8).

The text of *Edward II* establishes homoerotic overtones in the very first scene, as Gaveston reads a letter from the king, then muses on his relationship with Edward (see discussion of the extract in Chapter 1, pp.41–4). The speech is framed in unmistakably sexual terms, and the first time they appear on stage together the suggestions planted in Gaveston's opening soliloquy are developed further. In this extract, we find Edward being forced to sign the document that will banish Gaveston to Ireland.

CANTERBURY Nothing shall alter us. We are resolved.
LANCASTER Come, come, subscribe. 75
MORTIMER Why should you love him whom the world hates so?
EDWARD Because he loves me more than all the world.
　Ah, none but rude and savage minded men
　Would seek the ruin of my Gaveston.
　You that be noble born should pity him. 80
WARWICK You that are princely born should shake him off.
　For shame, subscribe, and let the loon depart.
MORTIMER SENIOR [*to Canterbury*] Urge him, my lord.
CANTERBURY Are you content to banish him the realm?
EDWARD I see I must, and therefore am content. 85
　Instead of ink, I'll write it with my tears.
　　　　　[*He writes*]
MORTIMER The king is lovesick for his minion.
EDWARD 'Tis done, and now, accursèd hand, fall off!
LANCASTER Give it me, I'll have it published in the streets.
MORTIMER I'll see him presently dispatched away. 90
CANTERBURY Now is my heart at ease.
WARWICK 　　　　　　　　And so is mine.
PEMBROKE This will be good news to the common sort.
MORTIMER SENIOR Be it or no, he shall not linger here.
　　　　Exeunt nobles. [*King Edward alone remains*]
EDWARD How fast they run to banish him I love!

They would not stir, were it to do me good.   95
Why should a king be subject to a priest?
Proud Rome, that hatchest such imperial grooms,
For these thy superstitious taperlights,
Wherewith thy antichristian churches blaze,
I'll fire thy crazèd buildings, and enforce   100
The papal towers to kiss the lowly ground,
With slaughtered priests make Tiber's channel swell,
And banks raised higher with their sepulchres.
As for the peers that back the clergy thus,
If I be king, not one of them shall live.   105

Enter Gaveston

GAVESTON   My lord, I hear it whispered everywhere
That I am banished, and must fly the land.
EDWARD   'Tis true, sweet Gaveston. O, were it false!
The legate of the pope will have it so,
And thou must hence, or I shall be deposed.   110
But I will reign to be revenged of them;
And therefore, sweet friend, take it patiently.
Live where thou wilt, I'll send thee gold enough;
And long thou shalt not stay, or, if thou dost,
I'll come to thee; my love shall ne'er decline.   115
GAVESTON   Is all my hope turned to this hell of grief?
EDWARD   Rend not my heart with thy too-piercing words;
Thou from this land, I from myself am banished.
GAVESTON   To go from hence grieves not poor Gaveston,
But to forsake you, in whose gracious looks   120
The blessedness of Gaveston remains,
For nowhere else seeks he felicity.
EDWARD   And only this torments my wretched soul,
That, whether I will or no, thou must depart.
Be governor of Ireland in my stead,   125
And there abide till fortune call thee home.
Here, take my picture and let me wear thine.

[They exchange lockets]

O, might I keep thee here as I do this,
Happy were I, but now most miserable.

GAVESTON   'Tis something to be pitied of a king.   130
EDWARD   Thou shalt not hence; I'll hide thee, Gaveston.
GAVESTON   I shall be found, and then 'twill grieve me more.
EDWARD   Kind words, and mutual talk, makes our grief greater;
    Therefore with dumb embracement let us part.
       [*They embrace. Gaveston starts to leave*]
    Stay, Gaveston, I cannot leave thee thus.   135
GAVESTON   For every look, my lord, drops down a tear;
    Seeing I must go, do not renew my sorrow.
EDWARD   The time is little that thou hast to stay,
    And therefore give me leave to look my fill.
    But come, sweet friend, I'll bear thee on thy way.   140
GAVESTON   The peers will frown.
EDWARD   I pass not for their anger, Come, let's go,
    O that we might as well return as go!

The barons and representatives of the church are united in their
determination to rid the country of Gaveston. Edward has made a
final, desperate plea, offering bribes to the assembled company, and
ending by (rhetorically, one presumes) offering the kingdom to
them, as long as he 'may have some nook or corner left / To frolic
with my dearest Gaveston' (I.iv.72–3). The Archbishop of
Canterbury speaks for them all when he replies that, 'Nothing shall
alter us. We are resolved' (74). Their disapproval is clear in the terms
they use to describe Gaveston and the hold he appears to have on
Edward. Gaveston's lowly social status is an obsession for the barons;
Warwick describes him as a 'loon' (which other editions print as
'lown') – a person of low birth (82). Mortimer refers to him as
Edward's 'minion' (87), a familiar epithet which translates from the
French as 'darling boy', and so has unmistakable homoerotic overtones. Mortimer asks, seemingly unable to comprehend why Edward
is so fixated on Gaveston, 'Why should you love him whom the
world hates so?' (76). Warwick's advice that Edward should 'shake
him off' (81) represents Gaveston as a kind of parasite, which is evidently how the barons view him. In act III, the same phrase recurs
in relation to Spencer, who takes Gaveston's place as Edward's
favourite at court after Gaveston's death. A herald speaking on behalf

of the barons to the king identifies Spencer as one of those 'smooth dissembling flatterers' that Edward must 'shake off' (III.i.169).

In the midst of this virulent opposition to their friendship, the depth of Edward's love for Gaveston is obvious. When Mortimer, perhaps incredulous, perhaps merely provocative, asks, 'Why should you love him whom the world hates so?', Edward's reply is poignant and, somehow, strikingly modern: 'Because he loves me more than all the world' (76–7). When Edward finally signs the document, he weeps: 'Instead of ink, I'll write it with my tears', he says, and Mortimer mocks him: 'The king is lovesick for his minion' (86–7). Edward, distraught, seems not to hear him, wrapped up in his own grief, cursing his own hand that has sealed Gaveston's fate: ''Tis done, and now, accursèd hand, fall off!' (88). When everyone else leaves the stage, hurrying away to spread the news of the barons' success and to enact the decree, Edward gives vent to his fury and distress in a soliloquy. The previously crowded stage has suddenly and rapidly emptied, leaving Edward a stranded, isolated and vulnerable figure. The passion in his verse, and the savage revenge he vows, are further evidence of his great love for Gaveston. There is a large measure of self-pity here, too, which becomes a more familiar aspect of Edward as the play progresses – observing how eagerly the barons set about the business of arranging Gaveston's banishment, he remarks, 'They would not stir, were it to do me good' (95). He is petulant when thwarted, and his frustrated cry, 'Why should a king be subject to a priest?' (96) is one of a series of irritable, childish responses to his own failure to face down challenges to his authority.

He proceeds with a menacing speech aimed at 'proud Rome' (the Catholic church) and the diatribe that follows is markedly ahistorical. The description of 'superstitious taperlights' and 'antichristian churches' (98, 99) is typical late sixteenth century invective against Catholicism: the more extreme Protestants at the time saw the Pope as the Antichrist. Edward announces his intention to burn and demolish the churches, and 'With slaughtered priests make Tiber's channel swell' (the reference to the river Tiber again identifies Rome as the target for his anger) (102). The impressive-sounding series of threats is delivered in a breathless, seven-line rant. In performance especially, the speech sounds hollow as it echoes around an empty stage. Tamburlaine issues orders to his followers and they run to obey him. Edward's declared intentions are roared into a vacuum. Without the support of his nobles, the king is left isolated and dangerously exposed.

With his opponents gone, Gaveston returns to the stage, and an emotional scene between him and Edward follows. Edward repeatedly addresses him with tender epithets – he is 'sweet Gaveston' (108) and, twice, 'sweet friend' (112, 140). In the first scene, when Gaveston kneels before him, Edward greets him with the cry, 'Knowest thou not who I am? / Thy friend, thy self, another Gaveston!' (I.i.141–2). This is a familiar image of the lover and the beloved, one that Edward invokes again now, as he faces the prospect of Gaveston's banishment; he declares that 'Thou from this land, I from myself am banished' (118). Their mutual exchange of miniature portraits is another ritual familiar to lovers who must part (127 s.d.). There is a marked emphasis on the gaze as they prepare to say goodbye. Gaveston laments that, 'For every look, my lord, drops down a tear' (136); Edward replies, since their time is short, 'give me leave to look my fill' (139). With a sensitive staging of this scene, there is considerable scope for conveying its intense emotions. It is difficult to see how it could be performed as anything other than a love scene. Nevertheless, in the midst of their loving exchanges, there is evidence of the gulf that inevitably remains between them – the king and his subject. Gaveston feels (or at least acts as if he feels) that gulf when he marvels, ''Tis something to be pitied of a king' (130). When he addresses Edward as the one 'in whose gracious looks / The blessedness of Gaveston remains' (120–1), it may be interpreted as a straightforward lover's declaration, but it also reminds us of Edward's royal status.

The movement of the verse is carefully controlled in this dialogue: Edward's first eight-line speech (108–15) is followed by an exchange of fairly long speeches (116–29), and as they prepare to say goodbye the dialogue moves into an exchange of single lines (130–3) expressing their sense of desperation. After an embrace, Edward lurches after Gaveston ('Stay, Gaveston, I cannot leave thee thus' [135]). Perhaps they embrace again, and Edward decides to accompany Gaveston for the first part of his journey (140). At that moment, however, they are interrupted by Isabella, and the scene that follows reveals much about Edward's relationships with her and with Gaveston. The extract below follows on immediately after the lines analysed above.

Edward II, I.iv.144–88

Enter Queen Isabel

QUEEN   Whither goes my lord?
EDWARD   Fawn not on me French strumpet; get thee gone.   145
QUEEN   On whom but on my husband should I fawn?
GAVESTON   On Mortimer, with whom, ungentle queen –
     I say no more; judge you the rest, my lord.
QUEEN   In saying this, thou wrong'st me, Gaveston.
     Is't not enough that thou corrupts my lord   150
     And art a bawd to his affections,
     But thou must call mine honour thus in question?
GAVESTON   I mean not so; your grace must pardon me.
EDWARD   Thou art too familiar with that Mortimer,
     And by thy means is Gaveston exiled;   155
     But I would wish thee reconcile the lords,
     Or thou shalt ne'er be reconciled to me.
QUEEN   Your highness knows it lies not in my power.
EDWARD   Away then, touch me not. Come, Gaveston.
QUEEN [*to Gaveston*]   Villain, 'tis thou that robb'st me of
     my lord.   160
GAVESTON   Madam, 'tis you that rob me of my lord.
EDWARD   Speak not unto her; let her droop and pine.
QUEEN   Wherein my lord, have I deserved these words?
     Witness the tears that Isabella sheds,
     Witness this heart that, sighing for thee, breaks,   165
     How dear my lord is to poor Isabel.
EDWARD [*pushing her away*]   And witness heaven how dear
     thou art to me.
     There weep, for, till my Gaveston be repealed,
     Assure thy self thou com'st not in my sight.

Exeunt Edward and Gaveston

QUEEN   O, miserable and distressèd queen!   170
    Would when I left sweet France and was embarked,
    That charming Circes, walking on the waves,
    Had changed my shape, or at the marriage day
    The cup of Hymen had been full of poison,
    Or with those arms that twined about my neck   175
    I had been stifled, and not lived to see
    The king my lord thus to abandon me.
    Like frantic Juno will I fill the earth
    With ghastly murmur of my sighs and cries,
    For never doted Jove on Ganymede,   180
    So much as he on cursèd Gaveston.
    But that will more exasperate his wrath.
    I must entreat him, I must speak him fair,
    And be a means to call home Gaveston;
    And yet he'll ever dote on Gaveston,   185
    And so am I for ever miserable.
      Enter the nobles [Lancaster, Warwick, Pembroke,
    Mortimer Senior, and Mortimer Junior] to the Queen

LANCASTER   Look where the sister of the king of France,
    Sits wringing of her hands, and beats her breast.

Isabella is the most interesting female character in the Marlowe canon, and that interest is aroused for the most part by the remarkable shifts in her attitudes, relationships and behaviour that take place over the course of the play. This extract gives us the 'early' Isabella, the passive, dependent, 'fawning' queen. When the audience first catches sight of her, she is hurrying 'Unto the forest ... To live in grief and baleful discontent', having been rejected by Edward on Gaveston's return (I.ii.47–8). Isabella appears to conform largely to a familiar early modern stereotype – the scorned female lover – and she plays the role efficiently in this encounter. Her dependence on Edward is palpable: the opening exchange, 'Whither goes my lord?' and 'Fawn not on me, French strumpet; get thee gone' (144–5), suggests that she attempts to embrace him, or at least place a restraining hand upon him as he attempts to leave with Gaveston.

In performance, Edward might physically recoil from her touch; certainly there is a sense of disgust, or at least distaste, in his vicious, 'get thee gone'. As he leaves, the Oxford edition adds a stage direction, '[*pushing her away*]' (166 s.d.), and he crushes her with a sarcastic invocation to heaven to witness 'how dear thou art to me' (167). When she is rejected, she falls into a lament – almost on cue, as Edward tells Gaveston to 'Speak not unto her; let her droop and pine' (162).

This is a dynamic three-way encounter, and Marlowe designs the cross-fire between the three characters to convey the excitement and emotional intensity of the conflict: Edward rejects Isabella (144–6); Gaveston interjects with an accusation that Isabella is unfaithful to Edward (147–8) and she turns on him (149–53), only to find Edward taking up the theme (154–5) and then attempting to blackmail her into persuading the barons to revoke Gaveston's sentence (156–8); Edward is then the passive centre of the scene as Gaveston and Isabella fight over him (160–66) and finally Edward pushes her away again and leaves with Gaveston (167–9), abandoning Isabella to mourn her loss (170–86). For Isabella's soliloquy, the play modulates out of the near-naturalistic style of the three-way confrontation into something more poetic. Isabella laments in formal terms, the shift signalled by the first line, where she addresses herself in the third person: 'O, miserable and distressèd queen!' (170). A long flight of fancy follows, as Isabella remembers her departure from France to come to England to marry Edward, and wishes that her wedding cup had been poisoned, or that Circe had changed her shape; the goddess Circe was famous for having turned the followers of Odysseus into pigs, and for having the ability to walk on the surface of the sea (171–4). The reference to changing shape may also suggest that Isabella wishes she had been transformed into a man, recognizing that this is the only way she could compete with Gaveston for Edward's affection. The classical allusions continue with references to Juno, Jove and Ganymede (depicted in Marlowe's *Dido Queen of Carthage*) (178–81). Again, the emphasis is on sexual orientation: the boy Ganymede was cup-bearer to Jove, king of the gods, and was prized by Jove for his beauty. This made him an object of jealousy for Juno, Jove's queen. The story was so familiar that 'Ganymede' was a common term for the younger partner in a homoerotic relationship.

Isabella's formal lament is prefigured by three lines she delivers during the preceding dialogue:

> Witness the tears that Isabella sheds,
> Witness this heart, that sighing for thee breaks,
> How dear my lord is to poor Isabel.
>
> (164–6)

The repetition of 'witness' implies ceremony, a formal declaration of her love, almost an offer of rededication to her husband. In its original performance context, it is most likely that the formal lines would have been matched by a stylized delivery, a 'telegraphic' acting style where her expression of grief and her declaration would have been accompanied by gestures signalling her breaking heart and her tears. The extract includes the return of the nobles to the stage, mostly for the interesting remark of Lancaster's: 'Look where the sister of the king of France, / Sits wringing of her hands, and beats her breast' (187–8). Again, this suggests a formal style of performance, where certain staged behaviour (wringing of the hands, beating of the breast) would be accepted as a convention that signified certain emotions.

Finally, it is important to pay some attention to the early suggestion of some kind of relationship between Isabella and Mortimer. Gaveston's accusation that Isabella is unfaithful could be played several ways. We have evidence elsewhere of his propensity for manipulating Edward and the apparently spontaneous way he lets the accusation slip is suspicious. There is something almost naturalistic in the artful articulation of his suspicion as he half-utters a thought, only to stop himself mid-sentence: when Isabella asks whom she should fawn upon if not Edward, Gaveston interjects, 'On Mortimer, with whom, ungentle queen – / I say no more' (147–8). In case Edward has missed the hint he turns to him, adding, 'judge you the rest, my lord' (148). The queen's response is surprisingly sharp, and she comes closer here than anywhere else to referring to the homosexual relationship between them – the accusation that he 'corrupts' Edward recalls the historian Holinshed's careful negotiation of the issue of sexuality in his account of Edward's reign and his relationship with Gaveston. The phrase 'bawd to his affections' has similar implications, and would strike an audience as acutely perceptive, particularly in the light of Gaveston's opening soliloquy, where he plans the entertainments he will lay on for his king.

There is nothing in the text to support Gaveston's accusation of Isabella's unfaithfulness at this point in the play. However, Isabella does focus her attention on him specifically, in the company of the barons, as she leaves the stage at the end of act I scene ii, and some critics and actors and directors have chosen to signal this as an early indication of a relationship between them. In that scene she refers to him as 'sweet Mortimer' (I.ii.80), implying a level of intimacy with him that she does not share with the other nobles. It is Mortimer in whom Isabella confides in act I scene iv (see 227, 229 s.d.s) and editors usually indicate that Isabella draws Mortimer apart to sit down and speak to him in private. The audience has now been primed to pay particular attention to the interaction between them, and the extract discussed below sees a very different Isabella emerging.

Edward II, II.iv.15–69

Marlowe places greater emphasis on the figure of Mortimer Junior than Holinshed does in his historical account. According to Holinshed, the relationship between Mortimer and Isabella began only after Isabella had given up hope of reconciliation with Edward and had returned to France. Moreover, the split between Edward and Isabella is seen more in political terms than personal ones. Marlowe streamlines the shape of the narrative and provides some intriguing (if inaccurate) additional dynamics to the way Edward, Gaveston, Isabella and Mortimer interrelate. When Isabella is repeatedly rejected by her husband she confides in Mortimer, and finally becomes his lover. Between the passages quoted above, and this extract from act II scene iv, we find her banished from court and ordered by Edward to seek the barons' consent to allow Gaveston to return from exile. In act I scene iv she attempts to persuade Mortimer to repeal Gaveston. 'Sweet Mortimer, sit down by me a while', she says, 'And I will tell thee reasons of such weight / As thou wilt soon subscribe to his repeal' (I.iv.225–7). We do not hear their conversation, but the other barons observe them closely, and their commentary reveals all we need to know about the conversation:

PEMBROKE   Fear not; the queen's words cannot alter him.
WARWICK   No? But mark how earnestly she pleads.
LANCASTER   And see how coldly his looks make denial.
WARWICK   She smiles! Now, for my life, his mind is changed.
                                                            (I.iv.234–7)

We are now in act II scene iv, however. Civil war has broken out and Edward is desperate to secure Gaveston's escape route. The extract begins just after a series of hurried farewells, and Isabella has suffered another rejection at the hands of the king.

QUEEN   Heavens can witness I love none but you. –   15
    From my embracements thus he breaks away.
    O that mine arms could close this isle about,
    That I might pull him to me where I would,
    Or that these tears that drizzle from mine eyes
    Had power to mollify his stony heart,   20
    That when I had him we might never part!
                Enter the barons [Lancaster, Warwick,
                Mortimer Junior, and others]. Alarums
LANCASTER   I wonder how he 'scaped.
MORTIMER   Who's this, the queen?
QUEEN   Ay, Mortimer, the miserable queen,
    Whose pining heart her inward sighs have blasted
    And body with continual mourning wasted.   25
    These hands are tired with haling of my lord
    From Gaveston, from wicked Gaveston,
    And all in vain, for when I speak him fair
    He turns away and smiles upon his minion.

MORTIMER   Cease to lament, and tell us where's the king?   30
QUEEN   What would you with the king, ist him you seek?
LANCASTER   No, madam, but that cursèd Gaveston.
    Far be it from the thought of Lancaster,
    To offer violence to his sovereign.
    We would but rid the realm of Gaveston.   35
    Tell us where he remains, and he shall die.
QUEEN   He's gone by water unto Scarborough;
    Pursue him quickly, and he cannot 'scape.
    The king hath left him, and his train is small.
WARWICK   Forslow no time, sweet Lancaster, let's march.   40
MORTIMER   How comes it that the king and he is parted ?
QUEEN   That this your army, going several ways,
    Might be of lesser force, and with the power
    That he intendeth presently to raise
    Be easily suppressed; and therefore begone.   45
MORTIMER   Here in the river rides a Flemish hoy.
    Lets all aboard, and follow him amain.
LANCASTER   The wind that bears him hence will fill our sails.
    Come, come aboard. 'Tis but an hour's sailing.
MORTIMER   Madam, stay you within this castle here.   50
QUEEN   No, Mortimer, I'll to my lord the king.
MORTIMER   Nay, rather sail with us to Scarborough.
QUEEN   You know the king is so suspicious
    As, if he hear I have but talked with you,
    Mine honour will be called in question;   55
    And therefore, gentle Mortimer, begone.
MORTIMER   Madam, I cannot stay to answer you;
    But think of Mortimer as he deserves.
            [Exeunt all but the Queen]
QUEEN   So well hast thou deserved, sweet Mortimer,
    As Isabel could live with thee for ever.   60
    In vain I look for love at Edward's hand,
    Whose eyes are fixed on none but Gaveston.
    Yet once more I'll importune him with prayers.
    If he be strange and not regard my words,
    My son and I will over into France   65

> And to the king my brother there complain
> How Gaveston hath robbed me of his love;
> But yet I hope my sorrows will have end,
> And Gaveston this blessèd day be slain.

There is a perceptible shift in Isabella's position in relation to the other characters in the play as this scene progresses. We are now in the midst of battle: civil war is raging between the king and the barons. At the beginning, Isabella is not very far removed from the weak, dependant woman of the previous extract. Edward urges Gaveston to flee, knowing that he is the barons' target, and as Edward takes his leave of Gaveston, his niece and Isabella, he refuses to bid his queen farewell – unless it is 'for Mortimer, your lover's sake' (II.iv.14). The pattern duplicates act I scene iv almost exactly: a parting, an accusation of Isabella's unfaithfulness, Edward's rejection of her declaration of love, and Isabella's lamentation in soliloquy. As the stage empties and Isabella is left alone, she turns to address the audience directly. Once more, the style is formal, from the choric commentary on the action – 'From my embracements thus he breaks away' (16) – to the rhyming couplet at the end of the speech, as she wishes that her tears 'Had power to mollify his stony heart, / That when I had him we might never part!' (20–1).

In conversation with Mortimer, as the barons arrive in hot pursuit of Gaveston, Isabella is weary and desperate. She describes her body as 'wasted' by mourning, and her heart 'blasted' by grief-stricken sighs (25, 24). 'These hands are tired with haling of my lord / From Gaveston', she complains (26–7). The speech crescendos with the repetition of the hateful Gaveston's name, and the despairing cry, 'And all in vain, for when I speak him fair / He turns away and smiles upon his minion' (28–9). 'Minion' is, as we have seen, a term that the barons use frequently to denigrate Gaveston, although Edward uses the same word once in non-pejorative fashion. At this stage, Isabella is still unable to overcome her misguided affection for Edward, and continues to play the role of the scorned female lover. Alarmed at the threat of violence, Lancaster has to reassure her that they seek to kill only Gaveston: 'Far be it from the thought of Lancaster, / To offer violence to his

sovereign,' he tells her (33–4). By contrast, Isabella has no compunction about guiding the barons on their way in their search and
destroy mission for Gaveston. The scene ends with her expressing
her desire to hear news of Gaveston's death – 'But yet I hope my
sorrows will have end, / And Gaveston this blessèd day be slain'
(68–9).

The scene contains one of the most moving expressions of
Isabella's love for Edward (15–21) and since these lines are spoken in
soliloquy, we are inclined to read them as a genuine expression of
her feelings: it is an unwritten rule in the drama of the period that a
character never lies in a soliloquy. At the same time, this scene acts as
a turning point for Isabella. It is a confused and urgent moment
(notice the short, breathless exchanges of lines from 46–52) for the
barons cannot afford to linger if they are to have any hope of over-
taking and arresting Gaveston. Mortimer first urges her to remain
where she is, and then, when she insists that she must follow the
king, he tries to persuade her to sail with him. She declines, still
reluctant to betray her husband and fearful lest her 'honour . . . be
called in question' (55). Mortimer can delay no longer, and she is
left alone again for a final brief soliloquy that finds her caught
between her sense of duty and enduring love for Edward, and her
recognition of the viable alternative that Mortimer represents: 'So
well hast thou deserved, sweet Mortimer, / As Isabel could live with
thee for ever' (59–60). She recognises the hopelessness of her situation, and seems to understand that there is no realistic possibility of
reconciliation with Edward: 'In vain I look for love at Edward's
hand, / Whose eyes are fixed on none but Gaveston' (61–2).

As the play proceeds, Isabella leaves the weak, pining, unrequited
lover of the first two acts far behind. A modern actress will probably
want to find a 'through line', a way of making the emotional and
intellectual connections that will thread her scenes together into a
consistent story. Such concerns were probably not primary for an
Elizabethan boy actor performing the role. However it may be
handled in performance, the Isabella of the fourth and fifth acts has
closed her heart against Edward and is content to go along with
Mortimer's plans for sealing the deposed king's doom: 'so the prince
my son may be safe', she says, 'conclude against his father what thou

wilt, / And I myself will willingly subscribe' (V.ii.19–20). She even participates in the deception of the imprisoned Edward, sending him a jewel and urging the messenger to assure him that 'I labour all in vain / To ease his grief and work his liberty' (70–1). To Edward she is 'unnatural', 'false' and 'unconstant', 'spot[ting] my nuptial bed with infamy' (V.i.17, 30, 31). Today, we are unlikely to take Edward's assessment of Isabella at face value, particularly in the light of his cruel treatment of her in the first half of the play. His accusations of adultery ring especially hollow. An Elizabethan audience may have had a more ambivalent response, or may even have condemned Isabella outright. In an age where female chastity was insisted upon, there were what we would today call 'double standards' with respect to a husband's fidelity to his wife. Edward is a more complex case, of course, particularly since his infidelity involves relationships with men rather than women. Furthermore, the dereliction of duty that his love for Gaveston has entailed, and the conflict with the barons that it has precipitated, make him even less sympathetic. As first he, and then Isabella and Mortimer meet their ends, an audience is most likely to find the death of each of them little more than what they deserve.

Conclusions

1. The study of these extracts has demanded a re-orientation of our understanding of sexuality and gender in relation to four-hundred-year-old plays. With societal beliefs, customs and practices being radically different then from what we are used to in our own time, any reading of the plays that fails to account for significant cultural differences is bound to be flawed. We also need to recognise that any conclusions we do draw about Elizabethan society (and the implications for readings of the plays) are not immune to 'historical contamination'.

2. This is not to say that we can find nothing analogous to our own experiences in Marlowe's plays. We have seen that some expressions of romantic love, for instance, seem strikingly modern: there is the agony of lovers forced to part (Edward and Gaveston)

and the gnawing pain of unrequited love (Isabella's for Edward). Attitudes to women, to marriage, and to homosexuality, however, have undoubtedly changed quite significantly since Marlowe's time. In a production a director and her actors have to make choices about how those changes will affect the performance. In reading the plays, we can more easily keep the two time frames in tension.

3. It is important to remember that these plays were written by a man for all-male companies. We have found that the study of Marlowe's representation of women is not as rich and provocative as, say, Shakespeare's or John Webster's. Zenocrate and Zabina are fleetingly placed centre stage, but even here they are doing little more than acting as analogues for their warring husbands. Abigail is chiefly on hand to be used in Barabas's plots against the Christian enemy. *Faustus* has no female characters of note, but the representation of Helen of Troy typifies early modern attitudes to women, and reveals certain anxieties deeply embedded in the culture. Such anxieties are readily identifiable in the figure of Queen Isabella, who moves from one 'safe' stereotype (the ineffectual scorned lover) to a more dangerous one (the duplicitous and adulterous female) during the course of the play.

Methods of Analysis

1. Close readings of the texts reveal layers of subtext, irony and *double entendre*. Once again, we have had to accept that there are unfamiliar words, and that certain words had specific meanings or connotations for Marlowe and his contemporaries that we may not be aware of today. This is particularly relevant to our study of *Edward II*. The play remains circumspect in its representation of homoeroticism, but close attention to the intimate scenes between Edward and Gaveston, in particular the language used by them (and about them by other, disapproving voices) reveals more about the nature of their relationship than a superficial reading would.

2. Imagery is also crucial in charting developing and deteriorating

relationships. Furthermore, we are able to draw some broader conclusions about the representation of women in Marlowe's plays by studying imagery more closely, and observing how images tend to cluster around a pair of binary opposites – the submissive, good, pure woman (Isabella in the first half of *Edward II*) and the rebellious, corrupt and dangerous woman (Isabella in the second half of the play, and Helen of Troy in *Faustus*).

3. When we are considering sexual and gender politics in the plays, staging can be crucial: in the critical confrontations between Edward, Gaveston and Isabella, for instance, the positions they occupy on stage, the way they move around one another, and their physical interactions, are all relevant to an exploration of the play's dynamics. Similarly, the positions of Zenocrate and Zabina in their confrontation in *Tamburlaine* are vital, as they act out their struggle for supremacy.

4. In intimate scenes, the texts often shift into something approaching naturalistic mode. There are far fewer extended speeches, and lengthy passages where exchanges are conducted in single lines, or less. The shifts in the rhythms of the scenes are important, as we move from long speeches into sharper dialogue, and, at other times, into formal soliloquies.

Suggested Work

Zenocrate's role in *Tamburlaine* is admittedly limited, but she does serve several important functions during the course of the two plays: her shock at Tamburlaine's cruelty is bound to impact on the audience's own perspective, for instance. At the end of act IV scene ii Zenocrate pleads for mercy for her home city of Damascus, a plea Tamburlaine disregards (I, IV.ii.123–6). She is horrified at the suicides of Bajazeth and Zabina (I, V.i.319–70). It is also worth comparing her interaction with her sons with Tamburlaine's at the beginning of *Tamburlaine II* (I.iii.17–111). Compare this with, for instance, Tamburlaine cutting his arm and demanding his sons imitate him to prove their bravery in Part II, III.ii.53–145. Finally,

Zenocrate's death is one of the key indications that Tamburlaine himself is not omnipotent and invincible, and his rage at her death is a critical point on the graph of his journey through the plays (see II, II.iv.78–142). In *The Jew of Malta*, Abigail is a fairly thin character, as we have already noted, but we can usefully compare her earlier compliance with Barabas's directions with her decision to turn against him. When her love for her father comes into conflict with her horror at his actions, the drama that is played out in her soliloquy is one of the play's more emotionally engaging (and, alas, fleeting) moments (III.iii.36–49).

Isabella is, of course, the richest female character in the Marlowe canon, and a close study of her progress through the play will fill in some of the gaps between the extracts I have chosen to examine in depth. See, for instance, her brief reconciliation with Edward when she engineers the return of Gaveston from banishment in act I scene iv (320–83), the pandemonium that ensues when he does return (II.ii.1–100), Isabella in self-imposed exile in France (IV.ii), arriving back in England to take part in the rebellion against Edward (IV.iv, IV.vi), and triumphant, with Mortimer, in act V scene ii. From that point, we move swiftly on to her attempt to influence her son, Edward III, in act V scene iv, and her arrest in the final scene (V.vi). It is also worth looking more closely at the figure of Gaveston to see whether it is possible to discover more about his motives in his relationship with Edward. Once you have formulated a more detailed reading of Gaveston, you can then look more closely at the shadowy figure of Spencer, Edward's favourite after Gaveston's death. Compare Gaveston's motives with Spencer's, and see if you can identify any differences in their approach (see act II scene i, III.ii.1–58, 89–183, and IV.vii).

6

Black Comedy and Black Humour

If we were to make a judgement simply by looking at the titles of Marlowe's dramatic works, each play would seem to fit fairly smoothly into the classical category of tragedy. The full titles of the texts are unambiguous: *The Troublesome Reign and Lamentable Death of Edward the Second, King of England; with the Tragical Fall of Proud Mortimer* is a good example. *Faustus* is *The Tragical History of Doctor Faustus*, and the publisher Richard Jones gave *Tamburlaine* the title of *Two Tragical Discourses* when he printed the play (although it is interesting to note that the Stationers' Register lists them as 'The two comical discourses of Tomberein [sic] the Scythian shepherd'; Jones remarks that he omitted some comic scenes which he considered to be inappropriate in 'so honourable and stately a history'. Some vestiges of humour remain in the version of *Tamburlaine* that survives and, judging by Jones's comment, it is likely that further comic business is now lost to us; indeed, it may have been improvised by the company rather than written by Marlowe. In any case, Jones's market was not theatre-goers but readers, educated enough to be able to read and wealthy enough to have the time to enjoy reading. *The Jew*'s full title is *The Famous Tragedy of the Rich Jew of Malta*. It is *The Jew* that seems to be the least clear cut case in terms of its genre, but it is important to bear in mind that words such as 'comic' and 'tragic' have evolved over the centuries, and it is worth pausing for a moment to define these terms a little more clearly.

161

Today, we understand the term 'comedy' to mean something that makes us laugh. In early modern times a comedy was, broadly speaking, something that had a happy ending. Furthermore, we tend to expect tragedy to be serious and meaningful, while comedy is dismissed (or celebrated) as something that is essentially frivolous and trivial, although we might be able to identify certain exceptions (black comedy and satirical comedy, for instance, are often valued more highly by some, since they can be politically or socially incisive or subversive). The theatre of the absurd – the plays of Eugene Ionesco, for instance, and Samuel Beckett – incorporates comic material and technique for what can be very serious philosophical explorations of human life. The categories of comedy and tragedy were relatively stable in early modern culture, but this is not to say that a tragic play could not incorporate humorous material. We also need to remember that performances of 'serious' tragedies in the Elizabethan playhouses would probably have been performed in the course of an afternoon's entertainment, which would have included appearances by clowns and other entertainers. This is very different from the standard theatre-going experience in the west, where a trip to see a performance of *King Lear* or *Edward II* will be anticipated as a serious 'cultural' experience.

Doctor Faustus is an interesting play in this respect. We know that it has a convoluted textual history, and there are comic (humorous) passages in the play that may seem out of place in a serious study of damnation. Some critics have explained the apparent inconsistency by arguing that the comic scenes are the work of another playwright. When the play is staged today, these scenes are often the first to be trimmed or else cut in their entirety. By contrast, during the eighteenth century, adaptations of *Faustus* into pantomime mode (a hugely popular form at the time) were common. Critics in the first half of the twentieth century were generally dismissive of the comic passages, and this no doubt had an impact on approaches to the play in the theatre. However, reassessments of Marlowe's work in the 1980s and 1990s have encouraged readers and theatre practitioners to revisit those passages. Today, a fully attentive and receptive reading of the text must devote more attention to the play's humour: a number of critics today insist that the comic interludes are not interpolations, but are rather integral to the design of the play as a whole.

The one play of Marlowe's that strains most obviously against its apparent classification as tragedy is *The Jew of Malta*. The play would more accurately be described as a scabrous black comedy, and although Barabas meets a terrible end, his villainy is delineated in such uncompromising terms that his end is likely to provoke a sense of satisfaction – even more so in Elizabethan times, when the audience would probably have been pleased to witness the agonizing death of a murderous Jew (the play seems to have been particularly popular in revival in 1594, around the time that a famous Jew, Roderigo Lopez, was executed for conspiracy to murder Elizabeth I, whom he served as a physician). This section looks at several extracts from *The Jew*, paying close attention to the way in which the text capitalizes, in comic terms, on the relationship the actor playing Barabas builds between his character and the audience. However, we begin with *Faustus*, and we will explore the ways in which the comic interludes, featuring Wagner and Robin the clown, can be understood as significant elements of the play as a whole rather than as additions commissioned or improvised at a later date to liven up a po-faced tragedy.

Doctor Faustus, I.iv.1–73

This interlude, featuring Faustus's servant Wagner and the clown figure Robin, comes immediately after Faustus has conjured Mephistopheles, and sent the devil back to bargain with Lucifer on his behalf, having offered his soul in return for twenty-four years of service from Mephistopheles. It is a difficult passage, mostly on account of its colloquial style and its frequent use of unfamiliar language. The colloquialisms are a sure sign that we are moving into comic territory: after the serious, steady verse of the previous scene, and its often grand poetry, this passage is fast, conversational, and sparking with low, often bawdy humour. The commentary that follows will explain some of the more obscure passages. In performance, actors can often make more sense of the lines for an audience unfamiliar with the language by inflection and physical gesture. When reading the play, we are more likely to move swiftly past scenes like this, but to do so is to fail to appreciate the varied texture of the play.

           Enter Wagner and [Robin] the Clown.

WAGNER   Sirrah boy, come hither.

CLOWN   How, 'boy'? 'Swounds, 'boy'! I hope you have seen
    many boys with such pickedevants as I have. 'Boy', quotha?

WAGNER   Tell me, sirrah, hast thou any comings in?

CLOWN   Ay, and goings out too, you may see else.   5

WAGNER   Alas, poor slave, see how poverty jesteth in his
    nakedness! The villain is bare, and out of service, and so
    hungry that I know he would give his soul to the devil
    for a shoulder of mutton, though it were blood raw.

CLOWN   How? My soul to the devil for a shoulder of mutton, 10
    though 'twere blood raw? Not so, good friend. By'r Lady,
    I had need have it well roasted, and good sauce to it, if I
    pay so dear.

WAGNER   Well, wilt thou serve me, and I'll make thee go like
    Qui mihi discipulus?

CLOWN   How, in verse?   15

WAGNER   No, sirrah, in beaten silk and stavesacre.

CLOWN   How, how, knave's acre? [*Aside*] Aye, I thought that
    was all the land his father left him. [*To Wagner*] Do ye hear?
    I would be sorry to rob you of your living.

WAGNER   Sirrah, I say in stavesacre.   20

CLOWN   Oho, oho, 'stavesacre'! Why, then, belike if I were your
    man, I should be full of vermin.

WAGNER   So thou shalt, whether thou beest with me or no. But
    sirrah, leave your jesting, and bind yourself presently unto
    me for seven years, or I'll turn all the lice about thee into 25
    familiars, and they shall tear thee in pieces.

CLOWN   Do you hear sir? You may save that labour. They are too
    familiar with me already. Swounds, they are as bold with my
    flesh as if they had paid for my meat and drink.

WAGNER   Well, do you hear sirrah? [*Offering money*] Hold,   30
take these guilders.

CLOWN   Gridirons! what be they?

WAGNER   Why, French crowns.

CLOWN   Mass, but for the name of French crowns, a man were
as good have as many English counters. And what should I
do with these?   35

WAGNER   Why, now, sirrah, thou art at an hour's warning
whensoever or wheresoever the devil shall fetch thee.

CLOWN   No, no, here, take your gridirons again.
[*He attempts to return the money*]

WAGNER   Truly I'll none of them.

CLOWN   Truly but you shall.   40

WAGNER [*to the audience*]   Bear witness I gave them him.

CLOWN   Bear witness I give them you again.

WAGNER   Well, I will cause two devils presently to fetch thee
away. – Balioll and Belcher!

CLOWN   Let your Balio and your Belcher come here, and I'll   45
knock them, they were never so knocked since they were
devils. Say I should kill one of them, what would folks say?
'Do ye see yonder tall fellow in the round slop? He has
killed the devil. So I should be called 'Kill-devil' all the
parish over.
*Enter two Devils, and [Robin] the Clown runs up and down
crying*

WAGNER   Balioll and Belcher! Spirits, away!   50

CLOWN   What, are they gone? A vengeance on them! They
have vile long nails. There was a he devil and a she devil.
I'll tell you how you shall know them: all he devils has
horns, and all she devils has clefts and cloven feet.

WAGNER   Well, sirrah, follow me.   55

CLOWN   But do you hear? If I should serve you, would you
teach me to raise up Banios and Belcheos?

WAGNER   I will teach thee to turn thy self to anything, to a dog,
or a cat, or a mouse, or a rat, or anything.

CLOWN   How? A Christian fellow to a dog or a cat, a mouse   60
or a rat? No, no sir, if you turn me into any thing, let it be

in the likeness of a little pretty frisking flea, that I may be
here and there and everywhere. O, I'll tickle the pretty
wenches' plackets! I'll be amongst them, i'faith!

WAGNER   Well, sirrah, come.   65

CLOWN   But, do you hear, Wagner?

WAGNER   How? – Balioll and Belcher!

CLOWN   O Lord, I pray sir, let Banio and Belcher go sleep.

WAGNER   Villain, call me Master Wagner, and let thy left eye be
diametarily fixed upon my right heel, with *quasi vestigiis*   70
nostris insistere.

Exit [*Wagner*]

CLOWN   God forgive me, he speaks Dutch fustian. Well, I'll follow
him, I'll serve him, that's flat.

Exit

Certain key contemporary readings of the comic scenes in *Doctor
Faustus* are heavily influenced by the work of the critic Mikhail
Bakhtin (1895–1975), whose book *Rabelais and his World* (published in 1965 in the Soviet Union, and first translated into English
in 1968) has taken on a kind of canonical status for many scholars
of the early modern period. The book investigates the festive life of
early modern Europe, concentrating on what Bakhtin refers to as the
'second life' or 'second culture' that existed in early modern society –
the popular culture of the common people. Bakhtin focuses on carnival, a tradition that reached its peak each year on Shrove Tuesday,
just before the period of Lent (a time of abstinence leading up to the
celebration of Easter). The Mardi Gras carnival preceding Lent was a
final blow-out before fasting began, and was marked by excessive
eating and drinking, and riotous behaviour. For Bakhtin, the festivi-
ties associated with carnival could be understood as challenges to the
practices and hierarchies established by the ruling class; the carnivalesque works by inversion, subversion, and debasement: the
emphasis is always on the physical and the bodily, as opposed to the
spiritual. Carnival also celebrates the grotesque; Bakhtin notes the
emphasis on an unashamed realism focusing on the parts of the
body usually not considered 'decent' – the mouth, the buttocks, the
genitals – and associated bodily processes, such as defecation, urina-

tion and copulation. Furthermore, laughter is crucial to carnival, in that it can work as a satirical, subversive force, parodying the hierarchies and the pretensions of authority that the dominant class clings to. It is in the light of these perspectives that we will consider the extract above.

The comedy of the scene is unsubtle and often overtly sexual. Much of the humour derives from the foolishness of the clown (the term used to designate a simple-minded and so unintentionally funny character, rather than the kind of entertainer we would label as a clown today). The foolishness often has its own wisdom – when Wagner remarks that Robin appears so hungry that he would give his soul to the Devil for a shoulder of mutton, Robin insists that he would 'need have it well roasted, and good sauce to it' if he were to pay so dear a price as his soul (11–12). The puns and quibbles are likely to be lost on a modern audience or reader: Wagner's reference to 'beaten silk and stavesacre' is a pun, with 'beaten' meaning 'embroidered', but carrying the implication that Robin deserves to be physically beaten, and 'stavesacre' being a reference to a treatment for lice, while at the same time punning on stave (stick) acre (ache) again, a veiled threat of physical punishment. The clown (probably deliberately) mishears Wagner's 'stavesacre' as 'knavesacre', a poor neighbourhood that had become a byword for poverty, and so manages to turn it into a joke at Wagner's expense. There is a pun on the word 'familiar' in lines 25–8: Wagner threatens to turn the lice infecting Robin into 'familiars', that is to say, evil spirits attending magicians, to torment him more. Robin retorts that the lice are already too 'familiar' (meaning 'intimate') with him. The misheard words and misunderstandings multiply: Wagner offers Robin money ('guilders'), which he takes as 'gridirons', instruments of torture (30–2), and he tries to refuse the payment. The joke about French crowns and English counters here is a reference to the common practice of forging French crowns; Robin implies that they are as worthless as 'counters', tokens used in counting money that had no value.

The sexual jokes and puns come in the second half of the extract. Robin's talk of the differences between male and female devils is the clearest example: 'all he devils has horns, and all she devils has clefts and cloven feet', he says, with a clear reference to sexual organs (52–4). When Wagner offers to teach Robin to turn himself into an animal, 'a dog, or a cat, or a mouse, or a rat', Robin insists he would rather be turned into a flea so that he can be 'here and there and everywhere' and 'tickle the pretty wenches' plackets [vaginas]' (62–4). Robin's aspirations may seem paltry when set against the magnificent achievements Faustus imagines for himself (I.i.80–99). However, as things turn out, Robin and Faustus may come closer than we would think.

On the surface, the humour of act I scene iv seems to derive from puns and wordplay, and the physical comedy of Robin being pursued around the stage by the devils Balioll and Belcher. However, the irony of the scene runs deeper. One of the subtexts is an analysis of the operation of authority. The previous scene has seen Faustus setting out the terms of the proposed pact with the Devil, giving the impression that he understands himself to be bargaining from a position of superiority, or at least equality. He addresses Mephistopheles as a servant: he uses the phrase 'I charge thee' twice, as he issues his orders, and is convinced that he is 'conjurer laureate, / That canst command great Mephistopheles' (I.iii.32–3); the audience would no doubt be aware of Faustus's self-delusion. Wagner's aim in the scene is to secure the services of Robin the clown, and he offers him money in exchange for his labour. When he first sees Robin, Wagner notes that he is 'bare, and out of service' (unemployed) (7). He asks him whether he has any 'comings in' (income), to which Robin replies that he has – but that he also has 'goings out too' (expenses), and these have left him in his present state. Wagner imagines he would sell his soul for a taste of raw meat, the reference to selling one's soul inevitably recalling Faustus, and there is a rich irony in the fact that the clown is more sensitive to the dangers of such a bargain than Faustus is. Wagner's terms of address are imperious ('Sirrah boy' in the first line is particularly condescending), and provoke Robin's sarcastic mimicry in lines 2–3; Robin refers to his 'pickedevant' (a short, pointed beard) as proof that he is no mere 'boy'.

Wagner comes up with a line of Latin in order to associate himself with Faustus, and assert his authority over Robin. However, the line he cites (which means 'you who are my pupil') has been noted by a number of editors as the opening line of a poem by William Lyly that would have been very familiar to grammar school children, and so presumably would not have sounded very impressive at all to the educated members of the audience (the other Latin line in the extract [70–1] translates as 'as if to follow in our footsteps'). Wagner's attempts to secure Robin's services are repeatedly frustrated by the clown's reluctance, and he even resorts to an appeal to the audience to bear witness that he has paid him (41). The use of Latin terms can be read as an ironic echo of Faustus's incantations in the previous scene, but the parody goes further than this. We have already seen some hints of other parallels between Wagner's recruitment of Robin and Faustus's attempt to secure the services of Mephistopheles, such as the reference to selling one's soul to the Devil. The connections are strengthened by Wagner's threat, demanding that Robin serve him ('bind yourself presently unto me') for a period of seven years – the standard duration of an apprenticeship. Wagner also insists that, having paid him, he must now be 'at an hour's warning / whensoever or wheresoever the devil shall fetch thee' (36–7).

The appearance of the devils Balioll and Belcher is another source of laughter. Their attacks on Robin may be vicious ('They have vile long nails', Robin remarks [51–2]), but the humorous tenor of the scene is too well established now for this to be played for anything but laughter. The bawdy joke about the horns of the he devil and the clefts of the she devil helps to maintain that tone. The devils themselves probably appear in stark contrast to Mephistopheles in the previous scene, whose first appearance is so terrifying that Faustus asks him to return in a more pleasing shape (I.iii.23–6). Even on his return, dressed as a friar, Mephistopheles is likely to be a powerful and imposing presence. Finally, Wagner's devils anticipate the more shocking appearances of demonic forces in the latter part of the play, when Mephistopheles threatens to 'in piecemeal tear [Faustus's] flesh', and dispatches others to torment the Old Man who has tried to lead Faustus back to salvation (V.i.68, 78–80).

The preoccupation with sex in the extract is, as we have already noted, characteristic of carnival. There is a strong emphasis on the body in the scene, with Wagner's assessment that Robin 'would give his soul to the devil / for a shoulder of mutton, though it were blood raw' (8–9). Robin is evidently one who would do much to satisfy his physical needs, both for food (10–12) and sex (61–4). Editors of the play have remarked on the names of the two devils Wagner summons, Balioll and Belcher (44); the latter's name is self-evidently carnivalesque, and there is a suggestion that the other name may be a pun on 'Belly-all'. The comedy is robustly physical, both literally and figuratively. The playing of the scene might find Wagner beating Robin, and the attack of the devils is also likely to involve physical violence. Elsewhere, there is talk of 'blood raw' mutton (9,11), the puns over 'beaten silk and stavesacre' discussed above (16), the threat of devils tearing Robin's flesh (26), the reality of the lice that, he says, 'are as bold with my / flesh as if they had paid for my meat and drink' (28–9), and the grotesque metaphor of Wagner's order that Robin's 'left eye be / diametarily fixed upon my right heel' (69–70).

If one of the functions of carnival is to debase, to replace the exalted and the spiritual with what is earthy and physical, then act I scene iv subverts the weighty, serious preceding scene, undercutting Faustus's pretensions, which he has poured out in great reams of poetry and Latin spells. The interlude gives members of the audience the room to find different ways of interpreting Faustus's behaviour. It may serve to spotlight Faustus's own foolishness in his dealings with Mephistopheles. It may also cut Faustus down to size: his heroic challenge of orthodoxy is less impressive when placed alongside Wagner's trivial games. Finally, and perhaps most importantly, our responses to the serious issues of salvation and damnation are complicated by the flashes of frivolous, bawdy humour. When it allows the audience to laugh at hell and its devils, the text is perhaps at its most subversive.

The Jew of Malta, I.ii.301–66

To investigate further the deployment of humour in Marlowe's plays, we will concentrate for the rest of the chapter on *The Jew of Malta*. We have already looked at the ways in which Barabas 'performs' in the play, taking on different roles for different situations. This next extract is perhaps the best example of his skilful role-playing, and of his exploitation of the complicity he nurtures with the audience. Most of the comedy derives from that complicity: Barabas knows that his audience is aware that his behaviour is a performance concealing his true feelings, one which allows him to further his own ends. The enjoyment, for the audience as well as for Barabas, comes from sharing that knowledge, and enjoying the ignorance of the other characters in the play. Here we find Barabas plotting to gain entrance to his house which has been confiscated by Ferneze and is being turned into a nunnery. Barabas has persuaded Abigail to pretend that she wishes to convert to Christianity, so that she can gain access to the house and retrieve a secret supply of treasure he has hidden there. The comedy of the scene is heavily dependant upon its staging, and it is important to try and imagine the traffic on-stage as it plays out.

ABIGAIL   Then, father, go with me.
BARABAS   No, Abigail, in this
    It is not necessary I be seen,
    For I will seem offended with thee for't.
    Be close, my girl, for this must fetch my gold.
        [*Barabas stands aside.*] *Enter two Friars* [*Jacomo*
        and Barnardine] *and* [*an Abbess and*] *two Nuns*
JACOMO   Sisters,   305
    We now are almost at the new made nunnery.
ABBESS   The better; for we love not to be seen.
    'Tis thirty winters long since some of us
    Did stray so far amongst the multitude.
JACOMO   But, madam, this house   310
    And waters of this new-made nunnery
    Will much delight you.
ABBESS   It may be so. But who comes here?
ABIGAIL [*coming forward*]   Grave Abbess, and you, happy
    virgins' guide,
    Pity the state of a distressèd maid.   315
ABBESS   What art thou, daughter?

ABIGAIL   The hopeless daughter of a hapless Jew,
    The Jew of Malta, wretched Barabas;
    Sometimes the owner of a goodly house
    Which they have now turned to a nunnery.   320
ABBESS   Well, daughter, say, what is thy suit with us?
ABIGAIL   Fearing the afflictions which my father feels
    Proceed from sin or want of faith in us,
    I'd pass away my life in penitence
    And be a novice in your nunnery   325
    To make atonement for my labouring soul.
JACOMO [*to Barnardine*]   No doubt, brother, but this
    proceedeth of the spirit.
BARNADINE [*to Jacomo*]   Aye, and of a moving spirit too,
    brother.
    But come,   330
    Let us entreat she may be entertained.
ABBESS   Well, daughter, we admit you for a nun.
ABIGAIL   First let me as a novice learn to frame
    My solitary life to your strait laws,
    And let me lodge where I was wont to lie.   335
    I do not doubt, by your divine precepts
    And mine own industry, but to profit much.
BARABAS (*aside*)   As much, I hope, as all I hid is worth.
ABBESS   Come, daughter, follow us.
BARABAS   [*coming forward*]
    Why how now Abigail? What mak'st thou   340
    Amongst these hateful Christians?
JACOMO   Hinder her not, thou man of little faith,
    For she has mortified herself.
BARABAS   How, mortified?
JACOMO   And is admitted to the sisterhood.
BARABAS   Child of perdition, and thy father's shame,   345
    What wilt thou do among these hateful fiends?
    I charge thee on my blessing that thou leave
    These devils, and their damnèd heresy.
ABIGAIL   Father, give me –
BARABAS   Nay, back, Abigail!

(*Whispers to her*)
And think upon the jewels and the gold;   350
The board is markèd thus [*making the sign of the cross*]
that covers it.
[*Aloud*] Away, accursèd, from thy father's sight!
JACOMO   Barabas, although thou art in misbelief,
And wilt not see thine own afflictions,
Yet let thy daughter be no longer blind.   355
BARABAS   Blind, friar? I reck not thy persuasions.
                    [*Aside to Abigail*]
The board is marked thus [*makes sign of the cross*] that
    covers it,
[*Aloud*] For I had rather die, than see her thus. –
Wilt thou forsake me too in my distress,
Seducèd daughter? (*Aside to her*) Go, forget not.   360
[*Aloud*] Becomes it Jews to be so credulous?
(*Aside to her*) Tomorrow early I'll be at the door.
[*Aloud*] No, come not at me! If thou wilt be damned,
Forget me, see me not, and so be gone.
(*Aside* [*to her*]) Farewell, remember tomorrow morning.   365
[*Aloud*] Out, out, thou wretch!

The plethora of stage directions in the extract are an indication of the complexity of the scene, particularly during Barabas's long speech (356–66). It is a scene that, in rehearsal, requires precise choreography. It is clearly not a 'realistic' scene: the convention of the aside requires the audience to accept that, though the character's lines are audible to them, and occasionally to a specific person on stage, they are unheard by the others. In this sense, it operates in a way akin to pantomime. So, although Barabas does not need to ensure that he is literally unheard by other actors on stage during his asides to Abigail, there needs to be a clear demarcation between lines spoken aloud and those spoken as asides.

Before this, Abigail proves herself very much her father's daughter. Her convincing portrayal of the Jew seeking forgiveness and conversion to the Christian faith easily dupes the abbess and the friars, in a performance that anticipates Barabas's own feigned conversion in act

IV scene i. The form of address she uses is deeply respectful: she begins her plea to the abbess by using the title 'Grave Abbess', and refers to the friars as 'you, happy virgins' guide' – these friars would have acted as confessors to the nuns. (Marlowe may well be inviting some knowing laughter at this point: the idea of sexual liaisons between friars and nuns was a very familiar one, a standard butt of anti-Catholic humour.) Abigail describes herself as 'The hopeless daughter of a hapless Jew' in a neat piece of wordplay (317). Her father is 'wretched Barabas', and the plea for mercy is cleverly founded on his misfortunes – as an unmarried woman, her own livelihood would have been entirely dependant upon the status of her father. Abigail draws on Christian doctrine as she describes her spiritual state – she claims to understand their afflictions as proceeding 'from sin or want of faith in us' (323), which is how Christianity understood Judaism at the time. Abigail's speech is heavy and sombre – 'afflictions . . . sin . . . want of faith . . . penitence . . . atonement . . . labouring soul' (322–6). It certainly impresses the friars, who respond to her plea with a private exchange in prose, which breaks in on the verse form of the rest of the extract. The friars seem convinced that it 'proceedeth of the spirit', meaning that the holy spirit has inspired her conversion. A number of editors of the text note that Barnardine's 'Ay, and of a moving spirit too' (329) implies that he is sexually aroused by her. Once again, the satirical slant of the scene makes such a reading quite plausible. Barnardine certainly seems eager to ensure that the abbess admits her to the nunnery. Having secured a place, Abigail moves swiftly to press home the advantage she has gained so easily. Her language remains deeply respectful, and she continues to push all the right buttons: she affirms her commitment to learning to frame 'My solitary life to your strait laws' (334). Her conclusion, 'I do not doubt, by your divine precepts / And mine own industry, but to profit much' (336–7) is clearly ironic: spiritual profit is the ostensible meaning, but Barabas's aside, 'As much, I hope, as all I hid is worth' underlines the fact that the imagined profit is actually financial.

The scene now moves into its dynamic section, as Barabas stages his performance of towering fury and grief at his daughter's apparent abandonment of the Jewish faith. Over the course of the next 25 lines, Barabas shuttles back and forth across the stage, swooping Abigail away from the others so that he can whisper orders to her, pushing her away again in feigned anger and disgust, snatching her back once more as the Christians attempt to take her into their protection. The scene requires the director and actors to be as nimble as Barabas in their negotiation of the space in order to capitalize on the scene's comic potential. He advances on the gathering with a snarling aggression ('What mak'st thou / Amongst these hateful Christians?' [340–1]) and, on hearing of her conversion, launches a bilious attack. Abigail is a 'Child of perdition' (345), 'accursèd' (352), a 'wretch' (366). In a neat reversal of Christian perceptions of Jews, the nuns and friars are 'hateful fiends' (346), 'devils' peddling 'damnèd heresy' (348). For Barabas, her conversion means her damnation (363) – again, the opposite of Christian doctrine, which saw the Jews as a doomed race. For Jacomo, Abigail's Jewish faith is a spiritual blindness that her conversion is healing (355). Barabas is a tornado of performed emotional responses: there is horror – the line 'Away, accursèd, from thy father's sight!' (352) begs for a dramatic gesture, as if Barabas were pushing something demonic away from him; there is the paternal response of disappointment ('thy father's shame' [345]), self-pity ('Wilt thou forsake me too in my distress' [359]), and shock at her faithlessness and gullibility ('Becomes it Jews to be so credulous?' [361]). Barabas also draws on the tradition of the father's formal disowning of a shamed child, moving from threat – 'I charge thee on my blessing' (347) – to dismissal: 'Away, accursèd, from thy father's sight! . . . Forget me, see me not, and so be gone' (352, 364).

There are, in fact, four distinct registers Barabas switches through in the final speech: the whispered, urgent instructions to Abigail alternate with rhetorical exclamations like 'Becomes it Jews to be so credulous?' (361), those aimed at the others on stage (such as 'Blind, friar? I reck not thy persuasions' [356]), and his feigned anger and grief in his words to Abigail (such as 'No, come not at me!' and 'Out, out, thou wretch!' [363, 366]). He moves from one to the other with ease, and the smooth performance by Barabas the *character* masks the extraordinary demands it places on the *performer's* energies and expertise. It is the kind of virtuoso turn that often provokes spontaneous applause from a dazzled audience. When done well, the scene is impressive not only for its showcasing of the actor's ability, but for its comedy: the pleasure experienced by the audience derives from their participation in a joke played by one character at the expense of other characters onstage. The device is so familiar it is easy to overlook its significance in this context. This scene is a fundamental one in terms of the establishment of Barabas's relationship to his audience. On the face of it, Barabas can be nothing but a villain: a murderous Jew, he is a stock Elizabethan bogeyman. Nevertheless, his manipulation of the audience into a kind of complicity with him in his villainy is likely to demand a reassessment of his status and, as the play continues, Barabas draws the audience more deeply into the crimes he enacts against the Christians.

The Jew of Malta, III.vi.1–52

This is one of those uncomfortably comic scenes that are scattered throughout *The Jew of Malta*. In terms of the development of the audience's response to Barabas, it seems to lead the audience in the opposite direction to the one established by the extract above. Act III scene vi depicts the death of Abigail, Barabas's daughter: having trusted her father and followed his orders faithfully, she has been horrified to discover how he has engineered the deaths of her two rival (Christian) suitors. She has consequently become a nun. Barabas in retaliation poisons the nunnery, killing all the inhabitants, including Abigail. The scene sheds some light on gender issues in the play, some simply satirical and comic, others more complex, and bound up with ideologies of religion and of the family. The scene is a very physical one, and it is important to try and visualize it being played out on stage in order to fully gauge its impact.

> *Enter [the] two Friars [Jacomo and Barnardine]*
> JACOMO   Oh brother, brother, all the nuns are sick,
>   And physic will not help them! They must die.
> BARNARDINE   The abbess sent for me to be confessed.
>   O, what a sad confession will there be!

JACOMO   And so did fair Maria send for me.   5
    I'll to her lodging; hereabouts she lies.
                Exit [Friar Jacomo.] Enter Abigail
BARNARDINE   What, all dead save only Abigail?
ABIGAIL   And I shall die too, for I feel death coming.
    Where is the friar that conversed with me?
BARNARDINE   O, he is gone to see the other nuns.   10
ABIGAIL   I sent for him, but seeing you are come,
    Be you my ghostly father; and first know
    That in this house I lived religiously,
    Chaste, and devout, much sorrowing for my sins.
    But ere I came –   15
BARNARDINE   What then?
ABIGAIL   I did offend high heaven so grievously
    As I am almost desperate for my sins,
    And one offence torments me more than all.
    You knew Mathias and Don Lodowick?   20
BARNARDINE   Yes, what of them?
ABIGAIL   My father did contract me to 'em both:
    First to Don Lodowick, him I never loved.
    Mathias was the man that I held dear,
    And for his sake did I become a nun.   25
BARNARDINE   So. Say how was their end?
ABIGAIL   Both, jealous of my love, envied each other:
    And by my father's practice, which is there
    Set down at large, the gallants were both slain.
               [She gives him a paper]
BARNARDINE   O, monstrous villainy!   30
ABIGAIL   To work my peace, this I confess to thee.
    Reveal it not, for then my father dies.
BARNARDINE   Know that confession must not be revealed;
    The canon law forbids it, and the priest
    That makes it known, being degraded first,   35
    Shall be condemned, and then sent to the fire.
ABIGAIL   So I have heard; pray therefore keep it close.
    Death seizeth on my heart. Ah, gentle friar,
    Convert my father that he may be saved,

And witness that I die a Christian.   40
                        [*She dies*]
BARNARDINE   Ay, and a virgin, too; that grieves me most.
     But I must to the Jew and exclaim on him,
     And make him stand in fear of me.
                        Enter Friar [*Jacomo*]
JACOMO   O brother, all the nuns are dead! Let's bury them.
BARNARDINE   First help to bury this, then go with me   45
     And help me to exclaim against the Jew.
JACOMO   Why? what has he done?
BARNARDINE   A thing that makes me tremble to unfold.
JACOMO   What, has he crucified a child?
BARNARDINE   No, but a worse thing. 'Twas told me in shrift;   50
     Thou know'st 'tis death and if it be revealed.
     Come, let's away.
                        Exeunt, [*bearing Abigail's body*]

Abigail plays the penitential convert: she confesses all to the friar,
and repents like a good Christian, while still trying to ensure the
protection of her father from retribution. We know that the conversion of young female Jews was not an unfamiliar fantasy in
Elizabethan England; we also see it rehearsed in the figure of Jessica
in Shakespeare's *The Merchant of Venice*. In this respect, Abigail (like
Jessica) is a 'good' Jew (in an Elizabethan context) for abandoning
her religious heritage and converting to Christianity. At the same
time, it is her apostasy that provokes the murderous and vengeful
wrath of the 'bad' Jew Barabas. We detect her conflicted sense of
duty, the agony of divided loyalty she evidently feels between her
father's trust (even in the full knowledge of his crimes), and the
demands of her new religion. She confesses all, but is anxious that
her confession remain confidential, lest she endanger Barabas. 'To
work my peace, this I confess to thee', she tells Friar Barnardine.
'Reveal it not, for then my father dies' (31–2). Her reason for con-
fessing is her fear for the fate of her own soul. Her anxious assertion
that she lived in the nunnery 'religiously, / Chaste, and devout,
much sorrowing for my sins' (13–14) cannot relieve the pressure she
feels on her soul – 'I am almost desperate for my sins', she declares

(18): the term 'desperate' is a technical one, implying that she is without hope of salvation (a comparison with Faustus's perception of his own state is not out of place here).

Abigail has been manipulated by Barabas for his own ends. The irony of his assertion earlier in the play that he holds Abigail 'as dear / As Agamemnon did his Iphigen; / And all I have is hers' (I.i.136–8) is borne out by the time we reach the end of act III: Agamemnon was forced to sacrifice his daughter to appease the goddess Diana, for an offence he committed himself. Barabas has no compunction about sacrificing his own daughter once she has 'betrayed' him. By contrast, Abigail's final plea is that the friar 'Convert my father that he may be saved' (39). Abigail maintains her duty to her father, and manages at the same time to remain true to her new faith: her penultimate line is a thought for her father's salvation, and her last line is, 'And witness that I die a Christian' (40). In this sense, she behaves as the ideal daughter and the perfect convert. However, all of this is undercut, in typical Marlovian fashion, by the behaviour of the friars. The scene has already been set up as black comedy. Friar Jacomo's opening lines are either weak, or else they deliberately invite the audience to laugh at the news of the poisoning of the nunnery: 'O brother, brother, all the nuns are sick, / And physic will not help them! They must die' (III.vi.1–2). Towards the end of the scene, after Abigail has confessed all to Barnardine and died, Jacomo returns with another inane announcement: 'O brother, all the nuns are dead! Let's bury them' (44). Similarly, the exposition Marlowe accomplishes via Abigail's confession is achieved via a series of prompts from Barnardine, which seem equally amateurish: 'What then? . . . Yes, what of them? . . . So. Say, how was their end?' (16b, 21, 26). The impression these awkward lines convey is that the scene is meant to be treated lightly; certainly it would be difficult for an actress playing Abigail to play her death seriously.

The other comic strand in the scene is the anti-Catholic satire evident in the representation of the friars. Any attempt at courting the emotional engagement of the audience in Abigail's painful death is bound to be undercut by Barnardine's speech. As she breathes her last, and asks that he 'witness that I die a Christian', the friar responds, 'Ay, and a virgin, too; that grieves me most' (40–1). The

portrayal of Catholic friars as lecherous would not have shocked an
Elizabethan audience; popular prejudice against the corrupt ministers of the Roman church had been accumulating for some time
(evidence is plentiful in Chaucer's fourteenth century *Canterbury
Tales*). With Catholicism now displaced as the official religion in
England, such prejudice was given a free rein. The satire on the
putative sex lives of the supposedly chaste friars continues in the following scene. Ithamore, in an attempt to emulate his master's murderous actions, remarks, 'But here's a royal monastery hard by; /
Good master, let me poison all the monks' (IV.i.14–15). Barabas'
reply is a sly, 'Thou shalt not need, for now the nuns are dead, /
They'll die with grief' (16–17). At the beginning of the scene Friar
Barnardine has marvelled at the 'sad confession' that the abbess will
make as she dies, implying that her sins are great and numerous (4).
Friar Jacomo seems to harbour similar concerns about 'Maria', who
has asked that he come to confess her (5).

As we have seen, Abigail is anxious to save her soul by confession,
while maintaining her father's safety. Friar Barnardine reassures her
with an elaborate invocation of the sanctity of confession, and the
terrible punishment that awaits any priest that fails to maintain its
confidentiality (33–6). Marlowe is taking liberties here, since there is
no evidence that a priest convicted of breaking this part of church
law would have been burned alive (though he may well have been
excommunicated). However, the poetic licence is in aid of a greater
comic 'pay off' at the end of the scene. Having insisted that
confession is inviolable, he hurries Jacomo away in order to use the
knowledge he has acquired in order 'to exclaim against the Jew' (46).
In the following scene, the two friars will attempt to blackmail
Barabas with their secret (see discussion on pp. 86–91). ''Twas told
me in shrift', he tells Jacomo. 'Thou know'st 'tis death an if it
be revealed' (50–1). But as they leave, carrying Abigail's body,
their intentions are fairly clear, and Barnardine's hypocrisy sets
them up for a fall in their ensuing encounter with Barabas. The
scene ends with another fairly familiar myth about the Jewish people
– that they crucified Christian children. As we have already seen, the
text's anti-Catholicism is matched and exceeded by its anti-
Semitism.

Abigail operates in this scene primarily as a cog in the comic mechanism. Her confession provides the friars with the information they need to blackmail Barabas: in the following scene, they display their hypocrisy (breaking the confidentiality of confession) and their greed (competing to be the one to convert Barabas and so inherit his wealth). Barnardine's aside about Abigail's status as a virgin reveals his lecherous nature. As so often in the drama of the period, the female characters are faint, sketchy and largely passive. In the first half of the play, she has done everything her father has asked her to do. Once she discovers his part in the deaths of Lodowick and Mathias, she rebels against him, submitting herself to Christian holy orders and renouncing her Jewish faith. In death, divided by a sense of loyalty to two competing patriarchies, her obedience to her father remains, while she does her best to do what is required of her by her newly adopted religion. It is only Isabella in *Edward II* who begins to transcend the customary stereotypes, and offers a richer and more diverse palette for a performer to explore.

The Jew of Malta, IV.iv.26–80

A number of critics have criticised the structure of *The Jew of Malta*, and it is fair to say that the play seems to have a false ending, the first coming halfway through act V scene i: Barabas's plots are discovered and he is arrested; we hear that he is dead, and his body is carried on stage, and Ferneze gives the order for the body to be thrown over the city walls 'To be a prey for vultures and wild beasts' (V.i.57). However, as soon as he is left alone, Barabas springs to life, informing the audience that he had drunk a potion that made him appear dead. The play then proceeds to chart his final act of *hubris*, as he betrays the Christian Ferneze to the Turk Selim Calymath, and then attempts a second double-cross, finally caught in his own elaborate trap. This extract sets up the first of the play's two climactic sequences. Ithamore has been persuaded by the prostitute Bellamira and her lover, the thief Pilia-Borza, to blackmail Barabas with his knowledge of Barabas's crimes. When he receives the letter from Ithamore demanding payment, and a second letter asking for even more money, Barabas decides to rid himself of all three of them, and visits Bellamira's lodgings disguised as a French musician.

BELLAMIRA   Come, gentle Ithamore, lie in my lap.
ITHAMORE   Love me little, love me long. Let music rumble,
    Whilst I in thy incony lap do tumble.
    Enter Barabas with a lute, disguised, [and a nosegay in his hat].
BELLAMIRA   A French musician! Come, let's hear your skill.
BARABAS   Must tuna my lute for sound, twang twang first.   30
ITHAMORE   Wilt drink, Frenchman? Here's to thee with a –
    Pox on this drunken hiccup!
BARABAS [*accepting a drink*]   Gramercy, monsieur.
BELLAMIRA   Prithee, Pilia-Borza, bid the fiddler give me the
    posy in his hat there.   35
PILIA-BORZA   Sirrah, you must give my mistress your posy.
BARABAS   *A vôtre commandement*, madame.
    [*He presents his nosegay, from which they all inhale*]
BELLAMIRA   How sweet, my Ithamore, the flowers smell!
ITHAMORE   Like thy breath, sweetheart; no violet like 'em.
PILIA-BORZA   Foh, me thinks they stink like a hollyhock.   40
BARABAS [*aside*]   So, now I am revenged upon 'em all.
    The scent thereof was death; I poisoned it.
ITHAMORE   Play, fiddler, or I'll cut your cat's guts into
    chitterlings.
BARABAS   *Pardonnez-moi*, be no in tune yet. [*He tunes*] So, now,
    now all be in.   45
ITHAMORE   Give him a crown, and fill me out more wine.
PILIA-BORZA [*giving money*]   There's two crowns for thee. Play.
BARABAS (*aside*)   How liberally the villain gives me mine own
    gold!   50
                [*He plays the lute*]
PILIA-BORZA   Methinks he fingers very well.
BARABAS (*aside*)   So did you when you stole my gold.
PILIA-BORZA   How swift he runs!
BARABAS (*aside*)   You run swifter when you threw my gold out of
    my window.
BELLAMIRA   Musician, hast been in Malta long?

BARABAS   Two, three, four month, madame.   55
ITHAMORE   Dost not know a Jew, one Barabas?
BARABAS   Very mush, monsieur, you no be his man?
PILIA-BORZA   His man?
ITHAMORE   I scorn the peasant, tell him so.
BARABAS [*aside*]   He knows it already.   60
ITHAMORE   'Tis a strange thing of that Jew, he lives upon pickled
   grasshoppers and sauced mushrooms.
BARABAS (*aside*)   What a slave's this! The governor feeds not as
      I do.
ITHAMORE   He never put on clean shirt since he was
      circumcised.
BARABAS (*aside*)   O, rascal! I change myself twice a day.   65
ITHAMORE   The hat he wears, Judas left under the elder when
   he hanged himself.
BARABAS (*aside*)   'Twas sent me for a present from the Great
      Cham.
PILIA-BORZA   A masty slave he is.
                    [*Barabas starts to go*]
   Whither now, fiddler?   70
BARABAS   *Pardonnez-moi*, monsieur, me be no well.
                    Exit [*Barabas*]
PILIA-BORZA   Farewell, fiddler – One letter more to the Jew.
BELLAMIRA   Prithee, sweet love, one more, and write it sharp.
ITHAMORE   No, I'll send by word of mouth now. [*To
   Pilia-Borza*]
   Bid him deliver thee a thousand crowns, by the same token
   that the nuns loved rice, that Friar Bernardine slept in his   75
   own clothes – any of 'em will do it.
PILIA-BORZA   Let me alone to urge it now I know the meaning.
ITHAMORE   The meaning has a meaning.
                    [*Exit Pilia-Borza*]
                              Come, let's in.
   To undo a Jew is charity, and not sin.   80
                    Exeunt.

This is another immaculate performance staged by Barabas the consummate actor. There is comedy of the broadest kind in the extract
– Barabas's painful, pidgin English being the most obvious – as well
as more subtle layers of irony. From his entrance, and his insistence
that he 'Must tuna my lute for sound, twang twang first' (30) it is
clear that Barabas will play the Frenchman role to the hilt, and there
are easy laughs in speeches like his opening line, above, and his
'*Pardonnez-moi*, be no in tune yet' (44). No less performative is his
role as the murderous villain – when Pilia-Borza, Ithamore and
Bellamira smell the poisoned flowers, he gloats, 'So, now I am
revenged upon 'em all. / The scent thereof was death; I poisoned it'
(41–2). Again, there is the turn to the audience, the sharing of a
secret hidden from the others on stage. The irony of the encounter is
underlined by Ithamore's question to the disguised Barabas, 'Dost
not know a Jew, one Barabas?' (56), whom Ithamore proceeds to
scorn as a 'peasant' (59). As Ithamore warms to his theme, Barabas
delivers a series of asides to the audience in response to the deroga-
tory remarks Ithamore makes about his character. The irony is
obvious – Ithamore is blissfully unaware that he is hurling these
insults into the disguised face of his own master – but no less effective; this is comedy at its broadest, but at the same time it is entirely
consistent with the way the play as a whole has been operating, dis-
playing Barabas's superiority in a game which pitches one schemer
against another, time and time again. On this occasion, however, the
secret has a sharper edge, since the deception will bring about the
deaths of Ithamore, Bellamira and Pilia-Borza. On the other hand, it
is fairly likely that none of these characters has sufficiently engaged
our interest for us to feel any pity for them, and their deaths serve
only as demonstrations of Barabas's ingenuity, particularly when he
himself springs back to life in act V scene i.

Ithamore has been enthralled by his master's machinations, and
his blackmailing of Barabas represents his attempt at independence,
a bid for recognition as a schemer in his own right. His pretensions
have already been undercut by the extent of the involvement of
Pilia-Borza and Bellamira in his plotting: his letter to Barabas has
been dictated for him, and Pilia-Borza has also undertaken to deliver
the letter to its recipient. Now, Ithamore is cocky, lording it over the

hired musician: 'Play, fiddler, or I'll cut your cat's guts into chitter-lings' (43) ('chitterlings' are animal intestines). He is prodigal with the money he has stolen from Barabas ('There's two crowns for thee. Play.' [47]), and when Barabas asks him whether he is Barabas's 'man', he responds, 'I scorn the peasant. Tell him so' (59). Here as elsewhere, Barabas's aside, 'He knows it already', is likely to provoke laughter, and serves as a reminder of Barabas's mastery of the situation.

The insults Ithamore aims at Barabas would have been familiar anti-Semitisms. Ithamore portrays Barabas as money-grubbing: ''Tis a strange thing of that Jew,' he remarks, 'he lives upon pickled / grasshoppers and sauced mushrooms' (61–2); the abstemious and unpleasant diet implies mean-mindedness. He is also characterized in Ithamore's speech as dirty ('He never put on clean shirt since he was / circumcised' [64]), and the text also makes reference to Judas Iscariot, the disciple who betrayed Jesus: 'The hat he wears, Judas left under the elder when / he hanged himself' (66–7). According to Christian doctrine at this time, the Jews were to blame for the death of Christ, and Judas, the disciple who handed Jesus over to the authorities, was the obvious focus for that belief. Ithamore, then, is depicted insulting his master, and not only failing to realise that his master is present, but remaining blissfully unaware that he is directing his remarks at Barabas himself. Pilia-Borza concludes the round of insults with 'A masty slave he is' (69), the word 'masty' meaning 'of swine' (and so, often, fat). The connection with swine would relate to the fact that Jews were forbidden to eat pork. Other editors dispute the text at this point, and suggest that the word is 'musty', or bad tempered. Whichever it may be, Barabas has clearly been used as a target for a series of slurs by the end of the encounter.

This is a level of irony that we have already identified elsewhere in the text. However, at the time the play was first performed, the comic pay off would have worked in other ways, too: the fact that the text has encouraged the audience to respond to Barabas's clever manipulation of other characters on stage would not prevent them from laughing at Barabas himself: after all, for the Elizabethan, he is a Jew, and consequently fit to be insulted and laughed at. Barabas is certainly in control, but, beneath the barrage of anti-Semitic remarks, he cannot enjoy his advantage, and there is presumably genuine hurt and displeasure at the aspersions Ithamore is casting upon him, and his parting line is worthy of some consideration in light of this. He excuses himself with the words, '*Pardonnez-moi*, monsieur, me be no well', (71) and while this could be nothing more than a straightforward exit line, it contains the potential for a more poignant interpretation. Barabas may well be smarting from the scorn that has been poured on him; his disguise has allowed him to engineer the deaths of those plotting against him, but his infiltration of Bellamira's lodgings in disguise has allowed him a glimpse of the contempt in which he is held by others, including the servant who had previously served him faithfully. The way in which he chooses to excuse himself ('me be no well') may allow an actor space to allow the audience a glimpse of something more human and vulnerable in Barabas. It is doubtful whether an audience of Marlowe's contemporaries would have been interested in seeing it, but if the play is revived today, this is one moment in the play that might allow space to subvert the dominant impression of Barabas as uncomplicated anti-hero.

Finally, note how the tone of the scene is established by its form: the scene is in prose, and the fact that we have the majority of the scene played in single lines of dialogue helps to maintain a conversational rhythm and a sense of 'realism'. The informal style is maintained in the choice of language – there is a higher than average proportion of colloquial and earthy terms, as well as an indecent joke: Ithamore's reference to Bellamira's 'incony lap' (28) means both 'sweet' and acts as a pun on 'cunny' ('cunt'). In the previous scene between Ithamore and Bellamira (IV.ii), the text switches from prose into verse, as Ithamore plays the part of the courtly lover attempting to woo his beloved. There, Pilia-Borza's exit (IV.ii.81) and re-entrance (99) act as cues for the text to move into verse and out again, as the love scene is broken up. The control of the poetic form is masterful, as we have seen elsewhere in *The Jew* and in other plays, particularly *Edward II*.

Conclusions

1. We have seen the importance of re-thinking genre distinctions, and thinking more carefully about what constitutes comic and tragic registers. We have also seen how the two modes can happily co-exist in the same text. In the case of *The Jew of Malta*, the sardonic humour that dominates the play, and the profoundly unsympathetic protagonist, make it difficult to identify it as a tragedy at all.

2. The comedy in a play like *The Jew of Malta* can serve a number of different functions: it may be simply satirical, and we have seen a number of instances of anti-Catholic satire and anti-Semitic propaganda in *The Jew of Malta*. In *Faustus* we have found that comic scenes that may seem out of place in a serious theological play can work not only to release the tension building up in the main plot, but to provide ironic reflections on that main plot.

3. Much of Marlowe's comedy depends on the exploitation of the gap between performer and role, and between performers and audience members. Barabas crystallizes these ideas: a successful production of the play will find director and actor making full use of the performative dimension of the character and making the most, too, of the frequent opportunities he is offered to make contact with the audience, drawing them into his plans, and encouraging them to see the other characters as dupes. In so doing, Barabas offers the audience the pleasure of seeing the foolishness of proud men such as Jacomo and Barnardine exposed, and the men being held up to ridicule.

Methods of Analysis

1. Close readings of extracts from two of Marlowe's plays show how he uses tragic and comic registers to make his drama provocative and engaging.

2. Once again, the comic potential of a scene relies heavily on the theatre practitioners rehearsing and performing the play: there is

a good deal of scope for making the humour in a play like *Doctor Faustus* accessible to a modern audience, even when the language is unfamiliar. When reading the play the task is more difficult, and recourse to footnotes and glossaries will bring enlightenment, even though the humour is likely to be lost in the process.

3. A full appreciation of the humour in the plays often requires a more detailed knowledge of the play's original context. There are times when jokes will be founded on topical reference; often they utilize colloquial language which has long since gone out of everyday use. A researched joke is unlikely to remain funny once the riddle of its meaning has been solved. It is important to try and re-imagine, then, the spontaneity and immediacy of those jokes, and try and appreciate how they would have been received by their first audiences.

Suggested Work

The comedy in *The Jew of Malta* often emerges from the dramatic ironies that are activated by Barabas's sense of complicity with the audience, the impression that his conspiracies against almost everyone else on the stage are being shared with audience members. Most frequently, this is grounded in Barabas's skills as a performer, his ability to take on and discard roles as necessary, and to be utterly convincing whenever he is 'in role'. We have seen how this works in three scenes – his performance as a potential convert to Christianity (IV.i); his grief and fury over his daughter's supposed apostasy earlier in the play (I.ii); and his more literal disguise as a French musician (IV.iv). Other examples include his apparent despair and rejection of the comradeship of his fellow Jews (I.ii.161–224); his engineering of the duel between Lodowick and Mathias in act II scene iii, convincing each one in turn that he will give him his daughter in marriage; and his trickery in convincing Friar Jacomo that he has murdered Barnardine (IV.i). Closer study of these scenes will also allow you to make an assessment of Barabas's status as villain or anti-hero on a broader base of evidence.

We have seen how one of the Wagner scenes in *Faustus* works as straightforward, broad comedy, but also operates as an ironic commentary on the 'serious' scenes, offering distorted mirror images of Faustus's necromancy. The other clown scenes work in a similar fashion, often challenging the dominant tone of the play. In act II scene ii, Robin steals one of Faustus's conjuring books. His motives are as base as ever ('Now will I make all the maidens in our parish dance at my pleasure stark naked before me', he declares [II.ii.3–4]), shortly after Faustus has claimed to be 'wanton and lascivious' and unable to live without a wife (II.i.140–1). Robin's promise to Rafe that he can 'make [him] drunk with hippocras at any tavern in Europe for nothing' is a conjuring trick not very far removed from Faustus's parlour games, such as conjuring grapes, out of season, at the request of the Duchess of Vanholt (IV.ii.16). Finally, the horse courser scene (IV.i) is also important in an assessment of the play's humorous interludes. It is the scene that is most overtly carnivalesque (it includes the sight of Faustus having his leg pulled off, literally, by an irate horse-trader whom he has swindled). An assessment of *Doctor Faustus* with its interludes read as integral to the work reveals the play to be a much richer and more provocative piece than might appear when read simply as a tragedy of damnation.

7

Endings and Exits

Tamburlaine II, V.iii.199–253

The inevitable conclusion of an historical play like this is the death of the protagonist, but the ending of the second *Tamburlaine* play is, in some senses, an anti-climax. Tamburlaine dies not in battle, but in old age. His dynasty, meanwhile, will continue, and the conclusion is as much about the coronation of his successor as it is about his own death. Marlowe deals with an undramatic set of circumstances by lavishing some grand poetry on this final scene, to match the impressive display of rhetoric that attended Zenocrate's death near the beginning of the play.

TAMBURLAINE   Let not thy love exceed thine honour, son,
    Nor bar thy mind that magnanimity   200
    That nobly must admit necessity.
    Sit up, my boy, and with those silken reins
    Bridle the steelèd stomachs of those jades.
THERIDAMAS [*to Amyras*]   My lord, you must obey his majesty,
    Since fate commands, and proud necessity.   205
AMYRAS [*as he ascends the chariot*]
    Heavens witness me, with what a broken heart
    And damnèd spirit I ascend this seat,
    And send my soul, before my father die,
    His anguish and his burning agony!
TAMBURLAINE   Now fetch the hearse of fair Zenocrate.   210

Let it be placed by this my fatal chair
And serve as parcel of my funeral.

[*Exeunt some*]

USUMCASANE   Then feels your majesty no sovereign ease,
Nor may our hearts, all drowned in tears of blood,
Joy any hope of your recovery?   215

TAMBURLAINE   Casane, no. The monarch of the earth
And eyeless monster that torments my soul
Cannot behold the tears ye shed for me,
And therefore still augments his cruelty.

TECHELLES   Then let some god oppose his holy power   220
Against the wrath and tyranny of Death,
That his tear-thirsty and unquenchèd hate
May be upon himself reverberate.

They bring in the hearse [*of Zenocrate*]

TAMBURLAINE   Now, eyes, enjoy your latest benefit,
And when my soul hath virtue of your sight,   225
Pierce through the coffin and the sheet of gold
And glut your longings with a heaven of joy.
So, reign, my son! Scourge and control those slaves,
Guiding thy chariot with thy father's hand.
As precious is the charge thou undertak'st   230
As that which Clymene's brainsick son did guide
When wand'ring Phoebe's ivory cheeks were scorched
And all the earth, like Etna, breathing fire.
Be warned by him, then; learn with awful eye
To sway a throne as dangerous as his.   235
For if thy body thrive not full of thoughts
As pure and fiery as Phyteus' beams,
The nature of these proud rebelling jades
Will take Occasion by the slenderest hair
And draw thee piecemeal like Hippolytus   240
Through rocks more steep and sharp than Caspian clifts.
The nature of thy chariot will not bear
A guide of baser temper than myself,
More than heaven's coach the pride of Phaethon.
Farewell, my boys; my dearest friends, farewell!   245

My body feels, my soul doth weep to see
Your sweet desires deprived of company;
For Tamburlaine, the scourge of God, must die.
                              [*He dies*]
AMYRAS   Meet heaven and earth, and here let all things end!
For earth hath spent the pride of all her fruit,   250
And heaven consumed his choicest living fire.
Let earth and heaven his timeless death deplore,
For both their worths will equal him no more.
          [*Exeunt in funeral procession, bearing in the hearse of*
          Zenocrate and the body of Tamburlaine, Orcanes and the
          king of Jerusalem drawing in the chariot of Amyras]

And so we see Tamburlaine finally defeated by his 'servant' Death, whom he now acknowledges as 'monarch of the earth'; in effect, he abdicates to his old enemy. The figure of Death has haunted the play: in act V scene i of *Tamburlaine I*, Tamburlaine, menacing the Virgins pleading for him to show mercy to Damascus, has imagined Death 'keeping his circuit by the slicing edge' of his sword (I, V.i.112), and he uses the specific term 'servant' to describe Death's relation to him (I, V.i.117). Death waits on him and does his will. Tamburlaine imagines him sitting on his horsemen's spears and feeding on their points (I, V.i.114–15). However, when Zenocrate dies, Death claims his first victory over Tamburlaine, who is left to rage and storm, demanding, with magnificent futility, that Techelles draw his sowrd 'And wound the earth, that it may cleave in twain', so that they might take their revenge on the Fates for depriving him of his beloved (II, II.iv.97). Having conquered Babylon and burnt the Moslem holy books, Tamburlaine is struck down with a sudden sickness, but he shakes off the attack with a dismissive, 'Whatso'er it be, / Sickness or death can never conquer me' (I, V.i.219–20). When he can fend off the illness no longer, he imagines Death haunting him, and his slighting of Death as his 'slave' sounds more like bravado than it did in the Damascus scene:

See where my slave, the ugly monster Death,
Shaking and quivering, pale and wan for fear,

Stands aiming at me with his murdering dart,
Who flies away at every glance I give,
And when I look comes stealing on.

(67–71)

His attitude swings from despair ('No, for I shall die' [66]) to defiance ('Then will I comfort all my vital parts / And live in spite of Death above a day' [100–1]). Now, in the final scene, the vision of Death is even more terrible: Tamburlaine refers to it as an 'eyeless monster that torments my soul', and claims that it is blind to the tears that are shed for him in his mortal sickness (217–18). Techelles picks up on Tamburlaine's vision, evocatively describing the tyrant Death as 'tear-thirsty' (222).

There is a dual focus in the play's closing moments. Although Tamburlaine's death itself is central, the matter of succession is also crucial, and the extract begins with Tamburlaine's invitation (or demand) that his son Amyras take his place in the chariot. The language is stately, the crowd of consonants necessitating a slow and careful delivery: 'Nor bar thy mind that magnanimity / That nobly must admit necessity' (200–1). The significance of the chariot is clarified when Tamburlaine invites Amyras to take up the reins to 'Bridle the steelèd stomachs of those jades' (203) the conquered kings that Tamburlaine has used to pull his chariot. The visual impact of the chariot and the yoked men remains undiminished in performance, a stark reminder of Tamburlaine's total, brutal authority. Tamburlaine orders him to 'Scourge and control those slaves, / Guiding thy chariot with thy father's hand' (228–9). The vision of the future under Amyras is depicted as no less steely and bleak than Tamburlaine's reign. The status of 'scourge' seems to be passed on from the father to the son. While 'Tamburlaine, the scourge of God, must die' (248), he must not die before he invites Amyras to 'reign, my son! Scourge and control those slaves' (228).

In death, Tamburlaine's speeches can still carry, in rhetorical terms, the blood and fire that has defined his career: the classical allusions refer, ominously, to Phaethon (son of Clymene) whose failure to control the sun-chariot scarred the sky and formed the Milky Way. The speech is studded with references to 'scorched . . .

Etna . . . breathing fire . . . as pure and fiery as Phyteus' beams' (232–7). There is a sharp irony in the use of the word 'pure': Tamburlaine's brutality has, in one sense, been pure in that it has remained untainted by any kind of pity and remorse; to have allowed any humanity to have mitigated his brutality would have been an impure act. Later in the speech, the allusion is to Hippolytus, dragged by his horses and battered to death on the rocks. Tamburlaine's speech is more of a threat than the traditional blessing a dying father would have bestowed on his son and successor. 'The nature of thy chariot will not bear / A guide of baser temper than myself', he warns him (242–3). Amyras's expression of his grief is an anguished cry, wishing that the heavens would inflict on *his* soul the 'anguish and . . . burning agony' (209) that his father is suffering. Likewise, Usumcasane's lament is couched in lurid, violent terms: 'our hearts, all drowned in tears of blood' (214). The only fleeting, redeeming moments are in Tamburlaine's vision of his longed for reunion with Zenocrate, when he imagines his soul, released from his body by death, will once more see his beloved. But note that even here the language is tainted with violence ('Pierce through the coffin' [226]) and framed in terms of conquest; 'glut your longings with a heaven of joy' is still acquisitive and possessive (227). Even the idea of seeing Zenocrate once more, finds expression in terms of Tamburlaine's masculine ('pierc[ing]') conquest of the passive, receptive female.

The visual impact of the final tableau warrants some attention. Earlier in the scene, Tamburlaine has made what he calls his 'last remove' and shifted from his position in the chariot to a chair (II, V.iii.180, s.d.). Tamburlaine has invited Amyras to take his position but, while Amyras has allowed them to crown him, '*he refuses to ascend the royal chariot*' (184 s.d.). Finally Amyras does take his place with a 'broken heart' and 'damnèd spirit' (206–7). At line 223, attendants bring Zenocrate's hearse onto the stage, Tamburlaine asking that it be placed 'by this my fatal chair' (211). The play concludes with a formal, conventional exclamation from Amyras, rounded off in typical fashion with a rhyming couplet: 'Let earth and heaven his timeless death deplore, / For both their worths will equal him no more' (252–3). In production, Tamburlaine may die sprawled across the coffin, as Albert Finney did in the National Theatre production in 1976. In the Royal Shakespeare Company production of 1992, the director Terry Hands cut Tamburlaine's final speech, instead leaving Tamburlaine (Anthony Sher) to reprise the line 'And shall I die, and this unconquered?' as he traced on a huge map all the territories outside the scope of his empire. It was an appropriately bleak reworking of the play's conclusion, redrawing the boundaries to circumscribe even the mightiest of human aspiration.

The Jew of Malta, V.v.51–123

The Jew of Malta's ending is more conventional in some respects than the conclusion to *Tamburlaine II*. Our anti-hero Barabas's death is as inevitable as Tamburlaine's, but has the inherent high drama that *Tamburlaine*'s final scene so patently lacks (and which is consequently laid over the play in the extravagant poetry of Tamburlaine's dying speeches). Barabas, having betrayed Malta to the Turks, now attempts a final double cross in which he will kill Selim Calymath and hand power back to Ferenze. Ferneze, however, out-manoeuvres him, and springs Barabas's elaborately prepared trap on its inventor.

CALYMATH   Come, my companion bashaws, see, I pray,
  How busy Barabas is there above
  To entertain us in his gallery.
  Let us salute him. – Save thee, Barabas!
BARABAS   Welcome, great Calymath.   55
FERNEZE [*aside*]   How the slave jeers at him!
BARABAS   Will't please thee, mighty Selim Calymath,
  To ascend our homely stairs?
CALYMATH   Ay, Barabas.
  Come, bashaws, attend.
FERNEZE [*Coming forward*]   Stay, Calymath!
  For I will show thee greater courtesy   60
  Than Barabas would have afforded thee.

FIRST KNIGHT [*Within*]   Sound a charge there!
    A [trumpet] charge [sounded], the cable cut [by Ferneze], a
    cauldron discovered [into which Barabas falls through a trap
            door. Enter Martin del Bosco and Knights.]
CALYMATH   How now, what means this?
BARABAS   Help, help me, Christians, help!
GOVERNOR   See, Calymath, this was devised for thee.   65
CALYMATH   Treason, treason! Bashaws, fly!
FERNEZE   No, Selim, do not fly.
    See his end first, and fly then if thou canst.
BARABAS   O, help me, Selim, help me, Christians!
    Governor, why stand you all so pitiless?
FERNEZE   Should I in pity of thy plaints or thee,   70
    Accursèd Barabas, base Jew, relent?
    No, thus I'll see thy treachery repaid,
    But wish thou hadst behaved thee otherwise.
BARABAS   You will not help me, then?
FERNEZE   No, villain, no.   75
BARABAS   And villains, know you cannot help me now.
    Then, Barabas, breath forth thy latest fate,
    And in the fury of thy torments strive
    To end thy life with resolution.
    Know, governor, 'twas I that slew thy son;   80
    I framed the challenge that did make them meet.
    Know, Calymath, I aimed thy overthrow,
    And had I but escaped this stratagem
    I would have brought confusion on you all,
    Damned Christians, dogs, and Turkish infidels!   85
    But now begins the extremity of heat
    To pinch me with intolerable pangs.
    Die, life! Fly, soul! Tongue, curse thy fill and die!
                        [*He dies*]
CALYMATH   Tell me, you Christians, what doth this portend?
FERNEZE   This train he laid to have entrapped thy life.   90
    Now, Selim, note the unhallowed deeds of Jews:
    Thus he determined to have handled thee,
    But I have rather chose to save thy life.

CALYMATH   Was this the banquet he prepared for us?
    Let's hence, lest further mischief be pretended.   95
FERNEZE   Nay, Selim, stay, for since we have thee here
    We will not let thee part so suddenly.
    Besides, if we should let thee go, all's one,
    For with thy galleys couldst thou not get hence
    Without fresh men to rig and furnish them.   100
CALYMATH   Tush, Governor, take thou no care for that,
    My men are all aboard,
    And do attend my coming there by this.
FERNEZE   Why, heard'st thou not the trumpet sound a charge?
CALYMATH   Yes, what of that?
FERNEZE   Why, then the house was fired,   105
    Blown up, and all thy soldiers massacred.
CALYMATH   Oh monstrous treason!
FERNEZE   A Jew's courtesy;
    For he that did by treason worked our fall
    By treason hath delivered thee to us.
    Know, therefore, till thy father hath made good   110
    The ruins done to Malta and to us,
    Thou canst not part; for Malta shall be freed,
    Or Selim ne'er return to Ottoman.
CALYMATH   Nay, rather, Christians, let me go to Turkey,
    In person there to mediate your peace.   115
    To keep me here will nought advantage you.
FERNEZE   Content thee, Calymath, here thou must stay
    And live in Malta prisoner; for, come all the world
    To rescue thee, so will we guard us now
    As sooner shall they drink the ocean dry   120
    Then conquer Malta or endanger us.
    So march away, and let due praise be given
    Neither to fate nor fortune, but to heaven.
              [*Exeunt*]

Throughout the play, Barabas has remained several steps ahead of
the opposition. However, in an hubristic attempt to betray
Calymath, he involves Ferneze in his plot; this is a fatal mistake that

leaves him open to the actions of one as skilled in policy and sub-
terfuge as he is himself. As Calymath arrives with his bashaws, he
hails Barabas with a friendly greeting, complacently noting 'How
busy Barabas is there above / To entertain us in his gallery' (52–3).
This image of Barabas reminds us of the performative aspect of the
character that we have noted during our discussion of extracts in
preceding chapters. He has opened this scene with an appearance,
according to the original stage directions, '*with a hammer above, very
busy*' (V.v.0, s.d.). He is part stage manager, part set designer, as he
makes the final adjustments to the trapdoor in the stage: 'How stand
the cords?' he asks his carpenters; 'How hang these hinges, fast?' (1).
However, Ferneze's aside as Barabas returns the greeting warns us
that the status relations that we are used to have altered significantly.
Now, it is not Barabas who nods and winks at the audience, but the
Christian governor. At the same time, the comment Ferneze makes –
'How the slave jeers at him!' (56) expresses amazement and, perhaps,
a sneaking admiration at the audacity Barabas displays as he greets
warmly the man he intends to betray.

Barabas continues with a customary show of deference; as usual,
he masks his supposed mastery over his intended victim with mock
humility, inviting the '**mighty** Selim Calymath' to 'ascend our
homely stairs' (57–8). The stage positions are instructive: Barabas,
up above in the gallery, over-confident and overly ambitious in his
plots, will soon be brought low. Ferneze, situated on the stage below,
literally undermines him. The action now moves in a blur: first, a
trumpet sounds; this is to signal for the detonation of the charges
beneath the outhouse where Calymath's soldiers are lodged, and its
significance is likely to be lost until Ferneze informs Calymath, and
reminds the audience, of what it signifies (105–6). It also functions,
presumably, as the signal to Ferneze's knights to come and rescue
him, as he warned them in the short scene V.iv. Next, Ferneze cuts
the cable to spring the trap not on Calymath ('Stay, Calymath!' he
warns him [59], presumably preventing the Turkish leader from
ascending to Barabas's gallery), but on Barabas himself while he is
still standing on the trapdoor. Barabas falls into a cauldron of
boiling oil, and the Spanish Admiral Martin del Bosco and Ferneze's
knights rush onto the stage.

There is uproar: barked orders, shouts of confusion and terror – note the profusion of exclamation marks and the short, broken, unmetrical lines. We have the knight's command to sound the charge (62), Calymath's bewildered 'How now, what means this?' (63) and then Barabas's scream for help as he falls into the cauldron. In the midst of Calymath's panic and Barabas's agony, Ferneze is calm and coolly ironic: 'No, Selim, do not fly. / See his end first, and fly then if thou canst' (67–8). He turns on Barabas with sardonic, pitiless spite and disdain. Once more, he is 'Accursèd Barabas, base Jew' (72), and Ferneze continues with standard issue anti-Semitisms, smugly remarking to Calymath, 'Now, Selim, note the unhallowed deeds of Jews' (91) and referring to Barabas's plan, sarcastically, as 'A Jew's courtesy' (107).

Barabas dies in conventional fashion. There is nothing realistic about this elongated dying speech. Presumably a man being boiled to death in oil would have neither the inclination nor the ability to reel off a catalogue of his crimes. It follows that it would be unwise for the actor playing Barabas to attempt any kind of naturalistic death in the midst of the speech. Such efforts invariably render the lines unintelligible, and it is important that the speech sounds loud and clear. There is only one half-line that might allow for something more true to life – the gasps or cries, 'Die, life! Fly, soul!' (88). For the rest, it is important that the audiences, onstage and off, are reminded of the extent of Barabas's crimes. We are also reminded that Ferneze, in killing Faustus, is actually avenging the death of his son. Boiling oil would have been seen as an appropriate execution for Barabas by the Elizabethans, since this was the customary way in which poisoners were executed. Barabas curses all and sundry in his dying moments: 'Damned Christians, dogs, and Turkish infidels!' (85); 'Tongue, curse thy fill and die!' (88). As in Thomas Beard's account of Marlowe's death, where he is depicted as having 'cursed and blasphemed to his last gasp', the irredeemably wicked die cursing and so are assured of eternal damnation.

Meanwhile, Ferneze is established as the consummate Machiavellian, having managed to outwit Barabas. He has chosen to spare Calymath's life, but only for his own advantage: he contrasts Barabas's wicked plan to kill with his own supposed mercy (90–3) but it is clear that he intends to hold him to ransom, releasing him only when Malta is firmly back in his hands: 'for Malta shall be freed, / Or Selim ne'er return to Ottoman' (112–13). Just as we have had the conventional death speech from the anti-hero/villain Barabas, so we must endure, also, the conventional speech that ties up the loose ends, with the inevitable rhyming couplet. However, there is something slyly subversive in Ferneze's appeal, in his final lines: 'So march away, and let due praise be given / Neither to fate nor fortune, but to heaven' (122–3). When Ferneze, in the midst of betrayal, double and triple cross, gives thanks to heaven, it is tempting to read the line as ironic. Or perhaps this is to fall into the trap of reading the author into his play, and to take on board the attractive Marlowe myth that we are familiar with from those romantic readings of the subversive playwright.

On the other hand, it is certainly possible to read the ending as stubbornly conservative. The Christians triumph over both the Jew and the Turkish infidel, and the status quo is restored. I find it difficult to imagine many members of that Elizabethan audience would have left the playhouse with anything other than a sense of grim satisfaction at having seen the evil Jew defeated, and the Ottoman empire fended off, with Ferneze and his knights left to fight another day. Today, the sight of a Jew being boiled to death in oil, crying 'But now begins the extremity of heat / To pinch me with intolerable pangs' (86–7), is likely to invoke far more disturbing cultural memories.

Doctor Faustus, V.ii.57–115

> *Exeunt Scholars. The clock strikes eleven.*

FAUSTUS   Ah Faustus,
    Now hast thou but one bare hour to live,
    And then thou must be damned perpetually.
    Stand still, you ever-moving spheres of heaven,   60
    That time may cease, and midnight never come!
    Fair nature's eye, rise, rise again, and make
    Perpetual day; or let this hour be but

A year, a month, a week, a natural day,
That Faustus may repent, and save his soul!   65
O lente, lente, currite noctis equi!
The stars move still; time runs; the clock will strike;
The devil will come, and Faustus must be damned.
O, I'll leap up to my God! Who pulls me down?
See, see where Christ's blood streams in the firmament!   70
One drop would save my soul, half a drop. Ah, my Christ!
Ah, rend not my heart for naming of my Christ!
Yet will I call on him. O, spare me, Lucifer!
Where is it now? 'Tis gone, and see where God
Stretcheth out his arm and bends his ireful brows!   75
Mountains and hills, come, come and fall on me,
And hide me from the heavy wrath of God!
No, no!
Then will I headlong run into the earth.
Earth gape! O, no, it will not harbour me.   80
You stars that reigned at my nativity,
Whose influence hath allotted death and hell,
Now draw up Faustus like a foggy mist
Into the entrails of yon labouring cloud,
That when you vomit forth into the air,   85
My limbs may issue from your smoky mouths,
So that my soul may but ascend to heaven.
                    The watch strikes.
Ah, half the hour is past!
'Twill all be past anon.
O God,   90
If thou wilt not have mercy on my soul,
Yet for Christ's sake, whose blood hath ransomed me,
Impose some end to my incessant pain.
Let Faustus live in hell a thousand years,
A hundred thousand, and at last be saved.   95
O, no end is limited to damnèd souls.
Why wert thou not a creature wanting soul?
Or why is this immortal that thou hast?
Ah, Pythagoras' *metempsychosis*, were that true,

This soul should fly from me, and I be changed   100
Unto some brutish beast.
All beasts are happy, for, when they die,
Their souls are soon dissolved in elements;
But mine must live still to be plagued in hell.
Curst be the parents that engendered me!   105
No, Faustus, curse thyself. Curse Lucifer,
That hath deprived thee of the joys of heaven.
                    The clock striketh twelve
O, it strikes, it strikes! Now, body, turn to air,
Or Lucifer will bear thee quick to hell.
                    Thunder and lightning
O soul, be changed into little waterdrops,   110
And fall into the ocean, ne'er be found!
My God, my God, look not so fierce on me!
         Enter [Lucifer, Mephistopheles, and other] Devils.
Adders, and serpents, let me breathe a while!
Ugly hell gape not. Come not, Lucifer!
I'll burn my books. Ah, Mephistopheles!   115
              [The Devils] exeunt with him

Doctor Faustus's final, lengthy speech is a *tour de force*. In the play's
time scheme, half an hour passes in the space of about thirty lines –
the clock strikes eleven at line 56, and half past the hour at line 87.
Twenty lines later, it strikes twelve. In the course of these fifty lines,
we witness one of the most powerful, agonizing journeys into
despair and terror ever staged. Although, during the course of the
play, we have seen some spectacular set pieces – Mephistopheles's
first entrance, the parade of the Seven Deadly Sins, the disruption of
the Pope's banquet, the appearance of Helen of Troy – this one
remains the most sensational, even when we have nothing but
Faustus on a bare stage.

    The drama inheres in the verse, which is wonderfully expressive of
Faustus's agony. Marlowe's daring experimentation with metre, in his
attempt to dramatize this spiritual crisis, is astonishing, with frequent disruptions of the iambic pentameter. Many of the lines are
fragmentary, and accurately convey the sense of Faustus's train of

thought as it twists, turns, halts and surges. The soliloquy begins with a fragmented line, the exclamation 'Ah Faustus' (57). As he faces up to his fate, the heavy stresses hammer home the reality of his fate ('Now hast thou but **one bare hour** to **live**' [58]), and he prays, '**Stand still** you **ever-moving spheres**' (60), the emphasis at the beginning of the line operating as a kind of brake, a *rallantando*. He implores the sun to return – 'Fair nature's eye, rise, rise again, and make / Perpetual day' (62 3), the effort in the middle of the line ('**rise, rise again**') almost physical. Similarly, at the end of the next line, the plosive sounds 'be but' serve to slow down the movement of the verse, as Faustus begs for 'A year, a week, a natural day' to 'save his soul' (64–5). The Latin line (66) is a quotation from Ovid's *Elegies*, meaning 'run slowly, slowly, you horses of the night'. In Ovid, the line is spoken by a lover, praying that the night will never end. As the critic Harry Levin notes, it is an appropriate quotation for Faustus, the 'scholar turned sensualist', who has demanded that Mephistopheles provide Helen of Troy as his lover as a final distraction from the gathering spiritual gloom.

The terrible, but inevitable realization comes in a line broken into three by semi-colons or commas – different editors make different choices, and those choices alter the impact of the line. Semicolons give the impression of the facts and their implications slowly seeping into his consciousness: 'The stars move still; time runs; the clock will strike;' (67). Commas make the line move more rapidly – 'The stars move still, time runs, the clock will strike' – and instead of slowing the verse, they quicken it, implying the swift passage of time. However this line may be interpreted and delivered, there is certainly a heavy fatalism in the next line: 'The devil will come, and Faustus must be damned' (68). Suddenly, almost as if Faustus is trying to escape the Devil by catching him off guard, he makes a desperate bid for salvation: 'O, I'll leap up to my God!' (69), but something pulls him down. The line cries out for the actor to move on the line, to enact physically the lunge for freedom and the invisible action of the Devil, clawing him back. Faustus catches a glimpse of his salvation in one of Marlowe's most famous lines, 'See, see where Christ's blood streams in the firmament!' (70). It is a startlingly vivid vision of redemption, but it remains infinitely beyond his reach, even though he knows that 'One drop would save my soul, half a drop' (71). When he calls directly, almost intimately on his Saviour ('**my** Christ'), the devils punish him: 'Ah, rend not my heart for naming of my Christ!', he cries (71–2). When he tries again ('Yet will I call on him') they presumably renew their attack, prompting his cry, 'O, spare me, Lucifer!' (73).

Faustus finds himself caught between a wrathful deity and the torments the devils are inflicting on him as he makes a final, now futile appeal to God to save him. The vision of Christ's redeeming blood is replaced with a sight more terrifying than anything Lucifer can conjure: there is a sense of dread in the slow, drawn out lines, 'see where God / Stretcheth out his arm and bends his ireful brows!' (74–5). Faustus wishes only to be hidden from the 'heavy wrath of God', and prays for the hills and mountains to cover him (76). As before, the repetition is expressive of his despair: just as we have 'rise, rise again' (62) and 'See, see' (70), we have 'come, come and fall on me' (76). The imploring cry, 'Earth, gape!' (80) is another intensely physical line. From the earth, Faustus's mind, spinning, turns to the element of air, imagining that, being drawn into a cloud by the planets of his horoscope, his body might be torn apart to free his soul to ascend to heaven (81–7). In his final moments before the devils come to fetch him away, he asks that his soul might be 'changed into little waterdrops, / And fall into the ocean, ne'er be found!' (110–11). A plea for redemption has turned into a plea for extinction. Faustus knows that his damnation is assured. As a human, he can expect only heaven or hell. Animals' souls are 'dissolved in elements', and Faustus's desire for his soul to be transported into 'some brutish beast' explains the reference to Pythagoras's *metempsychosis* – the transmigration of souls.

The clock strikes again and Faustus, realizing he cannot escape hell, begs that there may be some end to his torment. As moments before he has begged for a year, a month, a week, a day to try and save his soul, now he asks that he might live in hell 'a thousand years, / A hundred thousand, and at last be saved' (94–5). The pace quickens. Faustus curses blindly – his parents for engendering him, himself, Lucifer for depriving him of the joys of heaven (105–7). The final moments would presumably have been intensely theatrical.

There is a stage direction referring to '*thunder and lightning*'. We know that a stage prop existed at the time designated as a 'hell mouth'. Perhaps this was placed over the trapdoor in the floor of the stage, and the devils emerged from here, and dragged Faustus down into it after his last line. The devils may have crawled over his body, provoking his line, 'Adders and serpents, let me breathe a while!' (113). His final line will sound to the audience darkly ironic, as he makes a last ditch attempt at striking a bargain with a deity who seems to have absented himself; his promise that 'I'll burn my books' comes twenty-four years too late. His gasping 'Ah, Mephistopheles!' (115) can be interpreted in a number of ways: a scream of pain, an accusatory cry at having been betrayed by his companion, or a desperate, confused appeal for help. After the anguish of this 57-line soliloquy, the audience, if properly engaged in the experience, will by now be raw and ragged from the scene's overwrought, drawn out tension and emotion, and will find it a relief as he finally disappears beneath the stage.

At the moment of his destruction, it may be unclear exactly who is destroying Faustus – God, Lucifer, or both. Just before the devils enter, he cries, 'My God, my God, look not so fierce on me!' (112) and he has already seen God bending his 'ireful brows' and stretching out his arm against him. The matter is complex in theological terms, and those complexities are likely to be lost in the drama of the moment, when witnessed in performance. Nevertheless, the question has vexed generations of scholars, and one particularly provocative reading, from Jonathan Dollimore, can be found in the sample of critical views (see pp. 246–51). In any case, the awareness of God's wrathful presence in Faustus's last hour, and his apparent absence at his last living moment, cannot be passed over lightly.

Edward II, V.v.38–120

Edward's death is an emphatically physical event. It does not carry the spiritual freight that accompanies Faustus's end, but can be equally shocking for the audience when staged effectively. Lightborn is the assassin hired to carry out the murder, and his cold efficiency is set off against the weary, panicky Edward, whose unshakeable sense of impending doom only increases the sense of dread the scene evokes.

LIGHTBORN   So.
                    [*Exit Matrevis and Gurney*]
    Now must I about this gear. Ne'er was there any
    So finely handled as this king shall be.   40
    [*Lightborn opens the door or trapdoor of Edward's dungeon*]
    Foh! Here's a place indeed, with all my heart.
                    [*Enter King Edward*]
EDWARD   Who's there? what light is that? wherefore comes thou?
LIGHTBORN   To comfort you, and bring you joyful news.
EDWARD   Small comfort finds poor Edward in thy looks.
    Villain, I know thou com'st to murder me.   45
LIGHTBORN   To murder you, my most gracious lord?
    Far is it from my heart to do you harm.
    The queen sent me to see how you were used,
    For she relents at this your misery.
    And what eyes can refrain from shedding tears   50
    To see a king in this most piteous state?
EDWARD   Weep'st thou already? List a while to me,
    And then thy heart, were it as Gurney's is,
    Or as Matrevis', hewn from the Caucasus,
    Yet will it melt, ere I have done my tale.   55
    The dungeon where they keep me is the sink
    Wherein the filth of all the castle falls.
LIGHTBORN   O, villains!
EDWARD   And there in mire and puddle have I stood
    This ten days' space, and, lest that I should sleep,   60
    One plays continually upon a drum.
    They give me bread and water, being a king,
    So that for want of sleep and sustenance
    My mind's distempered and my body's numbed,
    And whether I have limbs or no I know not.   65
    O, would my blood dropped out from every vein

As doth this water from my tattered robes!
Tell Isabel the queen, I looked not thus
When for her sake I ran at tilt in France
And there unhorsed the duke of Cleremont.   70
LIGHTBORN   O, speak no more, my lord! This breaks my heart.
Lie on this bed, and rest yourself a while.
EDWARD   These looks of thine can harbour nought but death;
I see my tragedy written in thy brows.
Yet stay a while; forbear thy bloody hand,   75
And let me see the stroke before it comes,
That even then when I shall lose my life,
My mind may be more steadfast on my God.
LIGHTBORN   What means your highness to mistrust me thus ?
EDWARD   What means thou to dissemble with me thus ?   80
LIGHTBORN   These hands were never stained with innocent
      blood,
Nor shall they now be tainted with a king's.
EDWARD   Forgive my thought, for having such a thought.
One jewel have I left, receive thou this.
                    [*He gives a jewel*]
Still fear I, and I know not what's the cause,   85
But every joint shakes as I give it thee.
O, if thou harbour'st murder in thy heart,
Let this gift change thy mind and save thy soul.
Know that I am a king. O, at that name
I feel a hell of grief. Where is my crown?   90
Gone, gone, and do I remain alive?
LIGHTBORN   You're overwatched, my lord. Lie down and rest.
                    [*The King lies down*]
EDWARD   But that grief keeps me waking, I should sleep,
For not these ten days have these eyes lids closed;
Now as I speak they fall, and yet with fear   95
Open again.
                [*Lightborn sits on the bed*]
O wherefore sits thou here?
LIGHTBORN   If you mistrust me, I'll be gone, my lord.
EDWARD   No, no, for if thou mean'st to murder me

Thou wilt return again, and therefore stay.
LIGHTBORN   He sleeps.   100
EDWARD   [*starting*] O let me not die yet! Stay, O, stay a while!
LIGHTBORN   How now, my lord?
EDWARD   Something still buzzeth in mine ears
  And tells me, if I sleep I never wake;
  This fear is that which makes me tremble thus.   105
  And therefore tell me, wherefore art thou come?
LIGHTBORN   To rid thee of thy life. – Matrevis, come!
    [*Enter Matrevis and Gurney*]
EDWARD   I am too weak and feeble to resist.
  Assist me, sweet God, and receive my soul!
LIGHTBORN   Run for the table.   110
EDWARD   O, spare me, or dispatch me in a trice!
  [*Matrevis and Gurney bring in a table and a red-hot spit*]
LIGHTBORN   So, lay the table down, and stamp on it,
  But not too hard, lest that you bruise his body.
    [*The king is murdered*]
MATREVIS   I fear me that this cry will raise the town,
  And therefore let us take horse and away.   115
LIGHTBORN   Tell me sirs, was it not bravely done?
GURNEY   Excellent well. Take this for thy reward.
    Then Gurney stabs Lightborn
  Come, let us cast the body in the moat,
  And bear the king's to Mortimer our lord.
  Away!   120
    Exeunt [*with the bodies*]

It is hard to imagine audiences feeling anything other than pity for Edward by the time we reach this point in the play. The text does seem to invite sympathy by emphasizing the cruelty and vindictiveness with which Edward is treated. As Lightborn opens the door to his prison, Edward's first line is a confused, nervous flurry of questions: 'Who's there? what light is that? wherefore comes thou?' (42). He has been in solitary confinement, and it seems likely that he has been kept in darkness, hence the shock at the sudden influx of light. It may be that the scene was originally staged with Edward posi-

tioned beneath the stage, and hauled, blinking, into the light
through the trapdoor by Lightborn, so that the scene could be
played out on stage. We hear that the dungeon where he is kept is
the building's sewer – 'the sink / Wherein the filth of all the castle
falls' (56–7) and that he has been standing 'in mire and puddle . . .
This ten days' space' (59–60). Even before he appears, there is an
early warning in Lightborn's reaction as he opens the door; 'Foh!
Here's a place indeed, with all my heart' (41) is evidently an exclamation in response to the stench emanating from the dungeon.
Edward is deprived of sleep by the continual banging of a drum.
Although there is something self-dramatizing about Edward's pitiful
state – he begins the account of his treatment by assuring Lightborn
that his woeful tale will melt Lightborn's heart, were it 'hewn from
the Caucasus' (54) – there can be no doubt that his physical and
mental condition have deteriorated significantly: 'My mind's distempered and my body's numbed', as he says himself (64).

Marlowe finds other ways of ensuring that the audience have an
unmistakable sense of Edward as victim at this late stage in the play.
His collapse is all the more dramatic for his consciousness of the
traumatic loss of status. In the deposition scene (V.i), he put on his
crown for the last time with a defiant (and futile) challenge: 'See,
monsters, see, I'll wear my crown again' (V.i.74). Now he offers
Lightborn his last jewel, hoping it might persuade him to spare his
life. The attempt at asserting his authority is pathetic: now a filthy,
ragged and pale figure, he declares:

> Know that I am a king. O, at that name
> I feel a hell of grief: where is my crown?
> Gone, gone, and do I remain alive?
>
> (89–91)

Deprived of his crown, Edward is deprived of his identity. The
crown, as powerful a signifier in this play as it is in the *Tamburlaine*
plays, is what makes him a king, and without his royal status,
Edward has no reason to live. Indeed, Edward is acutely aware that,
under normal circumstances, a king would not lose his crown until
the moment of his death, when it would be passed on directly to his

successor. Jarringly, there is an odd reminiscence here of happier times with Isabel. This king whose words of affection for his queen have been few and far between – he loves her, it seems, only when she arranges Gaveston's return from banishment – displays his tattered robes and compares his present state with his magnificent appearance when he jousted at a tournament in France as her champion (69–70).

Lightborn performs his part efficiently. He delivers the queen's duplicitous message ('she relents at this your misery' [49]) and is equally convincing in his own expressions of sympathy: 'what eyes can refrain from shedding tears / To see a king in this most piteous state?' he declares (50–1). At Edward's description of his imprisonment, Lightborn exclaims, 'O, speak no more, my lord! This breaks my heart' (71). He insists that his hands 'were never stained with innocent blood, / Nor shall they now be tainted with a king's' (81–2). He invites Edward to lie down, and the image is reminiscent of Edward lying with his head in the abbot's lap in act IV scene vii. He assures Edward that he has not come to murder him: 'Far is it from my heart to do you harm' (47). Edward, however, seems to have had a premonition of his death, and nothing can persuade him that Lightborn is not his executioner; 'I see my tragedy written in thy brows', he tells him (74). As he hands over the jewel, his gift (or attempted bribe) he says that 'every joint shakes as I give it thee' (86). Even Lightborn's name itself is ominous, being a kind anglicized form of the name Lucifer, bearer of light. Critics have pointed out how Lightborn is also a literal bearer of light in two ways – he comes to Edward's prison carrying a lantern, but also bearing a red-hot poker – the murder weapon.

Edward, nevertheless, begins to trust Lightborn, though he still cannot sleep. His lines amplify for the audience his physical actions, since the subtleties may well have been lost in a large performance space:

> For not these ten days have these eyes lids closed.
> Now as I speak they fall, and yet with fear
> Open again.
>
> (94–6)

Just as he spells out the miserable conditions he has suffered during his imprisonment, Edward provides a kind of running commentary on his weariness, his attempt to sleep, his sudden reawakening, terrified. Reduced to this pitiable state, a prisoner awaiting execution, Edward reaches out to Lightborn as a fellow human being. There is a curious intimacy about the scene, an intimacy that some directors have exploited to play the scene as either subtly or explicitly homoerotic. In the Royal Shakespeare's staging in 1990 the death scene was played as sado-masochistic sex turning suddenly, fatally violent. The shift in the play from directly political concerns through most of the scenes, to the more personal dimension in the final stages, is revealing. We see more humanity in Edward in captivity than we ever did when he ruled. The play focuses on Edward's sexuality, and his love for Gaveston in particular, as the cause of his persecution. In act V scene iii, he exclaims,

> Gaveston, it is for thee that I am wronged;
> For me, both thou and both the Spencers died,
> And for your sakes a thousand wrongs I'll take.

> (V.iii.41–3)

Some have seen the method used to kill Edward as a kind of sick joke, an 'appropriate' punishment for Edward's sin of sodomy. There is actually nothing in the original stage directions that specifies the manner of his death. In productions in the first half of the twentieth century, the horror of the incident was airbrushed out, and although we cannot know how it was staged by the Elizabethans, the tale would have been familiar from Holinshed's account, and the audiences might well have felt cheated if it was not represented as described there. According to Holinshed, Edward was held down with a table or heavy mattress while one man thrust a hot spit into his anus and rolled it around, searing Edward's internal organs, then removing the spit and (supposedly) leaving the body unmarked. The execution can be seen as a cruel parody, a mockery of Edward's sexuality, a form of homosexual rape. It may well have shocked an Elizabethan audience – this was, after all, the staging of the murder of a king – but it is fairly safe to assume that a proportion at least would have found the spectacle thrilling. A taboo sexual practice has been turned into a horrifying act of violence.

The murder with the spit could be depicted with relative ease: it was certainly less of a challenge than other acts of violence that were regularly staged at the time. What is more important is the drama in the actors' speeches. Once Lightborn has, finally, admitted that he has come to kill Edward, the pace quickens. Lightborn barks an order – 'Matrevis, come!' and Edward, incapable of offering any resistance, manages a ragged prayer ('Assist me, sweet God, and receive my soul!' [109]). Lightborn probably holds Edward as Matrevis and Gurney leave the stage, briefly, and return with the table and the spit. Edward's death is agonizingly delayed by their absence and, helpless and doomed, he only wants an end to his suffering: 'O, spare me, or dispatch me in a trice!' (111). Holinshed describes Edward's last cry as having been audible throughout the castle and the town and, in performance, it is a truly horrifying moment. After this, Gurney's almost casual killing of Lightborn barely fails to register. By now, the audience is accustomed to such political assassinations, and Mortimer's attempt to cover his tracks by having the king's murderer dispatched will be no great revelation. As in *Tamburlaine* and *The Jew of Malta*, the world Marlowe has created on stage is one where death has become almost perfunctory. In the midst of deaths past and the death still to come, however – Mortimer's – the killing of Edward, both ideologically and psychologically, retains its power to shock and horrify.

Conclusions

1. All these plays, in their varied ways, conform to the pattern of tragedy, and the deaths of Tamburlaine, Barabas, Faustus and Edward are always anticipated as the narratives move towards their conclusions. Although the technique of maintaining suspense, of withholding information for the sake of an unexpected denouement, is standard issue in nineteenth and twentieth century drama, it is much less frequently used by early modern dramatists. The deaths of Faustus, Edward and Barabas are pow-

erful by virtue of being spectacular. When staged effectively, the deaths of Edward and Faustus can be difficult to bear, and Barabas's demise is finely balanced (for a modern audience, at least) between tragedy and the play's dominant mode of black comedy.

2. Some of the greatest poetry is reserved for the plays' final scenes. The visions of hell and the even more terrifying revelations of a wrathful God are the most devastating moments in *Doctor Faustus* and give rise to some of Marlowe's most famous lines. In *Tamburlaine*, a death that is inherently undramatic is enhanced by Tamburlaine's fiery dying speeches, and the trepidation Amyras feels as he prepares to succeed his father.

3. In each case, the death speeches do not constitute the closing speeches of the play, and the Suggested Work section below directs you to the true endings of each of the plays. In each case, the plays move towards a final position of equilibrium, with a restoration of some kind of status quo, whether it be restoration of Christian rule (*The Jew of Malta*), the establishment of a new monarch (*Edward II*, *Tamburlaine II*) or a moral judgement passed on a sinner (the Epilogue to *Doctor Faustus*).

4. Marlowe's plays retain their power partly because their endings are often still deeply unsettling. Edward's death is horrifying, and Marlowe manipulates audience response in the build up to the execution itself to intensify the horror, forcing us to respond to him with sympathy and pity. Equally disturbing is Faustus's death. Once again, whatever we make of his progress through the play, and however exasperated we may have become in the face of his blind pride and stupidity, his terrible end can provoke only pity and horror. *Tamburlaine* remains a difficult, in some senses unpleasant text: there is at Tamburlaine's death no quarter given to those he has conquered. If anything, his attitudes harden, and he takes his leave with a parting threat, rather than a blessing, for the son who succeeds him. Finally, *The Jew of Malta*, in an age sensitive to the terrible legacy of anti-Semitism, as well as many other instances of ethnic oppression, shocks audiences today in a way that is far removed from its original performance context.

Methods of Analysis

1. We have considered Marlowe's use of accepted conventions: notions of poetic justice, the punishment of *hubris* (overweening pride), and the restoration of the status quo. How Marlowe uses and experiments with these conventions has a significant impact on our often ambivalent responses to the protagonists at the ends of the plays.
2. The intensity and beauty of the poetry in some of the final scenes demands close attention, particularly in the expressions of Faustus's spiritual torment and Edward's fainting terror as he faces his assassin. We have seen how Marlowe's careful use of language, classical allusion and figures of speech contribute to the dramatic effect of these crucial scenes.
3. Marlowe is often bold in his manhandling of metre in order to achieve certain effects: at times, he seems to abandon the iambic pentameter altogether (without necessarily breaking into prose), finding a more naturalistic form to express more precisely the extreme mental, spiritual and emotional states of his protagonists as they face death.
4. Most of the plays feature spectacular endings or death scenes, and we have given some thought to how these scenes might have been staged in the Elizabethan playhouses, while also considering more recent production choices, and other possibilities for performance.

Suggested Work

In *Tamburlaine* the kingdom is passed on to Tamburlaine's son Amyras. In the drama as in life, the rule is, 'The king is dead, long live the king'. *Edward II* is the tale of the usurper as well as the tale of the deposed king, and the play does not conclude until Mortimer has fallen, Isabella has been sentenced, and Edward III established as monarch (see V.vi). After Barabas's death, Ferneze moves centre stage, takes Calymath as prisoner, and re-establishes Christian rule (V.v.89–123). *Faustus* concludes in the B-text version with a grotesque little scene depicting three scholars coming across Faustus's limbs 'All torn asunder by the hand of death' (B-text, V.iii.7), and it is worth having a look at this short scene, and considering whether it has any effect on the way we respond to Faustus's death. Although act V scene iii is missing from the A-text, both versions print an epilogue. The Chorus enters and declaims, in rigid, moralizing tones:

> Cut is the branch that might have grown full straight,
> And burnèd is Apollo's laurel bough
> That sometime grew within this learnèd man.
> Faustus is gone. Regard his hellish fall,
> Whose fiendful fortune may exhort the wise
> Only to wonder at unlawful things,
> Whose deepness doth entice such forward wits
> To practise more than heavenly power permits.
>
> (Epilogue, 1–8)

We cannot know for sure that this is Marlowe's work but, in passing uncompromising judgement, it certainly seems to resolve what might otherwise be considered ambiguous. The epilogue is often omitted from modern productions, and it is interesting to speculate how its inclusion might make us reassess what has gone before.

Finally, the fates of Isabella and Mortimer are sealed in act V scene vi of *Edward II*, following swiftly on the heels of Edward's death, and the scene requires attention before we can draw conclusions about the ways in which these two figures operate in the play, and the extent to which we engage with them. Our final impressions of Mortimer and Isabella are important in assessing not only their places in the drama, but the way we perceive Edward's death, and the establishment of Edward III on the throne as, typically, political instability is resolved into a new stasis. But even the sight of Mortimer's head, carried on as Isabella is led away to prison, is unlikely to provoke much of a response in the aftermath of Edward's terrible torture and execution.

PART 2

THE CONTEXT
AND THE CRITICS

8

Marlowe the Elizabethan

Introduction

Marlowe died at the age of twenty-nine, and his plays comprise a relatively slim volume when set against Shakespeare's complete works. But Marlowe was a phenomenally successful playwright, eclipsing Shakespeare during his lifetime. As he was enjoying huge success with *Tamburlaine* and *The Jew of Malta*, Shakespeare was working on his first set of history plays, the *Henry VI* cycle, and some early comedies like *The Comedy of Errors* and *The Taming of the Shrew*. Marlowe's works, in an approximation of chronological order, comprise the following:

Dido Queen of Carthage (1586)
   (possibly written in collaboration with Thomas Nashe)
Tamburlaine the Great (two parts, 1587–88)
The Jew of Malta (1590 or 1591)
Edward II (1592)
The Massacre at Paris (1592)
Doctor Faustus (1588? 1593?)

It is impossible to determine with any degree of certainty when Marlowe composed *Doctor Faustus*. It may have been written as early as 1588, although it may date from the tail end of Marlowe's career (he was killed in 1593). In addition to the plays, there is a collection of poetry, some translations of Ovid and Lucan, dating from his university years, an epic love poem (*Hero and Leander*) and a few other minor pieces, including a short, frequently anthologized pastoral piece, 'The Passionate Shepherd to his Love'. In this section, we shall see how these works fit into Marlowe's short but eventful life. Using biography as a backbone for the chapter, I will extrapolate from the details of his life to provide some more general discussion of the Elizabethan age, vital context for a full understanding of the meanings that inhere in his plays.

It is often said that, although we have some fairly solid facts about Shakespeare's life, we are able to deduce very little about his personality. It is as if he remains mercurial and aloof, detached from his work. By contrast, details of Marlowe's brief life are sketchy, but the scandal that surrounded his death seems to illuminate, suddenly and luridly, a larger than life character – a heretic or an atheist, a homosexual, a spy working for England's secret service in Europe during a series of extended absences from Cambridge University. In turn, stories of his atheism have led critics to see in *Doctor Faustus* an expression of Marlowe's own heresies. Some have chosen to read *Edward II* as a positive representation of homosexuality in the light of stories about his own sexual orientation, while the anti-Catholicism of *The Massacre at Paris* has been related to his work for Sir Francis Walsingham's secret service operations against the Catholic threat. Such direct links can be a little too facile. Part of the problem is the sheer proliferation of stories about Marlowe's death and the subsequent speculation on his life; there is no single true story of Marlowe's life, only a series of often contradictory accounts that we may piece together, and each configuration will produce a different picture. However, the extant documents that detail aspects of Marlowe's life and death are fascinating both for what they tell us about Marlowe and for what they reveal about the Elizabethan period.

Marlowe's Early Life

Marlowe's father, John, was a shoemaker in Canterbury. His mother, Katherine, had nine children, and Marlowe was the second born: the eldest did not survive infancy, and the other children that survived were all girls. Christopher Marlowe was born in February 1564 (the same year as Shakespeare) and we know that he attended King's School, Canterbury on a scholarship. At King's, his education would have been classically based: like all well-educated Elizabethan writers, the heritage of Greek and Latin history, literature and philosophy were fundamental components of his mindset. Incidentally, there is evidence that plays were regularly staged at King's School, and it is fairly likely that Marlowe himself would have taken part in performances.

Marlowe's student career began when he was sixteen (a couple of years older than the norm), and in 1580 he arrived at Corpus Christi College, Cambridge, on a scholarship established in the will of the former Archbishop of Canterbury, Matthew Parker. Marlowe's future (in principle) would have been mapped out for him from the time he arrived at Cambridge (and probably even earlier): a career in the church would have been the assumed 'calling' for a Parker scholar. But Marlowe was already writing; *Dido Queen of Carthage* and some of his extant poetry date from his student days. He may also have written most or all of the first part of *Tamburlaine* during this time. It seems that Marlowe was indulging in other, more intriguing extra-curricular activities, too. We know that there was a dispute over his progress from BA to MA status at university, based on his absence from Cambridge (students were generally obliged to remain in attendance for eleven months of the year). A number of scholars have examined college records and established that, after three years of mostly consistent attendance, Marlowe began to play truant for two months or more at a time. When the Cambridge college authorities attempted to block his progress to his MA, however, a letter from Elizabeth I's Privy Council was delivered which asserted that 'in all his actions he [Marlowe] had behaved himself orderly and discretely whereby he had done her Majesty good service, and deserved to be rewarded for his faithful dealing' (A. D. Wraight and Virginia F. Stern, *In Search of Christopher Marlowe*, Adam Hart Ltd, 1993, p. 88). This good service was, apparently, 'in matters touching the benefit of his country', an intriguing and tantalizing hint of what he may have been doing during this time. The letter talks of Marlowe travelling to Rheims in France, a city famous in England for the English College that had been established there, a seminary founded in Europe to train English men for the Catholic ministry. The reassurance that Marlowe had behaved 'orderly and discretely', and done the queen 'good service' is clearly a refutation of any suggestion that he may have defected from English Protestantism to Catholicism, and works to imply the opposite – that Marlowe had gone to Rheims 'undercover' to combat the forces of the Roman church from within.

Protestantism and Catholicism

Human conflict rooted in religious differences is something that continues to plague communities the world over at the beginning of the twenty-first century. Even in societies where religion plays a marginal role in the lives of the majority of its citizens, religious strife is still visible; at the time and place that this is being written, friction between the Catholic, Republican community and the Protestant, Unionist community in the North of Ireland remains the most obvious example. The Troubles also show how religious and political conflict are often intertwined. In Elizabethan England, religion and politics were much more deeply mutually implicated. In the sixteenth century, the country was a site of deep and savage religious controversy.

About thirty years before Marlowe was born, Henry VIII had established himself in the place of the Pope as Supreme Head of the English church via the Act of Appeals and Supremacy, a key moment in the movement known as the Reformation that swept across Europe during the sixteenth century, leading to the establishment of Protestant churches in Switzerland, the Netherlands, England, Scotland and elsewhere. The Pope had long been as much a political as a spiritual entity, and corruption in the church hierarchy was widespread and deep-rooted. The Reformation was a movement that, particularly on the continent, began as a revolution from the grass roots. In England, the decisive action taken by Henry VIII to break from the Catholic church was to some extent motivated by his desire to divorce Catherine of Aragon; the Pope had refused to annul the marriage. When Henry proceeded to marry Anne Boleyn (who would give birth to the future Elizabeth I) and had the divorce pronounced by his archbishop of Canterbury, he was excommunicated by the Pope, and from here the Act of Appeals and Supremacy was a logical step.

Edward VI succeeded to the throne at the age of nine. Born out of Henry's third marriage (to Jane Seymour) Edward was a sickly child, and he died when he was just sixteen. Lady Jane Grey lasted on the throne for less than a fortnight before Edward's sister Mary I ascended the throne in 1553. Edward had been an avid student of theology, and had continued his father's reformist tradition. But Mary had been raised a Catholic, having asserted her commitment to the cause of her mother Catherine of Aragon, and on taking the throne she began to reverse the religious laws established by her father and her brother. Opposition was ruthlessly put down, notably in the suppression of a rebellion led by Sir Thomas Wyatt, and in the execution of some three hundred Protestants burned at the stake between 1555 and 1558. When Mary died, she was succeeded by her half-sister Elizabeth, who was twenty-five when she became queen in 1558, six years before Marlowe was born. She had spent much of Mary's reign in virtual imprisonment, even though she had ridden at Mary's side on the latter's entry to London in 1553. Her Protestantism and her own claim to the throne had made her a potentially dangerous figure. When she did succeed Mary, she established a national Protestant church in England, and an act passed in 1582 left all Catholic clerics in England liable to be executed; about a hundred died over the next ten years. Nevertheless, Elizabeth brought a kind of stability, even though unrest still simmered, both between Catholics and Protestants, and between factions within the Reformist movement – notably due to the agitation of the extremist Puritans. Elizabeth spent much of her reign repelling Catholic threats from within and without, the Catholic Mary Queen of Scots being the most immediate threat, one Elizabeth neutralized by imprisoning her in 1568. Finally, and apparently reluctantly, Elizabeth signed a warrant for Mary's execution in 1587.

Anti-Catholic feeling had deep historical roots, and in

Elizabethan London a play like Marlowe's *The Massacre at Paris* had a broad appeal. *The Massacre at Paris* tells the story of the St. Bartholomew's Day Massacre which took place in Paris between 24 August and 17 September 1572, and involved the deaths of three thousand or more Huguenots (Protestants) at the hands of the ruling Catholics, apparently at the instigation of France's King Charles IX and his mother Catherine de Medici. The atrocity seems to have had a profound impact on the English mindset, being interpreted as proof of the monstrous cruelty of Catholic people. The kind of anti-Catholic satire we have found scattered throughout *The Jew of Malta*, *Doctor Faustus* and *Edward II* can be understood in a similar context. The Catholic threat was a real one (the queen was the target of a number of assassination plots and attempts). Elizabeth I's secret service, headed by Sir Francis Walsingham, though not an official body of the government, operated with surprising effectiveness. Marlowe's first extended absence from Cambridge comes shortly before the Spanish Armada sailed against England, and some scholars speculate that Marlowe may have been involved in the discovery of the so-called Babington Plot, a plan to assassinate Elizabeth in order to allow Mary Queen of Scots to succeed her (there are clear links between espionage activity at Rheims and the discovery of the conspiracy). The foiling of the plot was the final nail in Mary's coffin: she had authorized the plot herself, and it was this that finally precipitated her execution.

Of course, this is dealing with matters of state politics, and the ways in which these affairs impacted lower down the social strata are complex. The Reformation was a pan-European phenomenon that swept across the continent in a variety of different forms, some movements being more from the 'grass roots', others (as in England) more as a result of the business of monarchs and their governments. However, with literacy steadily on the increase, it may be that engagement with the issues was more widespread than it would have been earlier in the century. In principle, there was an opportunity, too, for the theatre to impact on people's thinking and their beliefs. There is one incident that is frequently offered as an example of the way in which theatre intervened directly in political affairs at the time: in 1601, the Earl of Essex led a march into London in an attempt to seize the throne from Elizabeth, and on the preceding day, some of Essex's followers paid the Lord Chamberlain's Men (Shakespeare's company) to perform Shakespeare's *Richard II*. The play features a scene in which Richard is deposed, and this scene was subsequently censored, probably as a direct result of Essex's rebellion. Play-going was certainly an immensely popular pastime in Elizabethan England, and the theatre culture grew in size and popularity very rapidly. Marlowe, by choosing a life as a playwright, was stepping into a volatile sphere.

The London Theatre

Whatever Marlowe's involvement in the affairs at Rheims may have been, we know that by September 1589 he was settled in London, living close by the Curtain Theatre, on the outskirts of the city. Although one might have expected a thriving theatre industry to be rooting itself firmly in the centre of the city, there was a good reason why the playhouses were being constructed in the so-called 'Liberties' – the areas were outside the jurisdiction of the authorities of the city of London. The authorities, the City Fathers, were predominantly Puritans, and Puritanism waged a constant legal war of attrition against the theatres and those who made their living in them. Fortunately, both Elizabeth I and James I were interested in theatre, and their willingness to be used as patrons helped to give the profession of acting, or playing as it was called, a degree of legitimacy, and presumably helped to stave off the efforts of the Puritans to close them down. However, both monarchs were also wary of the volatility of theatre in political terms, and a kind of state censor, the Master of the Revels, organized the visits of playing companies to court, and (in theory) checked all playscripts to ensure that nothing controversial was ever performed. Ben Jonson was just one of the more famous playwrights to serve time in prison for his hand in the writing of a play that was considered seditious.

Nevertheless, the City Fathers maintained their opposition to theatre performances. It was probably the influence of a strong Puritan element in parliament that caused the theatres to be shut down in 1642 for a period of eighteen years. The Puritans' complaints against the theatre industry were multiple. They argued that the playhouses functioned as convenient haunts for thieves and prostitutes. There was probably some truth in this accusation: bearing in mind that the theatres were built in the Liberties in order to remain outside city jurisdiction, criminal elements were bound to be rife in those areas for the same reasons. The Puritans also argued that the playhouses were unhygienic places, and that they bred disease. They had more specific, religious objections to theatre, too, believing that the plays endorsed immorality, and that the performances would lead both performers and audiences into sinful ways. Their obsession with the natural order of things meant they were horrified by the convention of cross-dressing (a necessary part of theatre practice at the time, since women were not allowed to perform). One famous tract, Philip Stubbes's *The Anatomy of Abuses* (1583, second edition) provides an extensive list of the kinds of immoral ways the plays supposedly advocated and taught, concluding that 'if you will learn to contemn God and all His laws, to care neither for Heaven nor Hell, and to commit all kind of sin and mischief, you need to go to no other school, for all these good examples may you see painted before your eyes in interludes and plays' (G. Blakemore Evans (ed.), *Elizabethan-Jacobean Drama*, 1989, p. 12).

At the time Marlowe was writing, careers in the theatre were precarious, for players, playwrights and theatre shareholders alike (usually the leading actors, occasionally playwrights and other personnel, would have a stake in the business, with other actors being hired for the minor roles, and being paid a wage for their work). The idea of the profession of playwright was still evolving: it was only in the late 1570s and the 1580s that purpose-built theatres started to appear, and up until that time (and later, particularly when plague closed the city theatres), companies of players would tour the provinces, performing in public halls and courtyards. The first purpose-built playhouse (the Theatre) was erected in London in 1576. About ten years later, the Rose was built, and the Lord Admiral's Men, the company led by Edward Alleyn, used it as their base. Marlowe was the equivalent of an in-house dramatist there, and Alleyn, perhaps the greatest actor of his day, played the roles of Tamburlaine, Barabas and Faustus.

The Theatre Profession

The relationship between a playwright and his text at this time operated rather differently from the way it tends to work today. Marlowe, once he had written his play, would sell it to his company, and would retain no legal rights of ownership over the work – rights that today are protected by laws of copyright. Marlowe's fair copy would have been transcribed by a book-keeper, who would have written out parts for each of the actors. These scripts (known as 'sides') would consist only of the lines, cues, entrances and exits for each part. It is quite likely that some of the actors covering minor roles would have had only a vague idea of the narrative of the entire play until the final rehearsals, or even its first performance. The company would have had about twenty-four hours total rehearsal time for a new play, and popular plays would have been kept in the repertoire and frequently revived. With a much smaller potential audience than a London West End production today, the turnover of new work had to be much more rapid to keep audience figures healthy.

It is also likely that the text of the play would have been altered during rehearsal, with lines cut and speeches or action improvised to suit the performers. Additional comic business in particular would have been worked out in rehearsal by the players. The clowns of the Elizabethan theatre, like Will Kemp and Richard Tarlton, were famous for their skills, including their talents for improvisation. We can only guess at how closely the texts of the plays that we have inherited resemble Marlowe's own final drafts. *The Jew of Malta* was first performed around 1590, and the oldest version of it we have dates from 1633. *Doctor Faustus* actually survives in two distinct versions, designated by scholars as the 'A-text' (1604), and the 'B-text' (1616). There is evidence that even the earlier version includes sections added by other writers – we know that the theatrical manager Philip Henslowe paid William Bird and Samuel Rowley £4 for additions made to the play in 1602.

There are many other crucial differences between the theatre-going experience of today and the practices and culture of theatre four hundred years ago. Although I do not have the space here to go into detail, it is important to outline some of the main differences in order to appreciate the way in which Marlowe's plays worked at the time they were first performed. There are all kinds of reasons why we might find aspects of the plays strange or inaccessible. Many of these depend on cultural and historical differences, which have been mentioned elsewhere in this book. Other problems will arise from archaic language or difficult syntax. However, a rudimentary under-standing of the conditions under which the Elizabethan companies performed will also help us appreciate the ways in which Marlowe presents his characters, or the opportunities he offers actors to exploit the relationship between themselves and the audience.

The first public playhouses were open air buildings: the two-tiered seating galleries around the perimeter were roofed, and the stage also had some protection from the sun and rain, but the central area was open, and it was here that the majority of the audience stood, crowding around three sides of the stage, which projected out into the centre of the roughly circular space (the Rose was a fourteen-sided polygon). Because there was no artificial lighting, perfor-mances would take place in the afternoon. There was no curtain to hide the stage for scene changes or to mark act or scene divisions, although the 'tiring house' at the back of the stage was used both as a dressing-room and as the stage wings, where props could be stored. A trapdoor in the stage led to the 'cellarage', and above the tiring house was a balcony, or gallery, which provided a third level. This might have been used, for instance, for the execution of the governor of Babylon, who is strung up and shot to death in *Tamburlaine II* (V.i), and for Abigail's appearance at a window with Barabas's gold in act II scene i of *The Jew of Malta*. The three levels also usefully repre-sented heaven, earth and hell (the cover above the stage was referred to as the 'heavens'). No doubt the staging of *Faustus* would have made use of all three levels, with the trapdoor used, perhaps, for the appearances of the Seven Deadly Sins, and the demons Balioll and Belcher – possibly even Mephistopheles. The Good Angel would probably have been placed on the gallery above the stage.

Set was minimal, although as the theatres improved the pillars and the wall at the back of the stage (the *frons scenae*) would have been richly decorated. When necessary, actors would impart essential information to the audience about the setting for a scene with a speech that provided all they needed to know: so, act II scene iii of *The Jew of Malta* begins with the First Officer announcing, 'This is the marketplace' (II.iii.1) and in act II scene ii of *Edward II*, we know that Edward is on the shore awaiting Gaveston's arrival when he begins the scene, 'The wind is good. I wonder why he stays; / I fear me he is wrecked upon the sea' (II.ii.1–2). Props were certainly used, and there is evidence to suggest that costumes were an important, often spectacular part of the performance. One list of props that has survived from the period includes a hell-mouth which may well have been used for the final scene of *Doctor Faustus*, when he is dragged down to hell.

It should be clear from this brief sketch that the Elizabethan theatre was not conducive to what we would call stage realism. There was no artificial lighting, so the division we are used to (actors lit, audience in darkness) would not have been present, and the breaking down of that invisible boundary at the edge of the stage inevitably reduces the scope for maintaining any illusion of 'reality' in the events depicted on stage. From what we can tell, the modern practice in traditional theatre of ignoring the presence of the audience, of keeping the focus of one's attention only on the other actors on stage, would have been alien to Elizabethan players. The most obvious example of interaction between actor and audience was in the frequent use of aside and soliloquy, where characters in the play address the audience directly, the convention dictating that their words are inaudible to other characters on the stage.

It is also unlikely that Elizabethan players would have applied themselves to the study of their stage personae with any of the psychological baggage that contemporary actors tend to bring with them as a matter of course. An Elizabethan (whether actor, playwright or member of the audience) would probably not have been concerned with character consistency and psychological realism, two principles which form the basis of the dominant acting systems in the west today, and the criteria by which plays and performances are often automatically and unthinkingly judged. These principles are inherited largely from acting systems derived from the work and writings of the Russian actor and director Konstantin Stanislavsky

(1863–1938) and are based upon understandings of human nature and society, as well as ideas about theatre and stage practice, that are worlds away from Marlowe's time. Acting styles in the Elizabethan playhouses were probably much more demonstrative than they are in mainstream theatre today: there was probably a repertoire of poses and gestures that would have been interpreted as signals of certain states of mind, or status relations between characters on stage. In *Edward II* we find, for example, this description of a conversation between Isabella and Mortimer being observed by three of the barons:

PEMBROKE   Fear not, the queen's words cannot alter him.
WARWICK   No? But mark how earnestly she pleads.
LANCASTER   And see how coldly his looks make denial.
WARWICK   She smiles! Now, for my life, his mind is changed.

                                                    (*Edward II*, I.iv.233–6)

Earlier, when the barons find Isabella in despair after Edward has abandoned her for Gaveston's company, Lancaster remarks: 'Look where the sister of the king of France, / Sits wringing of her hands, and beats her breast' (I.iv.187–8). This 'larger than life' acting style was probably necessary in the big public playhouses: recent experiments in a replica of the Globe Theatre, where many of Shakespeare's plays were first performed, have found actors drawn instinctively to a more gestural style of acting in terms of their movements and facial expressions. Furthermore, the acoustics of the open space means that volume has to be prioritized over subtleties of vocal tone. All these factors militate against the 'internalized' acting style that we are more familiar with today. As we read these plays, we need to be prepared to abandon any preconceptions about realism: just as the bulk of the plays is in verse – iambic pentatmeters – and we understand that this is not a 'natural' way to speak, so we also have to accept that the depiction of the characters on stage is to some extent symbolic, and not directly representational.

Marlowe's Career as a Playwright

Tamburlaine the Great was probably first staged around 1587 by the Lord Admiral's Men at the Theatre, with Edward Alleyn in the title role. *Tamburlaine* was a huge hit, revived numerous times over the next few years, and quite probably inspiring Marlowe to write the second part – it is likely that this would have been as much a commercial move as an artistic one. The two parts were brimming with spectacular set piece scenes, dressed in magnificent rhetoric. Marlowe seemed well aware of the pioneering nature of his work, and the prologue announces that, 'From jigging veins of rhyming mother wits, / And such conceits as clownage keeps in pay, / We'll lead you to the stately tent of war' (Part I, Prologue, 1–3). Dismissive of his rivals, deliberately provocative, Marlowe seems to be announcing his arrival on the London cultural scene with a brash self-confidence. He was one of a group of dramatists who were known as the 'University Wits', educated men who had, like Marlowe, abandoned the careers that would have been mapped out for them, and chosen instead to make their livings as writers. Neither Shakespeare nor Thomas Kyd (author of *The Spanish Tragedy*) were university graduates; others who were classed as wits are now less well known – they include George Peele, John Lyly and Robert Greene.

In 1589 Marlowe was involved in a street brawl that resulted in the death of a man by the name of William Bradley. Marlowe did not kill Bradley – the deadly weapon was wielded by Marlowe's friend Thomas Watson – but both men subsequently spent some time in Newgate Gaol. Marlowe was acquitted, and spent only a couple of weeks in prison. Watson had to wait several months for his full pardon. Such brawls and duels were not uncommon at the time (although, conversely, they probably did not occur as frequently as popular belief has it). The skirmish is ominous, however, and seems of a piece with Marlowe's proclivity for danger and controversy in various forms. Within four years, Marlowe would be dead.

The Jew of Malta was probably staged around 1590, another major commercial success for the young playwright. *The Jew* is a sharp black comedy, with both Catholicism and Judaism set up as targets for its satirical humour. The execution of Roderigo Lopez, a royal physician accused and convicted (very probably falsely) of conspiring to murder Queen Elizabeth, probably contributed to a revival of its popularity in 1594. Around 1592, Marlowe's two historical dramas, *Edward II* and *The Massacre at Paris* premiered. (The dating of *Doctor Faustus* is more difficult.) In the same year, it seems that Marlowe travelled to the Netherlands, where he was arrested in the English-occupied town of Flushing, along with fellow Englishman Richard Baines, for counterfeiting money. Marlowe's defence seems to have been that he was engaged in an operation similar to his work as a 'double agent' in Rheims. What happened when Marlowe returned to England, in custody, is unclear, but he seems to have been treated with leniency. It is notoriously difficult to document a life like Marlowe's, and it is perhaps unfortunate that he seems to leave his mark on documents that are extant today only when he is getting himself into trouble. Although we have records of some of the performances of his plays, too, the playwrights themselves were essentially dissociated from their work from the time they handed over the scripts to the company of players. In any case, in May 1593, Marlowe was fined and bound over to keep the peace after a scuffle with a couple of constables. This was in the middle of a lean time for those making their living from the theatre: for much of the year, the playhouses were closed due to plague epidemics, and approximately five per cent of the city's population died during that period. It may be that Marlowe, like Shakespeare, turned to poetry to pay his way at this time, writing his epic poem *Hero and Leander*. It is generally believed that Shakespeare's two narrative poems *Venus and Adonis* and *The Rape of Lucrece* date from around the same time.

On 30 May 1593 Marlowe spent the day in the company of three men, Ingram Frizer, a businessman, Robert Poley who, like Marlowe, had worked for Walsingham's secret service, and Nicholas Skeres, a shadowy figure with criminal connections. Settled in a room in a house owned by a woman called Eleanor Bull in Deptford, they had supper together, after which Frizer, Skeres and Poley played backgammon. Apparently suddenly and without warning, an argument erupted between Marlowe and Frizer – according to one account, the dispute was over 'the reckoning', the bill for the food and drink consumed during the day. In the fight that ensued, Marlowe beat Frizer around the head with Frizer's dagger, before Frizer wrested control of the weapon back and stabbed Marlowe in the eye. Marlowe died instantly. In scandal-ridden London, the stories that spread through the capital were legion. However, whether the inhabitants of the room concocted a story together or not, the coroner's report concluded that Frizer acted in self-defence, and that Marlowe was the aggressor.

Heresy and Atheism

One of the most fascinating aspects of Marlowe's unusual death is the proliferation of rumours and stories that quickly followed. Almost all of them launched attacks on Marlowe's reputation, often based on his supposed deviation from orthodox religious belief. Thomas Beard, a Puritan who had been at Cambridge at the same time as Marlowe, wrote in his *Theatre of God's Judgements* (1597) that Marlowe was 'by practice a playmaker, and a poet of scurrility' and a blasphemer who had 'denied God and his son Christ . . . affirming our Saviour to be but a deceiver . . . and the holy Bible but vain and idle stories, and all religion but a device of policy'. Beard found it particularly appropriate that the hand which wrote such heresies and blasphemies was used by God 'to be the instrument to punish him', and that the weapon went straight into his brain, 'which had devised the same'. To give Marlowe a helping hand on his way to eternal damnation, Beard embellishes the original story by adding that Marlowe 'even cursed and blasphemed to his last gasp', thus (like Faustus, perhaps) having no possibility of salvation (A. D. Wraight and V. F. Stern, *In Search of Christopher Marlowe*, 1993, pp. 306–7). Over the next few years, a number of writers followed Beard's lead. In William Vaughan's *The Golden Grove* (1600) we find a gratuitous (and probably quite fanciful) detail, describing how Marlowe lay dying with 'his brains coming out at the dagger's point'. Vaughan concurs with Beard's assessment when he concludes, 'Thus did God, the true executioner of divine justice, work the end of impious atheists' (Wraight and Stern, p. 307). Some time later, another tract in the Puritan tradition – *The Thunderbolt of God's Wrath against Hard-Hearted and Stiff-Necked Sinners* by Edmund Rudierd (1618) – took up the cudgels against blasphemers once more, only this time blasphemy is confounded with the theatrical profession. According to Rudierd, the 'profane wretch' Marlowe died in a street brawl; again, damnation is assured when we hear that, 'blaspheming and cursing', Marlowe 'yielded up his stinking breath'. Rudierd presents this as a warning to all 'brain-sick and profane poets, and players, that bewitch idle ears with foolish vanities', implying that it is a fate that should give pause to all those 'players, that live by making fools laugh at sin and wickedness' (Wraight and Stern, p. 307).

The rumours and accusations that sought to represent Marlowe as a heretic circulated widely after his death; however, there is some evidence to suggest that his reputation in this respect had a longer history. Although few documents survive that provide any criticism of the first performances of his work (an assessment of the plays' popularity is based largely on records of how frequently they were revived, and of box office receipts), there is an intriguing broadside against Marlowe in *Perimedes the Blacksmith* (1588). Both *Perimedes* and a deathbed pamphlet entitled *A Groatsworth of Wit* (1592) were the work of Robert Greene, another of the University Wits, and apparently a bitter and jealous rival of Marlowe's on the London theatrical scene. In *Perimedes*, he refers to 'two Gentlemen Poets' and contrasts his style with their own, referring to them 'daring God out of heaven with that atheist Tamburlan [sic], or blaspheming with the mad priest of the sun', and dismissing 'such mad and scoffing poets, that have prophetical spirits as bold as Merlin's race'. The reference to Tamburlaine is, of course, significant, and the identity of at least one of the 'Gentlemen Poets' is made even more certain by the reference to Merlin, since Marlowe's name was variously rendered as Marlowe, Morley, Marley and Marlin in different documents, with Marlin a familiar form during Marlowe's Cambridge days. In *A Groatsworth of Wit*, the slur that is implicit in *Perimedes* (which suggests the 'atheist Tamburlan' and his creator are both 'daring God out of heaven') is made more explicit:

> Wonder not, (for with thee will I first begin), thou famous gracer of
> Tragedians, that Greene, who hath said with thee (like the fool in his
> heart), There is no God, should now give glory unto his greatness: . .
> . Why should thy excellent wit, his gift, be so blinded, that thou
> shouldst give no glory to the giver? Is it pestilent Machiavellian policy
> that thou has studied? O peevish folly! What are his rules but mere
> confused mockeries, able to extirpate in small time the generation of
> mankind. . . . . The broacher of this diabolical atheism is dead, and in
> his life had never the felicity he aimed at: but as he began in craft,
> lived in fear, and ended in despair.

Greene, dying, repents of his atheism, though he writes of himself as
one who 'began in craft, lived in fear, and ended in despair' – one
not very dissimilar from Faustus, perhaps (Wraight and Stern, p.
192). The reference to 'Machiavellian policy' seems a clear indictment of Marlowe, who gave the ghost of Machiavelli a guest appearance as the prologue to his *The Jew of Malta* (Protestants
traditionally associated Machiavelli with atheism, too).

The most serious accusations on record came just days before
Marlowe's death. In a London seething with discontent at the rising
immigrant population (mostly refugees from Catholic oppression on
the continent), inflammatory, xenophobic notices were being pinned
up around the city. One, which has come to be known as the Dutch
Church libel, had been signed with the pseudonym 'Tamburlaine'.
The authorities, it seems, were particularly intent on identifying the
author of this notice and Thomas Kyd (who had shared rooms with
Marlowe) was arrested when heretical papers were found amongst
his belongings. The authorities described their contents as 'vile
heretical conceits denying the deity of Jesus Christ our Saviour'
(Wraight and Stern, p. 239). Kyd was interrogated (and probably
tortured), terrorized into confessions that claimed Marlowe to be the
owner of the documents, 'shuffled with some of mine (unknown to
me) by some occasion of our writing in one chamber two years
since'. Kyd goes on in another letter to give details of what he refers
to as 'Marlowe's monstrous opinions', including the notion that
'Christ did love him with an extraordinary love', and that St. Paul
was nothing more than a clever conjuror, 'a juggler' as he puts it. His
heresies seemed to consist largely of denials of the supernatural,

'things esteemed to be done by divine power might as well have been done by observation of men'. Although it appeared shortly after Marlowe's death, a testimony given by Richard Baines concerning Marlowe's character is even more damning. The casting of St. John as Christ's homosexual lover is improvised into a series of blasphemies with a sexual accent: 'That the woman of Samaria and her sister were whores and that Christ knew them dishonestly'; 'That St. John the Evangelist was bedfellow to Christ . . . that he used him as the sinners of Sodoma'; and 'That the Angel Gabriel was bawd to the Holy Ghost, because he brought the salutation to Mary'. Baines also accuses him (and Kyd hints at this, too) of attempting to persuade others to atheism, 'willing them not to be afeared of bugbears and hobgoblins, and utterly scorning both God and his ministers' (Wraight and Stern, pp. 308–9).

What are we to make of these claims about Marlowe's beliefs? The first thing to say is that we should not expect such stories to reveal the meanings behind Marlowe's plays. As I have noted before, it is tempting to associate Faustus's heresies with Marlowe's supposed unorthodox beliefs, and to see Edward's relationship with Gaveston as some kind of mirror for Marlowe's own sexuality. Nevertheless, it is clear that some of Marlowe's work walks a thin line between the conventional and the controversial. His anti-Catholic barbs and the anti-Semitism of *The Jew of Malta* would have found sympathetic ears in the audiences (and no opposition from the authorities who regulated the theatres as best they could). However, lines such as Faustus's 'I think hell's a fable' (II.i.127) are in a different category altogether. It is difficult to judge how an Elizabethan audience might have interpreted such a remark. In a society where heaven and hell were, for most people, as 'real' as the world around them, it may have sounded nonsensical. On the other hand, it may have been taken as an understandable response from a man clearly so set apart from godly knowledge that he conversed easily and eagerly with a devil: his search for truth from the 'father of lies' would have inevitably led to such 'monstrous opinions'. Similarly, Tamburlaine, to an Elizabethan, was a kind of bogeyman, representing the heathen, savage face of the Islamic empire. His challenging of the gods, and his own aspiration to godlike status, are likely to have been interpreted as the ravings of a man far removed from the true God and true faith.

Furthermore, in a society where disputes over doctrine easily spiralled into accusations and counter-accusations of heresy (a term often interchangeable with atheism), it is not surprising to find terms like 'atheist' bandied about more loosely than they are today, when atheism tends to have a more clearly defined meaning (a belief that God does not exist). In Elizabethan England heresy or atheism was often linked with political seditiousness, and in this context it is perhaps easier to understand how the Dutch Church libel could be linked to the heretical papers attributed to Marlowe. Furthermore, sexual deviancy, as defined in Elizabethan times, was often bound up with political and religious unorthodoxy: we can see traces of this in accounts of Marlowe provided by Kyd and Baines.

Gender and Sexuality

Another account, published five years after the event, sees Marlowe's death in slightly different terms, and the discrepancy is instructive. Francis Meres's collection of writings *Palladis Tamia* (1598) makes reference to Beard's account of Marlowe's death and describes how Marlowe was 'stabbed to death by a bawdy serving man, a rival of his in his lewd love' (Wraight and Stern, p. 307). Although the nature of that 'lewd love' is left vague, it is quite possible that Meres is picking up on rumours surrounding Marlowe's sexual orientation. We have already seen that testimonies obtained from Richard Baines and Thomas Kyd both make reference to Marlowe's supposed homosexuality, both in a blasphemous context, and Baines's account contains the infamous quip about 'tobacco and boys'.

The differences in customs, behaviour and language that we notice when looking at Elizabethan culture – how the word love, for instance, has different connotations at different times and places – are merely the outward signs of more deep-rooted differences in attitudes and understandings. In recent years, a number of critics (especially those working in the areas of new historicism, cultural materialism and queer theory) have devoted a great deal of attention to the issue of homosexuality in early modern England, and have reached a variety of conclusions. It is true to say that the kind of identity we would categorize as homosexual did not exist in the sixteenth century. In a society where companionate marriage (marrying for love) was still emergent, the idea of same-sex partnership really had very little to define itself against. At the same time, homoerotic practices were by no means unknown, particularly between masters and servants, and other relationships of similar status. In his first play, *Dido Queen of Carthage*, Marlowe portrays Jupiter, king of the gods, with his beloved boy cup-bearer, Ganymede. Valorized in classical literature, homoeroticism was a familiar theme in poetry of this period in particular. The consensus of opinion on Shakespeare's sonnets today is that they describe the poet's love for another man.

Matters are complicated further by the fact that sodomy, which today has a specific meaning, had a wide range of connotations in early modern times, embracing all kinds of sexual 'deviancy', as well as drunkenness and gluttony, and witchcraft. In this sense, once again, sexuality is seen to be bound up in political and spiritual transgression. The association of sodomy and the Devil is clear in *Edward II*, where the nobles understand Edward as one 'bewitched' by Gaveston (1.2.55). When Edward grieves at Gaveston's enforced departure Lancaster exclaims, 'Diablo, what passions call you these?' (I.iv.318); 'diablo', the Spanish word for 'devil', makes a similar association. It is not surprising, then, to find Marlowe accused of homosexuality and heresy in the same breath. The official punishment for the 'crime' of sodomy, incidentally, was death.

In the Elizabethan and Jacobean theatre, all roles were played by males, since women were not permitted to perform. Playwrights were resourceful and imaginative in their exploitation of the potential for 'gender games' arising from the ban on female performers. (For the playful use Marlowe makes of this in Gaveston's speech in the first scene, see pp. 43–4.) However, although gender is a key issue for many critics studying early modern drama, Marlowe is a less interesting case than, say, Shakespeare. The debates surrounding Marlowe's sexuality remain very lively – particularly in relation to *Edward II* – but his plays do not (with the possible exception of Isabella) feature female *dramatis personae* of the stature of some of

Shakespeare's heroines (particularly the comic ones, such as Viola in *Twelfth Night* and Rosalind in *As You Like It)*, or of the central figures in the revenge tragedies of the Jacobean period – Vittoria in *The White Devil*, the Duchess in *The Duchess of Malfi*, or Beatrice-Joanna in *The Changeling*.

The fact that all Elizabethan and Jacobean players were male did not escape the attention of the critics of the playhouses, who were outraged by the potential for sexual confusion it entailed. Philip Stubbes, one of the theatre's most vociferous opponents, argued that performances of plays incited audiences to vice and crime, and he deplored the practice of cross-dressing. 'Our apparel was given us as a sign distinctive to discern betwixt sex and sex,' he argued, 'and therefore one to wear the apparel of another sex is to participate with the same, and to adulterate the verity of his own kind' (cited in Russ McDonald, *The Bedford Companion to Shakespeare*, 1996, p. 319). Stubbes's insistence on difference is bound up with a concern for the maintenance of a status quo, an harmonious order in which every being knows its place. This social order included the placing of woman below man, and it is this sense of hierarchy that is threatened by the violation of dress codes (so-called sumptuary laws that were in place at the time actually determined what people of different social standing could wear, forbidding anyone outside the aristocracy from wearing fur or silk, for example). The marginalization of the female in Marlowe's work is itself a symptom of the situation of women at the time he was writing. The subordination of women was, of course, rooted in history and endorsed by both classical philosophy and Christian doctrine (from Adam and Eve to the traditional metaphor of the church, gendered female, as the bride of Christ). The role of women as child-bearers was vital to the social order, and something that generated a good deal of anxiety, since female infidelity risked the collapse of the patriarchal line of descent. Consequently the pure, virginal or chaste woman was highly valued, and the unfaithful woman was represented as deviant, evil and abhorrent. Something of that polarization, which is at the heart of plays like Middleton and Rowley's *The Changeling*, Shakespeare's *Othello* and countless others, can be seen, too, in Isabella, and the curious figure of Helen of Troy, as she appears in *Doctor Faustus*.

Conclusion

Marlowe's plays are deeply enmeshed in the cultural, political and religious cross-currents of his time. *Doctor Faustus* raises provocative questions about the nature of faith, of salvation and damnation. *Tamburlaine* can also be read as a meditation on the relations between God, 'fate' and the human. Both *Edward II* and *Tamburlaine* are profound explorations of the nature of power. *The Jew of Malta* is a daring black comedy that both panders to audience prejudice and subverts their expectations and challenges their values. All his major works, in different ways, push against the boundaries of what was orthodox and acceptable at the time, and a careful contextualization of the plays reveals the ways in which they intervened in their social and cultural environment at the time they were first performed.

9

A Sample of Critical Views

Christopher Marlowe has had a curious journey through the corridors of literary history. He was largely neglected during the eighteenth century, a period obsessed with classical models of drama and preoccupied with Shakespeare (whose work was often rewritten to suit contemporary tastes). Marlowe was seen as decidedly inferior to Shakespeare; Thomas Warton's criticism of Marlowe's 'tedious and uninteresting scenes' is representative (1781). Warton remarks that 'such extravagancies . . . proceeded from a want of judgement' and the 'barbarous ideas of the time', adding that 'it was the peculiar gift of Shakespeare's genius to triumph and predominate' over these defects – a typical slighting of Marlowe's work by comparisons with Shakespeare's. Marlowe was rediscovered in the nineteenth century by writers like William Hazlitt and Charles Lamb: the latter noted in 1808 that the death scene in *Edward II* 'moves pity and terror beyond any scene, ancient or modern, with which I am acquainted'. At about the same time, Edmund Kean, perhaps the greatest actor of his generation, staged a cut version of *The Jew of Malta* in 1818. Although the production led some critics to reassess Marlowe's reputation, it was still standard procedure to compare him unfavourably with his contemporary: as a dramatic character, Barabas was considered no match for Shylock in *The Merchant of Venice*.

Our sample of readings of Marlowe's plays all come from the twentieth century, a time when Marlowe had secured a place in the literary and dramatic canon and had, particularly in the later years, shaken off the burden of constant comparisons with Shakespeare.

We begin with a highly influential reading of Marlowe and his work dating from the 1950s, Harry Levin's *The Overreacher*. We shall then look at three more recent perspectives, one concentrating on *Doctor Faustus* and the other two on *The Jew of Malta*, showing contrasting views of the play in terms of its ideology, and in particular its representation of Barabas as a Jew.

Secondary reading is a very important part of studying literary and dramatic texts in depth. However, it can never function as a substitute for close reading of the texts themselves. It is vital that you ensure you are as familiar with the text you are studying as you can possibly be. Only then will you be in a position to assess your understanding of the play in the light of another's reading of it. Criticism can be very helpful, particularly the kind of specialized scholarship that facilitates a fuller understanding of the language or the ideas of the time that we might otherwise be unaware of. This kind of knowledge can often prevent us from misinterpreting the play, as well as open the text up for exploration from unexpected angles. However, always try and read criticism critically. Be prepared to disagree with the writer's interpretation of the play, or any argument she may develop out of that interpretation. By all means make use of insights the criticism provides (and be careful to acknowledge your sources if you refer to them in an essay or other work), but do not allow the opinions of another critic to replace what is most important – your own, unique understanding of the play.

Harry Levin

Harry Levin's work is distinctive for its fluent and often florid style, and he is always compellingly readable. Although I have certain significant reservations about some aspects of his approach to Marlowe, *The Overreacher* (1952) remains a seminal publication in the field, and was profoundly influential on a generation of critics. Levin has a very sensitive ear to the movement of the verse, and the kind of poetic effects we have looked at closely in some of the extracts in the first half of the book. He also makes frequent references to classical literature and other works of English literature, and cross-references his discussion of particular passages with other Marlowe plays, managing to piece together a coherent reading of all Marlowe's work. His study of *Faustus* also incorporates some discussion of the work in relation to its source (the *Faustbook*) and other works that deal with similar themes, such as Calderon's *El Magico Prodigioso* and Goethe's *Faust*. Incidentally, Levin was an early advocate for the superiority of the A-text (the 1604 quarto) over the B-text (1616) of *Doctor Faustus*, although it would be some time before the earlier version would find the fairly secure place it now occupies in scholars' consensus as the closest to Marlowe's 'original' vision of the play.

Levin's analysis of *Doctor Faustus* is the culminating point of his reading of Marlowe and his work as a whole. Throughout his book, Levin elaborates on the theme of Marlowe as an archetypal Renaissance figure, caught in a world of new discoveries, with the old order and its certainties crumbling away, eroded by the advance of new science and the redrawing of geographical boundaries via the discoveries of the new world. The image of Faustus in his study is the epitome of Renaissance man on the shores of a seemingly limitless ocean of new knowledge. 'His introductory soliloquy is no mere reckoning of accounts' Levin argues, referring to the different kinds of learning that Faustus turns to and then rejects one by one, 'but an inventory of the Renaissance mind' (p. 139). Levin sees Marlowe reverting to the tradition of the morality play for *Doctor Faustus*'s structure, but investing it with what he describes as 'the most personal of themes – an Atheist's tragedy, an Epicurean's testament, a mirror for University Wits' (p. 137). As he analyses the play, he periodically makes reference to its author: discussing the conjuring tricks that Faustus performs during the course of the play, such as his producing grapes out of season for the pregnant Duchess of Vanholt, Levin suggests that our scepticism as an audience about what Faustus manages to achieve as a result of his pact with the Devil mirrors Marlowe's scepticism about miracles; he notes how Marlowe is on record as having been dismissive of the saints of the Bible (calling them 'jugglers'). Levin devotes a good deal of attention to an interpretation of Faustus's heresies, suggesting that 'Faustus is more impressive as an Atheist than as an Epicurean [pleasure seeker]'.

Throughout, there is an implied reading that closely allies Marlowe's unorthodox opinions with Faustus.

The reading of Faustus himself in *The Overreacher* is generally more sympathetic than we might expect. We may also speculate that it is even more sympathetic to his plight than an Elizabethan audience would have been, since to them his heresies would have been all the more shocking and probably deemed worthy of swift and decisive punishment. At the same time, he chooses to identify Faustus as the chief (if not sole) architect of his own fate. According to Levin, Mephistopheles does very little to draw Faustus to his terrible fate: 'He proffers no tempting speeches and dangles no enticements; Faustus tempts himself, and succumbs to temptations which he alone has conjured up' (p. 143). Levin goes further, claiming that Mephistopheles 'does nothing to lure Faustus on; he suffers for him, he sympathizes with him, above all he understands him' (p. 144).

One of the most valuable elements of Levin's reading of the play is his assertion that the comic subplot of the play can be seen as an integral part of the whole design, and he identifies a couple of instances that support his argument – Wagner's mimicking of Faustus's behaviour by logic-chopping with his master's friends, and the talk of the clown bargaining for mutton directly after Faustus has made his own bargain with the Devil. Levin also anticipates those critics influenced by Bakhtin's work on early modern carnival when he refers to 'Victor Hugo's formulation for western art, the intermixture of grotesque and sublime,' as a useful way of viewing Marlowe's apparent decision to intersperse the tragic material with humorous interludes (p. 151).

Levin's reading of the final monologue is particularly acute, and perhaps manages to pinpoint what makes this play, so alien to us in many ways, a thrilling experience when performed well, or read with a full understanding:

> With every scene the pace of the drama accelerates, reaching a climax with the final monologue, which syncopates an hour into fifty-nine lines. This is much too fast, and we share the suspense with Faustus, whose contract expires at midnight; and yet, in a sense, it is slow enough to fathom – as it were – the thoughts of a drowning man. It

is a soliloquy in the profoundest sense, since it isolates the speaker; at the end, as at the beginning, we find him alone in his study. Tragedy is an isolating experience. To each of us, as to Proust on the death of his grandmother, it conveys the realization that we are truly alone . . .

(p.156)

My reservations about Levin's work chiefly concern his determination to read Marlowe's work as a single, coherent and consistent vision: he parallels Faustus with the protagonists of the other plays, arguing that 'magic is to Faustus what a crown was to Tamburlaine, gold to Barabas, or companionship to Edward' (p. 139). Elsewhere, he finds that each hero finds his counterpart in each play: 'Edward had his evil genius in Gaveston, Barabas his demonic familiar in Ithamore, and Faustus has in Mephistophilis [sic] an alter ego who is both a demon and a Damon' (a Damon being the epitome of a faithful friend) (p. 143). Both of these attempts require a certain stretch of the imagination. Furthermore, the impulse to distil from the work one clear vision is part of a specific, Romantic view of the artist, and is of a piece with the tendency to assume that the artist has a deep personal investment in his creative work. Time and time again, Levin confounds the art with the artist. Discussing the appearance of Helen of Troy in the play, he notes:

But metaphor is never enough for Marlowe; he must have the real thing, beauty in person; in *The Jew of Malta* policy was personified by Machiavelli himself; and the consummation of Faustus' desire – or the consolation, at any rate, for his regret – is to have Helen as his paramour.

(p. 152)

For Levin, the Icarus parallel is crucial. Faustus aspires to something greater than human nature, with all its limitations, can offer. Again, the Romantic inspiration for this vision of Faustus is evident, and Levin elides it with his interpretation of Marlowe himself:

If hell is destruction, it follows that heaven is creation; and perhaps the highest form of creation is that engendered out of the very forces of destruction, the imagination spanning beyond despair. Perhaps we may say of Marlowe what the Florentines said of Dante: this man has been in hell. As we broadly interpret that concept, many men have been there; but few have mastered their terrors and returned to communicate that mastery.

(p. 164)

This kind of reading is attractive: it paints a portrait of Marlowe as the tortured artist, and maintains his notional status as the archetype of the Renaissance man, both blessed and cursed by the dawning of new, dangerous knowledge. Critics have continued to cast Marlowe as the political and religious (or anti-religious) radical of Elizabethan theatre, although more recently his sexuality has made him a kind of icon for gay writers and artists; Oscar Wilde has been appropriated in a similar fashion. The most obvious example of Marlowe's canonization as a gay artist is the film version of *Edward II* directed by Derek Jarman in 1991 (Jarman's specific, clearly stated intention was to make a film that spoke out against the oppression of homosexuals). The work of a generation of critics in encouraging readers and audiences to identify Marlowe's work with what we know of his life and his personality has given us this indelible image of Marlowe as the subversive outsider figure. However, no matter how attractive this portrait of Marlowe might be, we need to balance it against other readings of his plays that emphasise their commitment to an orthodox line. The next critic we shall hear from, Jonathan Dollimore, has his own way of resolving the dichotomy between orthodoxy and subversion in Marlowe's work.

Jonathan Dollimore

Jonathan Dollimore's *Radical Tragedy* (first published in 1984) was an influential study of early modern drama offering a very different interpretation of *Doctor Faustus*. Dollimore was one of the key figures in the establishment of the school of criticism known as cultural materialism. Cultural materialism insists on the importance of situating texts within their contexts (social, political, religious) and also reminds us that no reading of literature is ever neutral: it insists

that we contextualize ourselves when we read those works of literature. Cultural materialism has traditionally denied that humankind
has any 'essential', unchanging nature, arguing instead that human
nature is largely (or even solely) the product of the culture that nurtures it, and so will always be culturally specific. Cultural materialists
also argue that literary criticism has traditionally hidden its political
agenda, consciously or otherwise, by insisting that literature tran-
scends the time and place in which it was first produced. Cultural
materialism, by contrast, adopts an unashamedly political stance,
and proclaims, in near-utopian terms, a 'commitment to the transformation of a social order which exploits people on grounds of race,
gender and class' (Jonathan Dollimore and Alan Sinfield (eds),
Foreword to *Political Shakespeare*, 1985).

Dollimore's book *Radical Tragedy* is a reading of early modern
tragedy that challenges the principles underpinning criticism like
Harry Levin's. According to Dollimore, literary criticism's traditional
insistence on essentialism – the idea that as humans we all share
something timeless, unchanging and 'natural' – is fundamentally
conservative, since it tends to universalize and naturalize a specific
cultural identity. Traditional criticism defends this 'one cultural formation, one conception of what it is to be truly human . . . to the
corresponding exclusion of others' (p. 258): so, for instance, the perspectives of women, homosexuals, blacks or the working class would
be marginalized in the name of essentialism. For Dollimore, the significance of early modern tragedy is its constant 'problematizing' of
that essentialism. One way in which these plays constantly raise
questions about the notion of essential human nature, Dollimore
argues, is by their interrogation of a certain kind of religious belief –
providentialism; that is to say, the idea that God is in control of
human destiny, and the course of invidual lives. Dollimore argues
that providentialism was a key component of the belief system (or
ideology) at this time, since it supported the idea of the monarch's
right to absolute power over his or her subjects. Since the monarch
was established by divine will (according to providential belief), any
questioning of the will of the monarch challenged not only the
queen or the king, but God as well. Like many other cultural materialists and new historicists (we shall come to new historicism, an

allied movement, shortly) Dollimore reads these plays in close con-
junction with other texts, and not just literary ones, but philosophical, religious and political texts also. Some of the writers he makes
reference to in the course of his investigation include religious
writers like John Calvin, philosophers like Francis Bacon and
Thomas Hobbes, and political thinkers like Montaigne and
Machiavelli (the latter we have already come across in discussions of
The Jew of Malta).

In his reading of *Doctor Faustus*, Dollimore's starting point is not
that far away from Levin's. Levin sees Faustus as the archetypal
Renaissance man, transfigured by new knowledge and new discoveries that threatened to overturn the established order and its understanding of the world, as well as the place of the human within that
world. For Dollimore, the elements of the equation are subtly but
crucially different. Dollimore notes how readings of *Faustus* traditionally interpret it either as a vindication of Faustus (the overreacher, if you like), or as a morality play that finally endorses
Faustus's fate as fitting punishment for his crimes against God.
Dollimore suggests a different perspective that breaks that deadlock,
arguing that we should read the play 'not [as] an affirmation of
Divine Law, or conversely of Renaissance Man, but [as] an exploration of subversion through transgression' (p. 109).

Dollimore sees the universe of *Faustus* as one 'violently divided',
going so far as to suggest that it owes much to the Manichean
heresy, the belief that there is an evil deity that exists in opposition
to God, and that the universe is constituted by the holding of the
two in tension. Dollimore suggests that 'not only heaven and hell
but God and Lucifer, the Good Angel and the Bad Angel, are polar
opposites whose axes pass through and constitute human consciousness' (p. 111). From here, it is not much of a stretch to see God and
Lucifer as 'equally responsible in [Faustus's] final destruction, two
supreme agents of power deeply antagonistic to each other yet tem-
porarily co-operating in his demise' (p. 111). Dollimore's quotations
seem to substantiate his point that in Faustus's final soliloquy, 'both
God and Lucifer are spatially located as the opposites which, *between
them*, destroy him' (author's emphasis) (p. 111):

O, I'll leap up to my God! Who pulls me down?

> see where God
> Stretcheth out his arm and bends his ireful brows

My God, my God! Look not so fierce on me!

Ugly hell, gape not! Come not, Lucifer.

(V.ii.69, 74–5, 112, 114)

Dollimore's reading of Faustus's status, then, is very different: he sees the indomitable Tamburlaine as the epitome of the 'self-determining hero bent on transcendent autonomy – a kind of Renaissance theme of aspiring man', while Faustus's transgression is born 'not of a liberating sense of freedom to deny or retrieve origin, nor from an excess of life breaking repressive bounds. It is rather a transgression rooted in an *impasse* of despair' (p.112). This reading of Faustus produces a figure 'at once rebellious, masochistic and despairing' (p.114). The implications of this line of argument should be becoming clear by now: the Protestant God that Dollimore is constructing in his reading of the play is something monstrous. Dollimore's trump card in his discussion of Faustus is his leap from the theological to the political (for all cultural materialist criticism tends to lead, finally, back to politics).

> The final chorus of the play tells us that Dr Faustus involved himself with 'unlawful things' and thereby practised 'more than heavenly power permits' (II.vi.8). It is a transgression which has revealed the limiting structure of Faustus's universe for what it is, namely, 'heavenly *power*'. Faustus has to be destroyed since in a very real sense the credibility of the heavenly power depends upon it. And yet the punitive intervention which validates divine power also legitimates power, it appears, by the end of the play, to be the other way around: power establishes the limits of all those things.
>
> (p. 118)

For Dollimore, Faustus is a precursor of the so-called 'malcontent' of Jacobean tragedy, the outsider figure, corrosively critical of the estab-

lished order, and at the same time intricately bound up in its struc-
tures and functions. Faustus's significance, finally, is in his work as a
kind of insurgent, and as a self-sacrificial victim of a tyrannical God.
His death, at the point where the powers of good and evil intersect,
expose the brutality of this aspect of the Protestant faith.

Dollimore's early work emerged from a specific set of cultural circumstances, as he himself would, no doubt, be the first to admit.
After all, it is one of the key principles of cultural materialism that
one must recognise and take account of the ways in which one's own
views have been formed or informed by one's social and political
context. At the time Dollimore wrote *Radical Tragedy*, Britain's prime
minister was Margaret Thatcher, and her Conservative government
was responsible for policies that many perceived as socially divisive
and culturally obtuse. The Conservatives were accused of disman-
tling much of the welfare system that had been put in place by the
Labour Party after the Second World War. In many universities at
the time, the rise of the New Right in Britain led to a corresponding
increased level of political agitation on the Left. Dollimore's work,
and the work of colleagues and associates like Alan Sinfield,
Catherine Belsey and Graham Holderness, was part of that movement of resistance to the dominant political climate at the time.
Fifteen years or more since *Radical Tragedy* was written, with the
social fabric showing less traumatic wounds (at least, on the surface)
a stridently left wing political stance is, paradoxically, less stable than
it was at a time when politics was more polarized. Furthermore, cultural materialists have tended to move away from an uncompromising rejection of essentialism, and are now, it would seem, more
ready to accept some sort of compromise between 'essence' and
'culture' in the debate about how human nature is constituted.

A familiar criticism levelled at cultural materialists is that they
devote too much attention to context; their critics often imply that
this kind of straying away from the central line of investigation is
accompanied by a corresponding failure to read the literary text itself
closely enough. There is certainly a tendency in some of Dollimore's
work to become engrossed in texts that are being read in parallel
with the literary text under investigation. While his subsection in
the *Faustus* chapter, 'Power and the Unitary Soul', is a lucid

summary of Augustine's doctrine of the nature of the soul, the extended discussion of Augustinian and Calvinist theology does tend to lead the reader some distance away from the play itself. However, Dollimore's work is always provocative, and his insistence on viewing Elizabethan society as one in crisis, spiritually, politically and culturally, was a badly needed corrective at the time *Radical Tragedy* first appeared. His reading of *Faustus* is richly suggestive in terms of the text's potential for subversion of dominant ideologies.

Stephen Greenblatt

This final section in the chapter will look at two contrasting readings of *The Jew of Malta*. The analysis will not be as full as the summaries of Levin and Dollimore above, but will instead present in concise form the arguments of each, Stephen Greenblatt and Emily Bartels. I will show how Bartels builds on Greenblatt's work to provide what is eventually a more 'optimistic' interpretation of Marlowe's problematic play *The Jew of Malta*.

Stephen Greenblatt, author of 'Marlowe, Marx and Anti-Semitism' (*Critical Inquiry*, 5, 1978), is in some ways the American equivalent of a figure like Jonathan Dollimore. Sharing some of the approaches we would associate with cultural materialism, but with some subtle, crucial differences, the genesis of new historicism can be traced back to the publication of Greenblatt's *Renaissance Self-Fashioning* (1980). Greenblatt's essay on *The Jew of Malta* actually predates this work by two years, and it takes as its starting point a fantasy: Barabas had two children; the eldest, Albigail, renounced her religion and entered a nunnery when she heard that her father had murdered her Christian suitor. The second, a son, wrote an anti-Semitic pamphlet denouncing Judaism as a religion based on greed and self-interest but, instead of converting to Christianity, insisted that Judaism was merely the 'practical essence of Christianity, the thing itself stripped of its spiritual mystifications' (p. 141). The son's name, Greenblatt concludes, was Karl Marx.

Greenblatt points out how both Marlowe and Marx used the Jew as 'a kind of powerful rhetorical device, a way of marshalling deep

popular hatred and clarifying its object' (p. 141). Perhaps surprisingly, Greenblatt insists that the Barabas portrayed in the play's
opening scenes is not the alien or outsider, but rather the 'true representative of his society . . . His pursuit of wealth does not mark him
out but rather establishes him – if anything, rather respectably – in
the midst of all the other [economic] forces in the play' (p. 145). He
shows how ideological considerations are always subordinate to economic ones, noting how, for instance, the knights only concern
themselves with Barabas's 'inherent sin' at the moment when they
wish to justify depriving him of his possessions. Greenblatt claims
that the play does not discredit anti-Semitism, but adds that it also
refuses to construct a binary between 'good' Christianity and 'evil'
Judaism. Furthermore, Greenblatt points out how Barabas's identity
is, to a large extent, 'the product of the Christian conception of a
Jew's identity' (p. 148). He continues:

> . . . Barabas's sense of himself, his characteristic response to the world,
> and his self-presentation are very largely constructed out of the mate-
> rials of the dominant, Christian culture. This is nowhere more
> evident than in his speech which is virtually composed of hard little
> aphorisms, cynical adages, worldly maxims – all the neatly packaged
> nastiness of his society . . . Barabas is inscribed at the centre of the
> society of the play, a society whose speech is a tissue of aphorisms.
>
> (p. 148)

Greenblatt proceeds to quote ten of these *sententiae*, showing how
'Barabas's own store of these ideological riches comprise the most
cynical and self-serving' of them (p. 149). The reliance on these
aphorisms, common currency in this mercantile community, serve
only to 'de-individualize' Barabas, making him more and more
typical of the world he inhabits. Having established that Barabas is
situated very much at the heart of the play, the latter part of the
essay shows how Marlowe does, in the final analysis, insist upon
Barabas's distinction from 'the world that has engendered him and
whose spirit he expresses', partly through Barabas's own insistence on
his difference from Turks, Christians and even other Jews (p. 150). It
would seem that Barabas is in fact more closely identified with the
audience than he is with any other characters on stage, via the com-

plicity he nurtures between himself and his audience, something we have discussed already at some length in analysis of key passages from the play. However, Greenblatt takes his argument one step further, and proposes that the playfulness that defines Barabas relates him to Marlowe himself. We seem to have reverted to something resembling Harry Levin's approach, as Greenblatt notes how

> There is some evidence for a similar dark playfulness in Marlowe's own career, with the comic (and extremely dangerous) blasphemies, the nearly overt (and equally dangerous) homosexuality, the mysterious stint as double agent, and, of course the cruel, aggressive plays themselves. The will to play flaunts society's cherished orthodoxies, embraces what the culture finds loathsome or frightening, transforms the serious into the joke and then unsettles the category of the joke by taking it seriously. For Barabas, as for Marlowe himself, this is play on the brink of an abyss, *absolute* play.
>
> (p. 154)

Greenblatt's reading of the play is, finally, a deeply pessimistic one. Despite the reversion to drawing parallels between the playwright and his characters, familiar in twenty years or more of Marlovian scholarship, the play remains, for Greenblatt, irredeemably anti-Semitic, and Barabas is 'a falsehood, a fiction composed of the sleaziest materials in his culture' (p. 153). His pessimism is characteristic of the new historicist approach, and signals a fundamental difference between new historicism and cultural materialism. The latter insists that there is always room for subversion of the dominant ideology. Texts are constant sites of struggle, where 'established' interpretations can be contested and revised. New historicists argue that, on the contrary, what is perceived as subversion is merely the dominant ideology's process of containing dissent. Any opposition is, in effect, already anticipated and already controlled.

Emily Bartels

Emily Bartels's discussion of the play, in her book *Spectacles of Strangeness* (1993) provides an alternative perspective that is closer to cultural materialism. According to Bartels, Marlowe's work operates to deconstruct traditional binaries, whether they be of race, gender or sexuality. In the case of *The Jew of Malta*, she argues that the established view of Barabas as vicious anti-Semitic stereotype is ill-founded, and proposes in its place a much more complex reading of the play's positioning of ethnic identities.

Bartels reminds us first of all that Malta was an important strategic outpost, a kind of sixteenth century Alamo, with the menacing Islamic forces of the Ottoman empire lurking within sight. Malta would have been familiar to the Elizabethans as the site of a siege by Turkish forces in 1565. In point of fact, the siege failed, but Marlowe rewrites history for the purposes of his play by showing the Turk Selim Calymath victorious (with a little help from Barabas). Bartels shows how the Spanish admiral del Bosco defines Malta as Christian, set against the heathen barbarism of the Turks, and argues that critics have traditionally taken that binary at face value: Malta as the Establishment, Calymath as the Outsider. In fact, Malta is a contested territory, and both the Spaniard Del Bosco and the Turk Calymath are interlopers and would-be conquerors. Ferneze, meanwhile, 'adopts the dictates of both imperializing powers' (p. 164):

> The Governor, in effect, exchanges a place as the colonized for a place as the colonizer, displacing his powerlessness onto an other (which he must create as other) as a strategic defence against his own disempowerment. . . . The colonized have access to power only by becoming colonizers themselves and, ironically, by reinscribing the kind of discrimination which has enabled their own disempowerment.
>
> (p.165)

The representation of Barabas as the stereotypical Jew comes, then, as a result of this internal colonization and domination. In effect, Bartels argues that the stereotyping of Barabas is Ferneze's act, not Marlowe's, although she does seem to acknowledge that Ferneze's strategy is one that draws on stage tradition ('the faithless, greedy, and deceitful Jews of the mystery plays') (p. 166), and would have been endorsed by the Elizabethan audience. However, she claims that the representation of the Christians as equally vicious and avaricious effectively defuses the anti-Semitic stereotype: 'because the stereotype signifies and therefore depends upon recognizable difference, the play's refusal to validate that difference has the effect of invalidating the stereotype and the discourses from which it derives' (p. 167). This is where she takes issue with Greenblatt, who insists that, however the Christians are portrayed, the text still endorses the anti-Semitic stereotype of the demonic Jew.

The final section of Bartels's chapter on *The Jew of Malta* considers more closely Barabas as stereotype, suggesting that he 'undermines his identity as the Jew by presenting himself in answer to different aspects of the stereotype, ultimately unfixing the stereotypical terms' (p. 169). So, his lament over his lost wealth in act I scene ii, his description of his supposed villainy in conversation with Ithamore (II.iii) and so on, all show him 'playing up' to the way others construct him. For Bartels, this is ultimately a 'tragedy of . . . "self-colonization"' (p. 170): Barabas is, finally, merely an absence – and it is here she comes closest to Greenblatt, who argues, similarly, that Barabas is 'a thing of nothing', his career 'a steady, stealthy dispossession of himself, an extended vanishing . . .' (Greenblatt, p.153).

My own view of the play is that we cannot turn a blind eye to its anti-Semitic content; neither can we excuse it by claiming that its representation of Christians is equally satirical. However, I would agree with Emily Bartels that the self-conscious aspect of Barabas's character – his awareness that he is role-playing other characters' construction of himself as a Jew – is crucial, and in this there is the potential to activate a reading of the play that might subvert its anti-Semitism. Our analysis of the extracts has revealed the 'performative' nature of Barabas's character – his performances of various different emotional states, his constant reminders to the audience that the whole play is merely a fiction (via asides and soliloquies, for instance), as well as his 'performance' as a stereotypical Jew. Barabas often comments, with sardonic humour, on his role as a stage villain, most obviously at the beginning of act II scene i (1–19) and in his speech to Ithamore in act II scene iii (175–202). At times, Barabas sounds more like a Chorus than a character. So, at one level, Barabas moulds his behaviour to the expectations of those who perceive him as a (stereo)typical evil Jew. At another level, there is a sense that the actor (not simply the character) is commenting ironically on the persona of Barabas himself. This kind of ironical approach may help us find a way out of the impasse that has traditionally been perceived as rendering *The Jew of Malta* unplayable: it is a play that has been almost entirely neglected in terms of performance over the past fifty years or so, largely, or even solely, on account of its anti-Semitic content. However, if we can recognize in reading and accentuate in performance this distance between character and performer, we may be able to move beyond the impression of Barabas as a pantomime villain fit only to be laughed and hissed at. This is not to say that Marlowe intended any such thing. We cannot know for sure, of course, but it seems more likely that Marlowe was working within the ideological parameters of his own time and his own society. But, if the play can be found to contain within itself the potential to subvert the kind of cruel stereotypes it is founded on, it is our responsibility to unlock that potential, whether in private study, discussion or performance.

Further Reading

Editions

I have recommended the Oxford World's Classics version of Marlowe's plays as the best single volume edition currently available, and all references in this book are taken from that version, edited by David Bevington and Eric Rasmussen (Oxford University Press, 1995). However, note that both *Dido Queen of Carthage* and *The Massacre at Paris* are omitted. For those requiring more scholarly editions, Oxford University Press has recently finished publishing the complete works, but these are hardback editions destined for library shelves. Fortunately, Manchester University Press has kept the Revels series fairly up to date (with the exception of *Tamburlaine*) and in print in affordable paperback. The Revels series is the best place to start for more in-depth commentary and other editorial apparatus. 'Student editions' of the Revels series have recently begun to appear, with more concise, up to date introductions. Of other single volume editions, the Penguin, by J. B. Steane, is over thirty years old (1969) and to be avoided; Mark Thornton Burnett's Everyman edition (1999) has all the plays, but is marred (in its first printing at least) by having a guide to further reading that fails to give full details of the books to which it refers. Marlowe's poems and translations appear in a Penguin paperback edition edited by Stephen Orgel (1979).

Biographical

The standard biography of Marlowe is now nearly sixty years old, J. Bakeless's two-volume *The Tragical History of Christopher Marlowe* (Harvard University Press, 1942). This is likely to be superceded by Lisa Hopkins's *Christopher Marlowe: A Literary Life* (Palgrave, 2000). Meanwhile Charles Nicholl's *The Reckoning* is a fascinating investigation of the circumstances surrounding Marlowe's death (Jonathan Cape, 1991). To be treated with a healthy degree of scepticism are the works of A. D. Wraight, who has dedicated herself to proving that Marlowe wrote those works commonly attributed to William Shakespeare: *Christopher Marlowe and Edward Alleyn* (Adam Hart, 1993), *The Story That the Sonnets Tell* (Adam Hart, 1995) and *Christopher Marlowe and the Armada* (Adam Hart, 1996). Her earlier work co-authored with Virginia F. Stern, which predates this obsession, is excellent, however: *In Search of Christopher Marlowe* (MacDonald & Co, 1965), reprinted in 1993 by Adam Hart (Publishers) Ltd.

Criticism

A brief study of Marlowe that is both readable and informative is Thomas Healy's *Christopher Marlowe* in the 'Writers and their Work' series published by Northcote House (1994). Roger Sales' study *Christopher Marlowe* in the 'Macmillan Dramatists' series (1991) is more challenging, and heavily indebted to postmodernist critical approaches. My own *A Preface to Marlowe* (Longman, 2000) looks at all of the plays, as well as the poetry, and provides more detailed coverage of Marlowe's life and times, as well as his legacy, than there is room for in this book. It pays considerable attention to stage history, and expands on the idea of the subversive potential of *The Jew of Malta* in performance, in particular.

Of the more specialized works, Sarah Munson Deats's *Sex, Gender and Desire in the Plays of Christopher Marlowe* (University of Delaware Press, 1997) wears its preoccupations on its sleeve (or spine), as does Simon Shepherd's very provocative *Christopher Marlowe and the Politics of Elizabethan Theatre* (Harvester

Wheatsheaf, 1986). Emily Bartels's study of *The Jew of Malta* is considered in the samples of critical reading, and her *Spectacles of Strangeness: Imperialism, Alienation and Marlowe* adopts similar approaches to the other works (University of Pennsylvania Press, 1993). *Re-Citing Marlowe* (Ashgate, 2000) finds its author, Clare Harraway, making a determined break from the author-centred criticism that has been discussed in Chapter 9.

There are a number of good collections of essays about Marlowe's dramatic works. There are two *Casebook* collections devoted to Marlowe: John Russell Brown has edited a selection covering *Tamburlaine the Great, Edward the Second* and *The Jew of Malta* (Macmillan, 1982) and John Jump oversees a volume devoted to *Doctor Faustus* (Macmillan, 1969). A *New Casebook,* reflecting more recent critical trends, was due imminently at the time this book went to press. Richard Wilson's *Longman Critical Reader: Christopher Marlowe* (Longman, 1999) includes three of the four essays discussed in Chapter 9. Other good collections include *Christopher Marlowe and English Renaissance Culture* (Scolar Press, 1996), edited by Darryll Grantley and Peter Roberts; and Kenneth Friedenreich (ed.), *A Poet and a Filthy Playmaker: New Essays on Christopher Marlowe* (AMS Press, 1988). Michael Mangan's *Doctor Faustus* in the Penguin Critical Studies series (1989) is perhaps the best one-volume introduction to Marlowe's most famous play. Also worth mentioning is Clifford Leech (ed.), *Christopher Marlowe: Poet for the Stage* (AMS Press, 1986). Other stage-oriented publications are George L. Geckle's *Text and Performance: Tamburlaine and Edward II* (Humanities Press International, 1988) and William Tydeman's book on *Faustus* for the Macmillan 'Text and Performance' series (1984). For those wishing to look more closely at Marlowe's sources, Vivien Thomas and William Tydeman's *Christopher Marlowe: The Plays and Their Sources* (Routledge, 1994) is an essential reference work.

Context

Russ McDonald's *Bedford Companion to Shakespeare* (St Martin's Press, 1996) is one of the best books I have found as an introduction to early modern culture, theatrical and otherwise, although (obviously) it generally relates the discussion to Shakespeare's works. It has a selection of original sources and documents, and these are keyed into the essays. *A New History of Early English Drama* (Columbia University Press, 1997) edited by John D. Cox and David Scott Kastan, is excellent, but more difficult and more detailed. Julia Briggs's *This Stage Play-World* (new edition, Oxford University Press, 1997) is also very good, now updated to take account of new historicist and cultural materialist readings in particular. Andrew Gurr's *The Shakespearean Stage 1574–1642* remains unsurpassed as a study of Elizabethan and Jacobean theatre history (Cambridge University Press, third edition, 1992). *The Cambridge Companion to English Renaissance Drama* (Cambridge University Press, 1990), edited by A. R. Braunmuller and Michael Hattaway, is starting to look a little long in the tooth, but is still a good one-volume guide.

For more in depth discussion of the issue of homosexuality in early modern culture, see Alan Bray, *Homosexuality in Renaissance England* (Gay Men's Press, 1982), Jonathan Goldberg, *Sodometries* (Stanford University Press, 1992) and Bruce R. Smith, *Homosexual Desire in Shakespeare's England* (University of Chicago Press, 1994). On the vexed issue of anti-Semitism, see James Shapiro, *Shakespeare and the Jews* (University of Columbia Press, 1996).

Critical Theory

There is a huge market in introductions to critical theory, and I cannot hope to cover it comprehensively here. Instead, I will simply mention three that students I have taught have found very helpful: Peter Barry's *Beginning Theory* (Manchester University Press, 1995), *A Reader's Guide to Contemporary Literary Theory* by Raman Selden and Peter Widdowson (Harvester Wheatsheaf, fourth edition, 1996), and Terry Eagleton, *Literary Theory* (Basil Blackwell, second edition, 1996).

Index